T. E. HULME

MICHAEL ROBERTS

T. E. Hulme

*with an introduction by
Anthony Quinton*

CARCANET NEW PRESS / MANCHESTER

Published in 1982 by
CARCANET NEW PRESS LTD.
210 Corn Exchange Buildings
Manchester M4 3BQ

First published in 1938 by Faber & Faber Ltd.

Roberts, Michael
T. E. Hulme
1. Hulme, T. E.   2. England-Intellectual life
—20th century
I. Title   II. Quinton, Anthony
942.081   DA566.4

ISBN 0-85635-411-2

*The publisher acknowledges the financial assistance of the
Arts Council of Great Britain*

Printed in England by SRP Ltd., Exeter

Anthony Quinton
INTRODUCTION

T. E. Hulme and Michael Roberts had a good deal in common. Both, to start with, were farmers' sons, on the whole. (On the whole, only because Hulme's father turned to the manufacture of ceramic transfers and Roberts's spent part of each year running a shop in Bournmouth.) Hulme was born in the village of Endon, North Staffordshire in 1883; Roberts in the village of Thorney Hill in the New Forest in 1902. Both went to Cambridge as exhibitioners to read mathematics; Hulme to St John's, Roberts to Trinity. Hulme's academic career ended abruptly in 1904 when he was sent down for some piece of boisterous misconduct. Roberts, even if he wound up as principal of an Anglican teacher training college, was clearly a lively and combative young man. Both were, one might say, unusually muscular intellectuals, not at a loss in the open air. Hulme spent a couple of years fending for himself in Canada, pretty much at the edge of subsistence. Roberts's favourite recreation was mountain-climbing, which he practised in a quite serious and distinguished way.

A more significant likeness is that in an epoch when the life of the mind in England was parcelled out between increasingly specialised academics and gentlemanly aesthetes who preserved their sensibilities intact from the tarnish of any definite knowledge, Hulme and Roberts were both generalists. Their education was in mathematics and natural science; their intellectual interests were in philosophy, widely conceived, religion, literature, above all poetry, which they both

i

wrote, art (Hulme), music (Roberts), politics and the social order generally. Both, since they ranged so widely and uncircumspectly, retained to the end a certain amateur status. That end came early in both cases. Hulme was killed in France in 1917 at the age of thirty-four; Roberts died of leukemia in 1948 at the age of forty-six. Hulme, in particular, never had time to get his ideas in order. His boldness animated a practice of unqualified utterance which time and reflection could usefully have modified. As it is, even to the most sympathetic reader he must seem to be constantly tripping over the furniture in the house of intellect.

As a matter of principle Hulme seeks to base all his views on a broadly philosophical foundation, a *weltanschauung* or view of the world, which he calls the religious attitude and whose opponent is humanism. Humanism, he holds, is so widely taken for granted that most of its adherents are unaware of it. For them, it is an underlying necessity of thought which functions in their thinking much as the laws of logic do in the thinking of rational people. It is strategically essential for the sake of effective controversy that the prevailing humanist assumptions should be dug out of their asylum of unthinking acceptance. At times Hulme says that his, 'religious', view of the world is 'demonstrably true', but that seems to be simply rhetorical excess, for he nowhere seeks to demonstrate it. More often he takes seriously the obvious implications of the word 'ultimate', in the description of views of the world as sets of systems of ultimate assumptions. One cannot, he says, directly prove to the holder of an opposed view of the world that his view is mistaken. All one can do is to drag it into the light and show carefully what follows from it, in the expectation that its unreflective adherent will then find that he is no longer attracted to it.

Humanism is, above all, a theory of human nature

which maintains that human beings are naturally good, that they are both perfectible and, by and large, on the way to becoming perfect. In politics this assumption implies democratic liberalism, the idea that all should participate in the work of government, where this is seen as a matter of freeing people from the customary and institutional fetters which have obstructed their natural impulse toward self-perfection. In ethics it implies that value is relative to human desires and feelings, more specifically it implies such doctrines as that value is derived from the contribution something makes to human pleasure or, more farsightedly, to the survival of the human race. The literary expression of the humanist principle is romanticism, which irrelevantly emphasises the importance of the subject-matter of poetry, seeks to express the infinite and to minister to the emotions. In painting and sculpture humanism leads to the glorification of the essentially inglorious human being, most notably the human body.

The religious attitude derives opposed conclusions from its assumption of human limitation and of the general fixity of human nature, an assumption whose symbol is the doctrine of original sin. The political consequence is that men need discipline and order, that the traditions of the past should be respected, that there should be authority and hierarchy, that it is desirable that nations, historically actual human groupings, should exist. Literature in general and poetry in particular should adhere to traditional forms, should seek a 'dry hardness', strive for accuracy and precision in the rendering of a freshly perceived world. In the visual arts representational enslavement to the human form should give way to a geometric art of the kind prefigured in Egyptian and Byzantine art in which that which is capable of perfection, the ideal order of abstraction, is the theme and not the essentially imperfectible topic of mankind.

The logical articulation of Hulme's opinions is dramatically characterised by human imperfection, but they have a kind of emotional affinity, if only as adding up to the comprehensive repudiation of a stuffy, *bien pensant* system of convictions about art, society and the universe. They are fresh, bold, agreeably immodest. It is not surprising that they were extremely influential. Commentators on Hulme fall over themselves in their eagerness to insist that his position was not original. Roberts says 'he was not an original thinker' in the second paragraph of the first chapter. No doubt most of the large ideas Hulme brought together have some sort of family likeness to ideas available at the time he was writing. But bringing them together in at least a rhetorically persuasive way was an original achievement. None of those he drew his ideas from could have brought it off because none of them, not even Sorel, had anything like his effective range. (Bergson wrote about everything, but often in a rather second-hand way.) Nearly all good ideas turn out to have been thought up by someone other than the person conventionally supposed to have first hit on them. But the anticipator did not know how to make the best use of his discovery.

Hulme's most direct influence was on art and poetry. He was the first theorist of abstract art in this country, fruitfully enthusiastic about Epstein at the crucial early stage of the latter's career, supplying a measure of stiffening for Wyndham Lewis, whose frequently unconvincing bluster showed a need for support. At much the same time he was the leading theorist of imagism, in this case reinforcing his aesthetic precepts with some practice. It now appears that the five short poems printed at the end of Herbert Read's edition of Hulme's *Speculations* as the 'complete poetical works' were seriously worked at and not just thrown off for instructional purposes. There are three more in Roberts's book

iv

and a total of twenty-eight pages of poems in Alun Jones's *The Life and Opinions of T. E. Hulme* (1960).

His political views are the least concrete and developed part of his corpus of convictions. In his introduction to Sorel's *Reflections on Violence*, seeking, apparently, to dissociate Sorel from the thinkers of the *Action Française* with whom he was for a while in sympathy, Hulme puts in an uncharacteristically pious footnote which states that 'no theory that is not fully moved by the conception of justice asserting the equality of men, and which cannot offer something to all men, deserves or is likely to have any future'. That is far removed in sentiment from the contentions of his lecture 'A Tory Philosophy', exhumed by Alun R. Jones from the pages of an obscure paper and republished in his *Life and Opinions of T. E. Hulme*, where Hierarchy, presented as the opposite of Equality, is associated as a political good with Constancy, Order and Authority, and Nationalism.

The most important single recipient of Hulme's influence is undoubtedly T. S. Eliot. It is clearly enough acknowledged in Eliot's famous self-classification of himself as 'classicist in literature, royalist in politics, Anglo-Catholic in religion'. Eliot takes over directly from Hulme both the rejection of humanism, understood in Hulme's way as liberal-romantic optimism, and the connected idea that the tenacity of its assumptions is much increased by the way in which they saturate the language we use, from which they can be squeezed out only by the most unrelenting vigilance and effort. In Hulme's spirit too is Eliot's early endorsement of poetic impersonality. And although Eliot does not seem to have become directly aware of Hulme's ideas before the publication of *Speculations* in 1924, seven years after Hulme's death, his own poetry in the pre-*Waste Land, J. Alfred Prufrock* period has marked affinities with the imagism Hulme was both defending and practising. That

practice received an almost hyperbolical approbation
from Eliot who wrote of Hulme as 'the author of two
or three of the most beautiful short poems in the
language'.

There is, for all Eliot's loyal acknowledgement of
indebtedness, a good deal of difference between the
two. Hulme's pessimism is breezy and vigorous; Eliot's
gloomy and listless. The central difference between
them, in thought rather than temperament, is in what
they understand by *religion*. For Eliot religion is straightforward Anglican Christianity, as defined by the creeds
of the Church, taken in a pretty literal sense. It is, to the
uninvolved, a religion of self-abasement and self-denial.
Hulme had little perceptible tendency to either of these.
When he talks of human imperfection it is the limitations of others that he has principally before his mind.
There is nothing to indicate any pangs of self-disgust.

Furthermore, the absolute values on which Hulme
insists are, to the extent that they are ethical, very far
from being Christian. His ideal of human excellence is
close to that of Sorel who was an uncompromising
affirmer of the claims of heroic virtue, an exponent of
the morality of honour, a less fetid and sickly Nietzsche.
Hulme was conspicuously devoid of the prime Christian
virtue of humility and his evident lack of qualms about
the fact suggests that he did not think much of it. For
one who saw all the debilitating spiritual weaknesses of
the age as stemming from the thinkers of the Renaissance,
he was curiously committed to the Renaissance ideal of
heroic *virtù*.

I have discovered no reference to Christ in Hulme's
writings nor does any characteristically Christian sentiment appear in them. Indeed in his frequent references
to the rightness and spiritually hygienic necessity of the
'religious attitude' he has very little so say about God.
In his essay on romanticism and classicism he says that

'part of the fixed nature of man is the belief in the Deity' but even here God is mentioned in the most abstract possible way. The real meat of Hulme's religious view of the world is the doctrine of original sin. But the belief that human beings are unalterably limited and imperfect is not associated in Hulme with any doctrine of redemption. His actual position comes out with genially ferocious clarity in the last section, The Religious Attitude, of the long chapter, 'Humanism and the Religious Attitude', with which *Speculations* begins. There he says that 'few since the Renaissance have really understood the dogma [*viz.* of original sin], certainly very few inside the Churches of recent years. . . . No humanist could understand the dogma. They all chatter about matters which are in comparison with this, quite secondary notions—God, Freedom, and Immortality.'

Hulme's religion, in short, is really half a religion, the bleak, negative part. In that it resembles Hobbes's religion. In both an absolute ideal, or, one could just as well say, an idealised Absolute, is set up with no definite positive characteristics, only the abstract, honorific ones of infinity and perfection, as a way to show up as sharply as possible the finitude and imperfection of mankind. Hulme is quite a bit like Hobbes in other ways. Both are unmitigatedly English. Both are impatient thinkers, with some mathematics in their mental constitution. They are writers of forceful knockdown prose, full of concrete imagery, ideal for use as an instrument of cheerful vituperation. (Wyndham Lewis, who seems never to have got over being held upside down over the railings in Soho Square by Hulme, described his writings as 'incredibly badly written'. This silly judgement comes as no surprise from the worst writer of English prose in the twentieth century, although Hulme is very often a *careless* writer.) Hobbes and Hulme agreed on the desirability of strong government, but for undisguisedly hard-headed, practical reasons. There is no Burkean nostalgia about them. Both took the whole life of the mind for their province. Both could make dreadful mistakes; Hobbes, most conspicuously, in his attempt to prove that the circle could be squared.

This inevitably raises the question of Hulme's status as a philosopher. By and large he has been completely ignored by exponents of that discipline. *Speculations* was reviewed in *Mind* not by a philosopher but by I. A. Richards. Hulme does not figure, as far as I can tell, in any history of recent philosophy, not even J. A. Passmore's highly detailed *A Hundred Years of Philosophy*, or in any encyclopedia of philosophy. That might be put down to his explicit attachment of himself to the hopelessly unfashionable Bergson. The fact is, however, that he was a complete philosophical amateur, not without shrewdness, but displaying no aptitude for sustained philosophical argument, perhaps, even, no awareness that such a thing existed or could be of some interest or value. The articles on some philosophers of his age that begin *Further Speculations*, brought together by Samuel Hynes in 1955, are wholly non-argumentative, being no more than the immediate emotional reactions of a sensibility reasonably familiar with philosophical literature to the works in question.

The shrewdness I mentioned comes out in the distinction he draws between the technical, more or less analytic philosophy practised by Russell, Moore and Husserl in the first decade of this century and *Weltanschauung*, the putting forward of general views of the world, attitudes towards human nature. The former, an 'investigation into the relations between certain very abstract categories', is a science; the latter is not. Sometimes he describes it as an art; at others, more compellingly, as autobiography or personal statement. Philosophy as a whole is, he asserts, 'a mixed subject', half science, half ideology. In the past philosophers have generally pursued the science because of the use they believed they could make of it to underwrite the ideology.

Something like this distinction has been very widely accepted by philosophers, in the English-speaking world at any rate, in the twentieth century. It is clearly drawn in the closing paragraphs of Russell's *History of Western Philosophy*. The type of analytic philosophy he himself practises is, he writes,

> able, in regard to certain problems, to achieve definite answers, which have the quality of science rather than of philosophy. . . . Its methods . . . resemble those of science. I have no doubt that, insofar as philosophical knowledge is possible, it is by such methods that it must be sought. . . . There remains, however, a vast field, traditionally included in philosophy, where scientific methods are inadequate. This field includes ultimate questions of value. . . . (p. 834)

Most philosophers of Russell's kind have regarded questions about ultimate values as not being susceptible of rational demonstration. One who did not was G. E. Moore, about whom Hulme made some admiring remarks and whom he may have encountered in either of his two periods at Cambridge. Moore held that goodness is a simple quality, as simple as yellow, whose incidence must just be perceived, in some non-sensory fashion. Its presence in 'states of consciousness', where alone it is to be found, is a matter of brute, objective fact. Such a theory makes values objective, but at the cost of leaving disagreement about them barely intelligible.

Moore supposed his theory about value to be part of technical philosophy, a matter of discriminating the relations between certain very abstract categories. Like other philosophers he went on in his last chapter (in

Principia Ethica) to set out his results; that is, to reveal the findings of that power of ethical intuition which his technical inquiries had shown to be valid, to his satisfaction, at any rate. Those findings were not very Hulmean, being the morality of the Bloomsbury group, elevating the contemplation of beauty and affectionate personal relations above everything else. It would have been objectionable to Hulme for its 'humanist' assumption that nothing could be of value but states of human consciousness and for the sedentary, unheroic nature of the states ennobled. But at least he would have preferred it to the 'compassionate' or 'caring' moral outlook of modern social Christianity.

Hulme's real concern in this area is that one's *Weltanschauung* or ultimate system of values should be *absolute*, not subordinated to human desires and feelings, rather than that it should be *objective*. It is perfectly consistent to take certain things to have value independently of their capacity to minister to human desires and feelings without believing that their value is objectively demonstrable or a matter of truth or falsity at all. Such a voluntarist kind of scepticism about value is congruous both with Hulme's temperament and his endorsement in principle of tension and struggle.

The conversational informality of Hulme's writing on philosophy leaves it open to a good deal of technical criticism and objection. Is his theory of three levels or orders of reality—inorganic, organic and ideal—part of scientific philosophy, as it certainly seems to be? (It is very close to the Trinitarian ontologies of Bolzano and Frege, the two greatest scientific philosophers of the nineteenth century, neither of whom had any perceptible ideology whatever.) If it is, what is it doing as the foundation of the religious attitude, in opposition to the 'principle of continuity' adhered to by humanists? For in that case it is being used to prop up a system of values in defiance of Hulme's belief in the absolute distinction of scientific philosophy from ideology.

The point can be made in another way by considering Hulme's notion of a critique of satisfaction. Attitudes to the world or ultimate value-systems, he says, owe much of their power to their latency. What is needed is to bring them out into the open and then to ask what particular human desire or partiality they serve. They need to be subjected to a 'critique of satisfaction' which he seems to conceive as an objective way of adjudicating between basic emotional biasses. But no way of going about the adjudication is suggested. In the end it seems that once a system of values is brought fully into the open, with its emotional roots and its ideological consequences fully traced out, its acceptance or rejection becomes a matter of personal decision.

Hulme's philosophical activities were seriously interfered with by his early involvement, at first intellectual and then personal, with Bergson. (Bergson helped him to get readmitted to Cambridge with an elegant testimonial and he translated Bergson's *Introduction to Metaphysics*.) Bergson's thought, with its depreciation of the analysing, scientific intellect, was calculated to provide relief from that nocturnal disquiet of the later nineteenth century, the 'nightmare of scientific materialism'. But Hulme soon got over the distress occasioned by that metaphysical spectre. The humanism that became his principal enemy numbers Bergson among its adherents. The fear of finding man to be a part of nature, which could be said to be the emotional source of his philosophy, is just the sort of wet, suburban state of mind which Hulme wants to bring his critique of satisfaction hard down on.

The firmness and definiteness of Hulme's own convictions and his cheeky indifference to academic pieties minimised the ill effects of his Bergsonian involvement.

INTRODUCTION

A good tune was played, even if on a curiously inappro-
priate instrument, a march-tune for quick-stepping
riflemen on a leaky church organ. Michael Roberts made
somewhat idiosyncratic use of Hulme, coaxing him in a
Christian, democratic direction, but to nothing like the
same extent as Hulme manipulated Bergson. Much of
Hulme's anti-humanism survives in Roberts's more considered exposition of his own beliefs in *The Recovery of
the West*, and Roberts's positive doctrines are not more
than half way along the road that leads from Hulme to
T. S. Eliot.

Michael Roberts is still, no doubt, best known as the
highly capable impresario of the socially conscious
British poets of the 1930s, that group whose members
now seem to stand to Auden as the poets of the Rhymers'
Club do to Yeats. First, he edited selections from their
works, in *New Signatures* in 1932 and in *New Country*
the year after. In the *Faber Book of Modern Verse* the
1930s poets found themselves placed in a coherently
assembled tradition of modernist poetry in English.
Ahead of them were Hopkins, Yeats, Eliot, Pound,
Ransom, Tate, Cummings, Graves. Georgians, however
good in themselves, were excluded, so no de la Mare
and no Blunden. Following them was a representative
advance-guard of the more lurid and imaginative poets
of the (early) 1940s: Dylan Thomas, George Barker,
David Gascoyne. That anthology, which no one who
was young in its first years can remember without grati-
tude, was anatomised in an excellent long introduction.

Between the two smaller anthologies and the *Faber
Book* Roberts had published his first extended prose
work: *Critique of Poetry*. A chapter towards the middle
of the book is called 'T. E. Hulme's Speculations' and
serves to introduce a discussion of four different world
views, which are an elaboration of Hulme's binary
system of humanism and the religious attitude. At right

angles to that distinction Roberts introduces another between world views that exalt reason and those that exalt the emotions. The four resulting combinations are classicism (religion, or rather absolute values, plus reason); fundamentalism (absolute values plus emotion, the position of Tolstoy and D. H. Lawrence); romanticism (merely human values—for Roberts that comes to taking human survival to be the *summum bonum*—plus emotion); and, finally, humanism, in an only half-Hulmean sense (human values plus reason). At that stage Roberts plumped for humanism as he defined it, still unwilling to make even the very negative religious commitment of Hulme.

It is a more sensitive classification than Hulme's, as, being twice as complex, it ought to be. It certainly avoids various implications of Hulme's insistence on identifying the view that values are human with romanticism which fail to compel assent, such as that the French *philosophes* of the eighteenth century are romantics. But Roberts made no further use of it, since, by the time he came to write *T. E. Hulme*, which came out four years later in 1938, he had returned to Christianity. The anti-religious naturalism that had caused him, in the earlier book, to keep Hulme at a respectful arm's length had evaporated and he could recognise Hulme as a forerunner without serious reserve.

Roberts's *T. E. Hulme* gives a thorough, sympathetic, moderately digressive exposition of almost all Hulme's views except those on painting and sculpture, which are very summarily handled. After an 'analysis of Hulme's position' in the middle of the book, Roberts turns to criticism and development of Hulme's ideas. He accepts the point I made earlier that Hulme's notion of religion is peculiar and admits that Hulme is more a stoic pessimist than a Christian. But at the end of the ninth chapter on religion and the critique of satisfaction, he says that to avoid a purely wayward and impulsive individualism 'some authoritative road to the absolute values' must be found. 'It is difficult to see', he goes on, 'how, for a Western European, the authority could be any other than that of the Christian Church'. In other words, Hulme's assumptions entail the acceptance of institutional Christianity, although Hulme did not realise it.

Roberts sees that there is a discrepancy between Hulme's loyalty to the ideas of Bergson, who was a relativist and, for all his opposition to the claims of science, a humanist, the actual content of Hulme's basic principles. Against the view of Hulme as a man of the Right, rather forcibly suggested by Hulme's description of his doctrines as a 'Tory philosophy', he says that Hulme had the deepest sympathy 'with the working-class demand for more equitable economic conditions'. That, perhaps, is more what he feels Hulme *ought* to have felt, rather than what he actually did. Generally, in the second, more freewheeling half of the book, it is as if Roberts is using Hulme as a quarry for the construction of a system of beliefs of his own, more than assembling them in an orderly way.

Hulme's terminological excesses are taken calmly in Roberts's stride. He points out that romanticism is not the same thing as sentimentality, that classicism is not always religious, that Christianity is more than a conviction of original sin, that heroism is not the same as a Sorelian commitment to violence, nor the only alternative to a blind faith in automatic progress. Generally, he recognises that Hulme was too impatient to pick his enemies out one by one, he rolled them all together into one great Loathly Opposite. In Roberts's last chapter, on 'the tragic view', he praises Hulme for emphasising certain crucial features of the human condition: that men are limited beings, acting under uncertainty, pursuing unattainable ideals, but reaffirms his main point about Hulme, that sentimental optimism can be rejected and Hulme's view of the place of man in the world accepted, without his lapse into stoic pessimism. The Christian alternative he had in mind was presented in 1941 in *The Recovery of the West*, less as philosophy than as general social doctrine and so in the aptest form to collide with the hallucinated leftism of the age.

PREFACE

Since Hulme's *Speculations* appeared in 1924, an increasing number of readers have found in them an articulate statement and a justification of their growing dislike of romanticism in literature, utopianism in politics and hedonism in ethics, and if Hulme had no other title to consideration, it would still be remarkable that he saw this coming change so clearly more than twenty-five years ago. His influence on English critics and poets is far from exhausted, and my object in writing this book has been to expound some of Hulme's ideas, to offer some references that may be useful in understanding and judging them, and to add some comments of my own. I have given as much of Hulme's personal history as seems relevant to a discussion of his work, and I am deeply grateful to Hulme's sister, Mrs. Auchterlonie, and to his friends, Sir Edward Marsh, Sir John Squire, Mr. Richard Curle, the Rev. James Fraser, Mr. A. Haigh, Mr. F. S. Adams, Mrs. Charles Baty (Halszka Bevan), Mrs. Kibblewhite, Mr. Ezra Pound, Mr. Ashley Dukes and others for the help that they have given me in this matter. I thank Mrs. Auchterlonie for permission to use a number of Hulme's letters, notes and poems that have not previously been printed, and I also thank Mr.

7

PREFACE

Herbert Read and the editor of *The Criterion* for permission to reprint some *Notes on Language and Style* that were not included in the *Speculations*. In these notes I have incorporated a number of others taken from Hulme's manuscripts, and I have also added a *Lecture on Modern Poetry* that appears to have been delivered some time before the lecture mentioned on p. 21, and then slightly modified for that occasion.

I am deeply indebted to Messrs. Kegan Paul for permission to make such quotations from *Speculations* as were necessary, and I must also thank Messrs. Eyre & Spottiswoode for allowing me to use a passage from *Blasting and Bombardiering* by Wyndham Lewis. Finally, I am specially grateful to Mr. T. W. Eason and Bro. George Every, S.S.M., for reading my typescript and making some very useful suggestions.

CONTENTS

CONTENTS
Appendices

Chapter One

BIOGRAPHICAL SKETCH

Pascal's place in philosophy has always been a matter for dispute between those who hold him no philosopher at all, and those who see in him a precursor of Kant, and one who came upon important truths through intuition rather than through reasoning. Certainly Pascal, who began as a mathematician, ended by doubting the adequacy of the kind of reasoning that is used in logic and in mathematics; his aim was not to show the structure of reality or to analyse the forms of thought, but to assert important truths that were liable to be overlooked. In this, he stood against the current of his time, for he opposed ideas and habits of thought that were ingrained in the common outlook of the age as deeply as in its academic philosophy. The French Syndicalist, Georges Sorel, was another man of the same kind: as Pascal opposed the doctrines of Montaigne, so Sorel fought against those of nineteenth-century liberalism. Both were prophets rather than philosophers; they were more concerned with the persuasive statement of fundamental truths than with constructing a logical system on truths already accepted. Pascal preached the doctrine of Original Sin and of Redemption through Christ; Sorel preached the non-perfectibility of man and the regeneration of society through the General Strike. However different these men may have been in personal character and in intellectual ability, they resembled each other in their conception of the nature of man, in their opposition to the general outlook of their time, and in their unsystematic manner of writing. T. E. Hulme, who was a disciple of Sorel's, and who said that everything he wrote was to be regarded as a prolegomenon to a reading of Pascal, was of the same type.

The cutting of Gordian knots is not a philosophical activity; but the assertion of salutary truths may be valuable even when it is not systematic. A hostile critic might say that Hulme's sole merit was that he could read French and German. He was not an original thinker, he solved no problems and made no startling observations or distinctions, and his ideas were sometimes expressed untidily and incoherently. But his writing was racy and energetic, and the ideas he put into circulation certainly needed asserting in England. In his attacks on romanticism, pacifism, and the utopian conception of progress, Hulme was trying to make people understand that they were looking at things through one particular pair of spectacles. He was neither a selfish reactionary nor a fire-eating militarist: he believed that the liberal and romantic outlook coloured nearly all political and philosophical thought in England; and he claimed that this outlook was mistaken and could be abandoned without any sacrifice of generosity or intellectual integrity. The fact that there is scarcely an argument or instance in Hulme's writing that does not come from Pascal, Sorel,

Lasserre, Worringer, Husserl or Bergson does not lessen the value of his work. Hulme's influence has grown steadily since the publication of his *Speculations* in 1924, and it is still increasing.

Hulme has sometimes been represented as a mathematical genius; this is certainly a wild exaggeration, but it is equally certain that his early interests, like those of Pascal and Sorel, were mathematical and mechanical; even at the top-spinning age he was engrossed in a book of gyrostatics. His sister tells how, as a small boy, he would play draughts with his mother, while she was doing something else, on these terms: that it did not matter whether she thought about the game or not—he would be quite satisfied to go away for an hour or so and consider all the possibilities, and then come back for another equally aimless move to be made.

This small mathematical monster, Thomas Ernest Hulme, was born on 16th September 1883, at Gratton Hall, Endon, North Staffordshire. His father, Thomas Hulme (the name is pronounced *Hume*) had been a farmer at one time, and although he gave this up to become a ceramic-transfer manufacturer, he remained passionately fond of shooting and fishing all his life. His mother was a woman of strong character, a keen cyclist at a time when cycling was unusual for ladies; and her friends still remember her sense of humour and her command of repartee. In January 1894 Hulme entered the High School, Newcastle-under-Lyme. Those who knew him at this time say that he was original, humorous, and speculative. His best subject was mathematics ('he never seemed to forget a formula'), but he also took a keen interest in the school debating society and in natural history. The school Natural History Society was affiliated to the North Staffordshire Field Club, and notices of the Field Club Excursions were always displayed on the school notice-board. No one had ever heard of any boy joining them, till one day Hulme suggested to two of his friends[1] that they should go to the Victoria University College Museum with the club. This meant asking the headmaster for leave off for the Saturday morning, and Hulme's friends were sceptical about getting this leave; but he made them muster up their courage, and they went.

Hulme went up to St John's College, Cambridge, in October 1902 as an Exhibitioner. His rooms were in Third Court, by the Bridge of Sighs, and there he would entertain his friends with his persistent examination of every idea they expressed. No subject was beyond question, and no one escaped who had anything to do with him. He would start an argument with the coach of his boat during an outing, with a lecturer in the middle of his lecture, or with a waiter in Hall. A good deal of his criticism took the form of banter, and most of it was destructive, but there was no malice or superiority in his manner. 'I liked Hulme though some didn't,' says one of his friends of that period.[2] 'He was entirely without side, and however provocative he might be, he was

---

[1] A. Haigh and F. S. Adams, to whom I am indebted for most of my information about Hulme's schooldays.

[2] Rev. James Fraser.

14

always entertaining and kind, and at bottom serious. He was certainly interested in mathematics, but he cared more for philosophy and art. Though his method of arguing was coldly mathematical, with terms of fixed value, his judgments seemed to be mostly intuitive and aesthetic. He didn't seem to work much at College, but he did talk.'

Hulme's fundamental seriousness was not apparent to the college authorities, but they observed the perpetual rows in his rooms. Hulme himself was a teetotaller, eating a lot of sugar, but some of his friends were drunken rowdies. There were disturbances at the local theatre, where Hulme with his Staffordshire voice corrected the pronunciation of the actors, and in March 1904 he was sent down, together with other undergraduates, for 'over-stepping the limits of the traditional licence allowed by the authorities on Boat Race night'. According to J. C. Squire, Hulme was given 'the longest mock funeral ever seen in the town'.[1] He was at this time a big fellow with a genial open face; he walked with a rather heavy bouncing step, leaning slightly forwards. At school he had shown no special skill at games; and he did not get very far as an oarsman, though he did not give up, as many do, at an early stage. When he had settled in London after being sent down, he sometimes walked home, sleeping in barns and under hedges.

In July 1906 he went to Canada, working his way out and back, and doing labouring work on farms and in lumber-camps for eight months. Little seems to be known

[1] J. C. Squire: *The Honeysuckle and the Bee* (Heinemann, 1937).

about this period, except that while in Toronto he used to go to St. Thomas's, a church of Anglo-Catholic tendencies. He came back to England with £70 in his pocket: his physique had become first-rate; he was 6ft. 2in. and weighed about 13st. 7lb. He stayed in England only a few weeks, and early in 1907 went to Brussels, where for seven months he taught English and learned French and German. When he returned to London, he began a more systematic study of aesthetics and the history of philosophy, and in 1909 he published a number of essays on Bergson's philosophy. From this time onwards, he lived mainly on a small allowance from one of his relatives. In April 1911 he attended the Philosophical Congress at Bologna, and spent the next three months travelling in Italy. At Bologna Hulme hesitated whether to go and hear Professor Enriques's opening paper on 'Reality' or to stay and hear the bands and watch the dignified, brown-cloaked crowds that were waiting to welcome the Duke of the Abruzzi. 'I regard processions as the highest form of art. I cannot resist even the lowest form of them. I must march even with the Salvation Army bands I meet accidentally in Oxford Street on Sunday night.'

On his return to England, Hulme told his friends that there had been a free fight in the Ethical Section; whether this was true or not, the report illustrates Hulme's liking for mischief. In some notes on the Congress he explained that his own attitude to conferences was not that of an undergraduate whom he once knew. This young man thought that the nature of the ether could be settled once and for all if only Larmor, Poincaré, J. J. Thomson, Kelvin and the others could be brought together in one room and kept there for a month; and he used to worry about it so much that he could not sleep. 'That is one attitude toward congresses. The other is, I think, best explained by a conversation I had with Bergson last July. I told him I was going to Bologna. "I don't know", he said, "whether these meetings actually do any good, but sometimes when you have been puzzled by a man's philosophy, when you have been a little uncertain as to his meaning, then the actual physical presence of the man makes it all clear. And sometimes, as William James used to say, one look at a man is enough to convince you that you need trouble no further." '[1]

In October and November 1911, Hulme published a series of articles on Bergson in *The New Age*, and about this time he wrote some short poems, five of which were printed in *The New Age* (25. i. 12) under the heading, *The Complete Poetical Works of T. E. Hulme*. They were meant to convey clear visual images rather than romantic emotions, and they used cadence rather than metre. This was the kind of thing that Hulme thought young poets ought to be doing; and the poems were typical of what afterwards came to be known as Imagism.[2] There is a story that Hulme wrote them all in about three minutes, to show how easy it was; but this seems to be

[1] *The New Age*, 27. iv. 11.
[2] J. G. Fletcher has some references to Hulme's relations with the Imagists in his autobiography *My Life is My Song* (Farrar & Rinehart, 1937).

belied by his manuscripts, which show very careful corrections and improvements.

Hulme was already beginning to make the acquaintance of a number of critics and philosophers. 'On the way to Italy, I stopped two days at Dieppe with Jules de Gaultier, about whom I have already written a little in this Review.' He was particularly interested in the French syndicalists and in the neo-royalists of *L'Action Française*. 'I noticed early this year that one of the most interesting of the group, M. Pierre Lasserre, had made an attack on Bergson. I was very much in sympathy with the anti-romanticism of his two books, *La Morale de Nietzsche* and *Le Romantisme Français*, and I wondered from what point of view exactly he was attacking Bergson. I was in agreement with both sides, and so I wondered whether there was any real inconsistency in my own position. When I was in Paris, then, last April, I went to see Lasserre and talk to him about it. . . .'

Hulme's views were now taking a definite form: Bergson's doctrine of intuition, and the anti-romanticism common to the syndicalists and the neo-royalists, were combining in Hulme's mind to form a new compound: '. . . I can find a compromise for myself, however, which I roughly indicate by saying that I think time is real for the individual, but not for the race'—a statement that recalls Baudelaire's argument that there is no real progress, that is to say moral progress, except for the individual. At this time Hulme seems to have shared the anti-democratic views of syndicalists and royalists, and he rejected the arguments of those who found support for the democratic ideal in Bergson's philosophy. 'Bergson no more stands for Democracy than he stands for paper-bag cookery.' Later, in his articles on the war, Hulme tried to dissociate the democratic ideal from the romantic faith in personality and the inevitability of progress.

Early in 1912 he was readmitted to St John's, partly on the personal recommendation of J. C. Squire, and partly owing to a letter from Bergson: 'Je me fais un plaisir de certifier que je considère Mr. T. E. Hulme comme un esprit d'une grande valeur. Il apporte, à l'étude des questions philosophiques, de rares qualités de finesse, de vigueur, et de pénétration. Ou je me trompe beaucoup, ou il est destiné à produire des œuvres intéressantes et importantes dans le domaine de la philosophie en général, et plus particulièrement peut-être dans celui de la philosophie de l'art.'

Hulme had already given a course of lectures on Bergson at a private house in Kensington (November and December 1911), and at Cambridge he gave a lecture on the same subject to a society in Girton. In the same month (February 1912) he addressed the Heretics on 'Anti-romanticism and Original Sin'. He remained at Cambridge only a short time; something happened again, and down he came once more, without taking a degree. He next spent nine months in Berlin, where he attended the Berlin Aesthetic Congress and talked with Worringer. Rupert Brooke happened to be in Berlin at the same time; Hulme did not like him very much because he did not like any romantics, but the two used to meet and talk at the Café des Westens. In view of the place that religion held in Hulme's philosophy, it is worth mentioning that while in Berlin he attended the American Church. Apart from this, few of his friends ever knew him to attend a place of worship, although he always called himself a member of the Church of England.

After his return to London he lived for a time with Ashley Dukes in Mortimer Street, and with the help of some of his friends he produced a translation of Bergson's *Introduction à la Métaphysique*, and this appeared in 1913. Meanwhile he had become interested in the new geometrical art of Picasso, Wyndham Lewis, David Bomberg, William Roberts and Jacob Epstein. It seemed to him that this art was the expression of an attitude very like his own. It was anti-romantic, and had nothing to do with vitality and delight in nature. According to P. G. Konody's report of one of Hulme's lectures, Hulme maintained that this new art 'creates certain geometrical abstract shapes, rigid lines and crystalline forms, which are the refuge from the confusion and accidental detail of existence'.

Romantic art, as Hulme saw it, was an expression of faith in man's natural power of development. Classical art (presumably Hulme would have called Tura and Veneziano 'classical') expressed a sense of man's limitations and a feeling for the *tension* that is fundamental to all valuable activity. Romantic art, being divorced from this sense, was slack and disorganized: it was based on a false view of human nature, and it recklessly indulged in emotion for emotion's sake without criticizing the quality of the emotion itself. Hulme maintained that the classical view needs to be expressed through the rigidity of geometrical form, and against Roger Fry's 'pure' formalism he argued that form cannot be used properly unless its use corresponds to an underlying conviction. To imitate Egyptian sculpture without some sympathy with the attitude that demanded that kind of expression was humbug, or at best a useful exercise. Hulme therefore had no sympathy with the 'chocolate-box Cézanne' of Roger Fry's paintings or with the work of Duncan Grant, in which 'elements taken from the extremely intense and serious Byzantine art are used in an entirely meaningless and pointless way'.[1] He denounced sham archaism as he denounced the Nietzschean philosophizing of A. M. Ludovici, 'because I consider it a duty, a very pleasant duty and one very much neglected in this country, to expose charlatans when one sees them'.

In April and May 1914 a series of lectures on new developments in art and literature was given at the Kensington Town Hall, and at one of these meetings Hulme read a paper on modern poetry. 'Hulme was not a good lecturer', says one of the audience, 'and Wyndham Lewis read a paper supporting Hulme and came off pretty badly himself, mumbling in a husky voice, with his head buried in his manuscript. The audience felt as if they could snatch the papers from the poets and read them for themselves—there was so obviously something very worthwhile buried in all their

[1] *The New Age,* 25.xii. 13.

abstract mumbling. To end it all, Ezra Pound stood up,
all self-possessed, complete in velvet coat, flowing tie,
pointed beard and a halo of fiery hair. Lolling against
the stage, he became very witty and fluent, and with his
yankee voice snarled out some of his and Hulme's
poems. Somehow, such a voice rather clowned verse.'

Hulme was more impressive in his conversation and
his casual writing than in the lecture-hall, and his knowledge and critical sensibility combined with his personal
charm and his brilliance as a talker to make him a centre
of the new movements in art and criticism: 'to hear
Hulme develop general ideas and abstractions was like
studying an elaborate pattern whose inner lines and
texture emerge gradually as you gaze'.[1] There were
weekly discussions at 67 Frith Street, and among those
who went were Epstein and Gaudier-Brzeska, Ezra
Pound, J. C. Squire, Ashley Dukes, Wilfrid Gibson,
Ramiro de Maeztu (afterwards Spanish Ambassador to
Argentina), Middleton Murry, Richard Curle (the
friend and biographer of Conrad), and A. R. Orage.
Edward Wadsworth and C. R. W. Nevinson often
came to these meetings, and Rupert Brooke turned up
once or twice. Hulme's talk bubbled with imagery.
Sometimes he would lead people up the garden path,
make them agree to things, and then leave them in the
cart, simply for the fun of the thing; but he was intolerant of affectation and obscurantism, and Edward Marsh,
another of the visitors to Frith Street, tells how 'There
was a fashion at that time for nosing out unexpected

---

[1] Richard Curle: *Caravansary and Conversation* (Cape, 1937.)

22

racial strains in the pedigrees of great men, and crediting these with their qualities—Hulme was ridiculing this with his usual energy and finished up with comical gusto: "I decline to revise my opinions on the basis that Dostoievsky was an Italian".'

Hulme was at his best in monologue: 'I have seen him in the clutches of a little university professional, with Kant at his finger-tips, whom he had provoked by his dialectical truculence,' says Wyndham Lewis.[1] 'Hulme floundered like an ungainly fish, caught in a net of superior academic information.' Perhaps Wyndham Lewis is a prejudiced witness, with an eye for the picturesque, but he tells one or two likely stories against Hulme, including one in which Hulme appears in the character of the frustrated amorist in a kind of *tableau vivant*. At the only bookshop from which Hulme could get philosophical books on credit there was a girl assistant who was (or so says Wyndham Lewis) beautiful but far from frivolous. Hulme was interested both in her and in maintaining his credit; but the proprietor sat in the room above and had a hole drilled in the floor, so that whenever Hulme began to make a little headway on the first account, there would be a frantic stamping overhead and the enterprise would go back to starting point. 'This awful stability of things appalled him. No Heracletian flux. An implacable *status quo* reigned in the bookshop—dominated the world. And he would discuss this problem—sandwiched in between the doctrine of Original Sin and the Fascism of the Frenchman, Sorel, whose

[1] *Blasting and Bombardiering* (Eyre & Spottiswoode, 1937).

Réflexions sur la violence he was translating—in his nagging, nasal, North Country voice, until he induced in his listener a sensation of the cussedness of things that really was in its way a novel cocktail. He was an excellent gossip.'

Against this, we may set the story of Hulme emphasizing an argument with Lewis himself by holding him upside down on the railings in Soho Square. This was early in 1914, about the time when Gaudier-Brzeska was threatening to sock Bomberg on the jaw, and Epstein and Bomberg were engaged in a quarrel that ended with a ceremonial kiss of reconciliation in the Goupil Galleries. Hulme persuaded Gaudier-Brzeska to make him a knuckleduster, carved out of solid brass, and this he afterwards carried about with him wherever he went. He was interested in the quarrels, but more concerned to illustrate his own theories of aesthetics, even when dealing with knuckledusters, and in the course of some articles in *The New Age* he defined his own position as a critic:

'As in these articles I intend to skip about from one part of my argument to another, as occasion demands, I might perhaps give them a greater appearance of shape by laying down as a preliminary three theses that I want to maintain.

'1. There are two kinds of art, geometrical or abstract, and vital and realistic art, which differ absolutely in kind from the other. They are not modifications of one and the same art, but pursue different aims and are created to satisfy a different desire of the mind.

24

'2. Each of these arts springs from, and corresponds to, a certain general attitude towards the world. You get long periods of time in which only one of these arts and its corresponding mental attitude prevails. The naturalistic art of Greece and the Renaissance corresponded to a certain rational humanistic attitude towards the universe, and the geometrical has always gone with a different attitude of greater intensity than this.

'3. The re-emergence of geometrical art at the present day may be the precursor of the re-emergence of the corresponding general attitude towards the world, and so of the final break-up of the Renaissance.'[1]

Epstein's drawing, 'The Rock Drill', as well as his carvings in flenite, and some of the early sculpture of Gaudier-Brzeska, might be taken to show the influence of these theories. Hulme had a genius for harnessing the energies of other people: just as he cajoled or bullied his friends into doing most of the work of his translations, so he tried to persuade the sculptors to do work that would illustrate his theories, and he was annoyed when Epstein spent much of his time modelling realistic busts. Hulme's relations with Ezra Pound and Wyndham Lewis were sometimes strained, but he always liked and admired Gaudier, and his enthusiasm for Epstein was unbounded. He persuaded Orage to reproduce some of the drawings of Epstein, Gaudier, Nevinson, Roberts and Bomberg in *The New Age*, and later he wrote a book about Epstein, but this was lost in 1917.

The painters and sculptors used to have a show every

1 *The New Age*, 12. ii. 14.

week in Fitzroy Street (later it was held near the Cumberland Market) and after this they would all dine together at the old Sceptre eating-house. One of the strongest memories of those days concerns Hulme's passion for suet-pudding and treacle: 'there used to be hours of anticipation and imagination of that succulent sweet before we settled down to it at the Sceptre'. Afterwards the party would go on to the Café Royal. Hulme was still a teetotaller ('I was fervently implored on his first kiss never to drink whisky'), and did not need any artificial stimulus to make him comical and entertaining. Once he was making water in Soho Square in broad daylight when a policeman came up and said: 'You can't do that here.' Hulme turned around and buttoned himself up, saying: 'Do you know you are addressing a member of the middle classes?' The policeman said, 'I beg pardon, sir', and went on.

Hulme, although he did not value unconventionality for its own sake, had very little respect for habits that were merely conventional, and he always insisted that in England the popular notion of morality was restricted almost entirely to sexual morality, most of which was really nothing more than convention. He saw no inconsistency between his concern with moral problems and his own personal affairs. Girls found Hulme very attractive; often his Staffordshire accent (of which he was proud—he always pointed out that Dr. Johnson, the greatest of English scholars, also had one) made them take him for a German, and there was something Prussian-looking about him that confirmed this impression. Hulme was rather proud of these adventures, and perhaps he exaggerated their number and variety. At any rate, they were not characteristic of his later years. Marriage he regarded as a sacrament, and his views on the home were patriarchal. For a woman to argue with him was not only useless; he thought that it was wrong, and he would make use of Gaudier's knuckle-duster with a strength only tempered by a kind of fierce kindliness: 'Anyone, man or woman, would flounder badly on first acquaintance with Hulme.'

When the war broke out, Hulme joined the Honourable Artillery Company, and on 29th December 1914, he went to France. For a few days he was stationed at a Rest Camp, 'a fearful place, deep in mud, where we have to sleep in tents, which makes me very depressed.... I thoroughly enjoy all the events, like being seen off at the docks, except that there were only about ten people to cheer us as the ship left the side, but it's all very amusing—and the girls at the windows.' Early in January, his battalion was moved up nearer to the front: 'In the evening I went round to see some of the people I used to know in the 1st Battalion. All looked very different, their faces and clothes a sort of pale mud colour, all very tired of it and anxious to get back.'

Before the end of the month, he was in the trenches. At first their part of the line was quiet, and on January 27th Hulme wrote in his diary: 'I had to crawl along on my hands and knees through the mud in pitch darkness, and every now and then seemed to get stuck altogether. You feel shut in and hopeless. I wished I was about four

feet. This war isn't for tall men. I got in a part too narrow and too low to stand or sit and had to sit sideways
on a sack of coke to keep out of the water. We had to
stay there from about 7 p.m. till just before dawn next
morning, a most miserable experience. You can't sleep
and you sit as it were at the bottom of a drain with nothing to look at but the top of the ditch slowly freezing.
It's unutterably boring. The next night was better because I carried up a box to sit on and a sack of coke to
burn in a brazier. But one brazier in a narrow trench
among twelve men only warms about three. All through
this night we had to dig a new passage in shifts. That in a
way did look picturesque at midnight—a very clear starry
night, this mound all full of passages like a molehill and
three or four figures silhouetted on top of it using pick
or shovel. The bullets kept whistling over it all the time,
but as it's just over the crest of a hill most of them
are high, though every now and then one comes on
your level and is rather uncomfortable when you are
taking your turn at sentry. The second night it froze
hard, and it was much easier walking back over the
mud.

'In reality there is nothing picturesque about it. It's
the most miserable existence you can conceive of. I feel
utterly depressed at the idea of having to do this for
forty-eight hours every four days. It's simply hopeless.
The boredom and discomfort of it exasperate you to the
breaking point.'

Hulme found nothing romantic or attractive in the
war, and he had no liking for the technical business of

warfare; but since the job had to be done he thought it might as well be done efficiently. In his diary he speaks of inefficiency and muddle, but there is no personal complaint; and when he mentions that the tennis-player, Kenneth Powell, has been killed carrying up corrugated iron, he says: 'It seems curious the way people realize things. I heard a man say: "It does seem a waste, Kenneth Powell carrying up corrugated iron." You see, he was interested in games.'

At times Hulme wrote with the detachment of a poet or a painter, describing actual physical sensations that everybody shared. 'The only thing that makes you feel nervous is when the star shells go off and you stand out revealed quite clearly as in daylight. You have then the most wonderful feeling as if you were suddenly naked in the street and didn't like it. . . . It's really like a kind of nightmare, in which you are in the middle of an enormous saucer of mud with explosions and shots going off all round the edge, a sort of fringe of palm trees made of fireworks all round it.'

The censor complained of the length of these letters, but Hulme went on writing sketches of life behind the line and in the trenches: 'We had to spend the night in the open air as there were very few dug-outs. There was a German rifle trained on a fixed part of the trench just where we were. It's very irritating to hear a bullet time after time hit the same spot on the parapet. About lunch time this rifle continually hitting the same place, spattered dirt from the parapet over my bread and butter. It gets very irritating after a time and everybody shouts out "Oh stop it". It showed however that it was a dangerous corner. . . .'

On February 10th they came under heavy shell-fire: 'It was a dangerous trench for shelling because it was very wide and gave no protection to the back. An N.C.O. told us to shift to a narrower part of the trench. I got separated from the others in a narrow communication trench behind with one other man. We had seen shells bursting fairly near us before and at first did not take it very seriously. But it soon turned out to be very different. The shells started dropping right on the trench itself. As soon as you had seen someone hurt, you began to look at shelling in a very different way. We shared this trench with the X Regiment. About ten yards away from where I was a man of this regiment had his arm and three-quarters of his head blown off—a frightful mess, his brains all over the place, some on the back of that man who stands behind me in the photograph. The worst of shelling is, the regulars say, that you don't get used to it, but get more and more alarmed at it every time. At any rate, the regulars in our trenches behaved in rather a strange way. One man threw himself down on the bottom of the trench shaking all over and crying. Another started to weep. It lasted for nearly one and a half hours and at the end of it parts of the trenches were all blown to pieces. It's not the idea of being killed that's alarming, but the idea of being hit by a jagged piece of steel. You hear the whistle of the shell coming, you crouch down as low as you can, and just wait. It doesn't burst merely with a bang, it has a kind of crack with a snap in it, like the crack of a very large whip. They seemed to burst just over your head, you seem to anticipate it hitting you in the back, it hits just near you and you get hit on the back with clods of earth and (in my case) spent bits of shell and shrapnel bullets fall all round you. I picked up one bullet almost sizzling in the mud just by my toe. What irritates you is the continuation of the shelling. You seem to feel that twenty minutes is normal, is enough—but when it goes on for over an hour, you get more and more exasperated, feel as if it were "unfair". Our men were as it happened very lucky, only three were hurt slightly and none killed. They all said it was the worst experience they have had since they were out here. I'm not in the least anxious myself to repeat it, nor is anyone else I think. It was very curious from where I was; looking out over the back of the trench, it looked absolutely peaceful. Just over the edge of the trench was a field of turnips or something of that kind with their leaves waving about in a busy kind of way, exactly as they might do in a back garden. About twelve miles away over the plain you could see the towers and church spires of an old town very famous in this war. By a kind of accident or trick, everything was rather gloomy, except this town which appeared absolutely white in the sun and immobile as if it would always be like that, and was out of time and space altogether. You've got to amuse yourself in the intervals of shelling and romanticizing the situation is as good a way as any other. Looking at the scene, the waving vegetables, the white town and all the rest of it, it looks quite timeless in a Buddhistic kind of way and you feel quite resigned if you are going to be killed to leave it just like that. When it ceased and we all got back to our places everybody was full of it.'

Early in March, Hulme was wounded, and sent home; and two months later Gaudier-Brzeska was killed at Neuville Saint-Vaast. Hulme had been one of Gaudier's nearest friends: he was the first to hear of his death, and it was he who sent Mrs. Bevan to break the news to Sophia Brzeska.[1] After Hulme had recovered from his wound, he was 'lost' by the War Office for some months, and walked about London telling his friends that he didn't see why he should go back till they asked him. Meanwhile, however, he was trying to get a commission in the Royal Marine Artillery. He did not want a commission in the infantry, that would have been 'too much the same thing', nor did he want to go on serving in the ranks. 'It would be extremely depressing to me to start again as a private at this stage of the war. It was very

[1] Horace Brodzky: *Henri Gaudier-Brzeska* (Faber & Faber 1933). There is a reference to this period in Ezra Pound's *Canto* XVI:

And Henri Gaudier went to it,
    and they killed him,
And killed a good deal of sculpture,
And ole T.E.H. he went to it,
With a lot of books from the library,
London Library, and a shell buried 'em in a dug-out,
And the Library expressed its annoyance.
    And a bullet hit him on the elbow
. . . gone through the fellow in front of him,
And he read Kant in Hospital, in Wimbledon,
in the original,
And the hospital staff didn't like it.

different in the first months of the war, when one was excited about the thing. Besides, even impersonally, I do think I am suited to have a commission of this kind. Mathematics was always my subject and I should pick up the theoretical part, the calculations, etc., of which there is quite a lot in connection with the very big guns of the R.M.A., more easily than most people, and should enjoy the work. I am also about the build for heavy gun work. . . .'

In a series of War Notes published in *The New Age* (November 1915 to March 1916) and *The Cambridge Magazine* (January to March 1916) over the signature 'North Staffs', Hulme put forward a temperate and reasoned defence of the war based not on any liking for the excitement of war, and not on any belief that the war would achieve any great positive good, but on his conception of 'the heroic values' and his dislike of the prospect of German domination in Europe. In the course of these articles, he engaged in a controversy with Bertrand Russell and other pacifists, and tried to show that their arguments rested on a romantic conception of progress and an over-valuation of 'life' as against the absolute ethical values that make life worth while.

The commission came in March 1916, and Hulme spent the next six months in barracks at Portsmouth, going up to London frequently to sit to Epstein for the bronze head now in the possession of Ashley Dukes. About this time, he published his translation of Sorel's *Réflexions sur la violence* together with an introduction that he had already printed in *The New Age* (14. x. 15).

In 1924 Herbert Read reprinted this essay together with the lectures on Bergson and a number of essays on humanism, romanticism and the philosophy of modern art, in the volume called *Speculations*. Since that collection was published more of Hulme's papers have come to light, and some of them are reprinted in the appendix to the present book.

It would be ridiculous to judge Hulme's work mainly in the light of his passion for processions, knuckledusters and suet pudding. It is always interesting to trace the relation between a man's conduct and his ideas, but if the ideas have any value at all, they must be judged on their own merits. To some of his friends, it seemed that Hulme was a genius, but without the faith that makes geniuses think it worth while to express themselves and justify themselves. To others, it seemed that all his public truculence and exhibition of ingenuity for ingenuity's sake was nothing more than youthful exuberance. They believed that there was another side to Hulme, a side that seldom appeared in argument but found expression sometimes in his writing and sometimes when he was talking to one or two friends in Mrs. Bevan's house at Hampstead or in his old room above Harold Monro's Poetry Bookshop. 'He had a very powerful brow and nose, and then a mouth kind and small compared to the other features, and a chin that did not reinforce the brow and nose. His eyes had a quick, almost projecting, glance, and the lids could become heavy and the eyes veiled in contemplation, giving him quite a different expression.'

Hulme believed that the work he was doing was important, but he knew that he had added very little to the ideas he had borrowed, and that his real work remained to be done. Some verses written by his friend Francis Tancred show that he could carry off his attitude without priggishness:

UPON A GENTLEMAN ENGAGED IN THE SERVICE OF ATHENE

With tousled head
And mien distraught—
As from an over-plus of thought
Discomforted—
Here sits and sits
Stout Yeoman Hulme,
And sternly pits
His staunch Phoebean wits
To radiate the Stygian gloom
That rests to-day
On all the nincompoops who play
At poising of the philosophic plume.

Here,
Fortress'd round
From roof to ground
With tier on tier
Of magic and mysterious gear,[1]
He doth compound
Those dynamite-cum-shrapnel shells,

[1] These are my boxes of grenades and apparatus for sorting notes.— T.E.H.

BIOGRAPHICAL SKETCH

With which—
Discharged six times in weekly spells—
He hopes to very shortly clear
The philosophic atmosphere.

From dawn to dusk,
Brandishing a blade of elephant tusk,
With corrugated brows he broods
At marshalling a vast array
Of foolscap sheets in some new way
To please his million moods:
First will he deal a hand, and then
Shuffle and deal round again;
This process now he will repeat
Until the thousandth turn's complete;
Then, pausing, some slips, for their sins,
He'll savagely transpierce with pins,
Whereafter with his pen, perhaps,
He'll draw crude chess-boards in the gaps.
This labour done he'll seek relief
In sundry sandwiches of beef
Which he'll discover nestling 'mid
More foolscap slips, or deftly hid
Between the boards of some machine
Now serving as a sandwich screen.
For e'en philosophers have need
Their fevered cerebrums to feed:
Yet would it be indecent should
They gulp a meal of vulgar food
At table, like plebeian folk;

In fact they probably would choke.
But sandwiches, discovered thus,
As by some charm miraculous,
No way deserve the sophist's scorn,
But savour of manna, heaven born.

Thus then, we see
Heroic Hulme
Assiduously
Striving to dissipate the gloom
Wherein the mind of man is wrapped,
What time his friend in verses apt
Now celebrates some Duchess, now
Relates in studied stanzas how
The Empire's whole affairs are run
From dawn until the set of sun.
Or leaving London at command
Of sister-folk who hold whip-hand,
Forsakes the old Parnassian clubs
For Buxton's Hydropathic tubs.

Hulme's outlook as expressed in his notes was incomplete and perhaps not wholly self-consistent, and the papers that he left behind ranged from 'a collection of hundreds of loose notes, varying in size from pieces of paper no bigger than a postage-stamp to complete folios of notes on one subject'. A 'Notebook on Notebooks' gave some clue to the use to which he intended to put these notes, but the work was never completed. He went back to the front towards the end of 1916, taking the book on Epstein with him, and still full of the work that he was going to do. The batteries of the Royal Marine Artillery were situated at Oost-Duinkerke Bains, on the coast behind Nieuport, and they confined themselves to shelling German long-range batteries near Ostend, mostly at regular and conventional hours. Ashley Dukes, who was with the First Division when it came into that part of the line in June 1917, says that Hulme viewed this entry with great disfavour because the coastal sector had been quiet under the French, and Hulme preferred a quiet war. 'He had never in fact walked up as far as Nieuport, a mile in front of his guns, because he objected to coming under rifle fire. He explained the barbarous character of close-range warfare and one evening when we were walking together up the road because I had to go into the line, he turned back at a ruined dairy and said that was the utmost limit of his constitutional.'

Perhaps this was nothing more than the usual pose of the artilleryman, but those who met Hulme when he came home on leave say that his outlook was greatly changed: 'I remember Hulme remarking that the war had made him more tolerant, and that he was growing more and more democratic. I thought it wiser to ask no question on this remark as the knuckleduster was near at hand.' Certainly Hulme was as disputatious as ever. 'What a man!' said an officer who met him while he was serving with his battery. 'He'd argue a dog's hind leg off.' On September 28th, just when everybody seemed to have knocked off for lunch, there was an unexpected burst of shell-fire, and Hulme was killed.

Chapter Two

HUMANISM AND THE PERFECTIBILITY OF MAN

'Put shortly, these are the two views, then. One, that man is intrinsically good, spoilt by circumstance; and the other that he is intrinsically limited, but disciplined by order and tradition to something fairly decent.'—T. E. HULME, *Speculations*, p. 117.

It is a plain fact that man has made no appreciable moral progress in historical times. People are still as selfish, intolerant and insensitive as they were two thousand years ago: their manners may be less violent and their cruelty less obvious, but there has been very little sign of any real increase in the moral effort of the individual. He is still torn between impulses towards good and towards evil; he is still pushed one way or the other by his own needs, and those of his near friends, and by the opinions of people round about. No doubt there have been changes in physique and mental power, but those changes are no guarantee of moral progress; and often our apparent progress in manners is due to a change in the way we make or buy the things we need. Piracy has died out not because people are better, but because nations that are skilful in the use of machinery have come to depend on overseas trade for their livelihood, and therefore refuse to let anyone interfere with it. Any new attempt at piracy would be repressed by all the forces at their command, and if those forces were not strong enough to stop it, it would return. Meanwhile, the wickedness that once went into piracy now finds an outlet in antisocial action on the exchanges.

These tendencies may sometimes be driven underground by custom and tradition, but they are not destroyed: a civilized state is always precarious and needs to be maintained by constant effort. All that we can safely say is that the real progress in invention has made short-sighted selfishness far more dangerous to the world in general than it was three centuries ago, and that some kinds of selfishness are therefore more strongly repressed. A higher standard of truthfulness, honesty and kindliness to strangers may have become so ingrained that it would not easily be lost; but it is not a permanent gain: it does not correspond to a change in the hereditary physical structure. In the same way, the improved standard of knowledge is due not to any increase in mental skill, but partly to inventions, such as writing and printing, which have made knowledge more readily available, and partly to changing methods of production, which have made knowledge more necessary. That the brain of modern man is better than the brain of Neanderthal man is evident: but there is no evidence either for or against the belief that the brain is still evolving by imperceptible steps; and there is certainly no reason to suppose that a higher standard of education for everybody would lead to any very general increase in kindness, sensibility and intelligence.

The view that humanity is naturally sliding uphill, and needs only a little education to accelerate the process, is dangerous and misleading. Some actions are good in themselves, and some produce good results; but these actions do not automatically increase with the mere passage of time. There is no progress except through the conscious effort of individuals; and however deeply and earnestly people may look into themselves, they do not always agree on the actions that are good and progressive and those that are bad and reactionary. Nevertheless, the belief that humanity, in spite of occasional setbacks, is moving towards a goal, the attainment of which will justify all past and present suffering, is so widespread and so deeply rooted that any attempt to question it is dismissed as reactionary and pessimistic. The critic is regarded either as an enemy of all moral and material improvement, or else as a cynic disparaging all that is fine and noble in humanity. People who oppose those ideals for selfish reasons are likely to make the same mistake; and the critic will often find himself surrounded by embarrassing allies who have mistaken the nature of his criticism and the ultimate aim of his work as completely as the indignant idealists. When Hulme, for example, questioned the inevitability of progress, he was not trying to oppose desirable changes: he was simply trying to discover the truth. But it is always dangerous to question a deeply rooted idea: people do not see it as an assumption at all; they see it as an obvious truth, and they cannot help regarding the critic as an enemy of their *ideals*. The notion that he is sincerely and thoughtfully denying the accuracy of their *ideas* is totally incomprehensible to them.

Hulme was not an enemy of social or intellectual progress. He was not a diehard fighting to maintain Capitalism or Imperialism, nor was he trying to absolve the well-to-do from their responsibilities in the face of poverty and misery. He was pointing out that the modern idea that man is perfectible and that progress is inevitable is based on confused thinking, and is therefore unlikely to produce the results to which it seems to point. Ideals are not likely to be effective if they are formulated in a framework of mistaken ideas; and the greatest obstacle to any real advance is the self-righteous indignation of the muddle-headed idealist whose ideas are called in question. Hulme does not assert that there never has been any progress in the biological sense: the notions of 'progress', 'evolution', and 'adaptation' are quite definite scientific concepts in their proper field; and Hulme protests only against their unjustified use in quite different fields, those of morality and political history. It is not enough, he claims, to drift with the stream, nor even to strike out in the direction in which the stream appears to be moving. To do that would be to substitute one god for another, to trust in the guiding hand of a kind of providence called Progress, and to sacrifice the power and right of moral judgment.

All Hulme's criticism is based on the belief that man is fundamentally and inherently imperfect: that he can apprehend perfection, but can never attain it. Man's apprehension of perfection gives him a right and necessary aim in life; but the aim is unattainable, and must be recognized as unattainable, both for the individual and the race. This is expressed in theology by means of the distinction between things that are human and things that are divine. Perfection belongs to the region of the divine. All human progress and virtue are relative: they are improvements on previous human conditions, but they bring us no nearer to perfection. Hulme calls this outlook religious, and the opposite outlook he calls humanist.

To the humanist, it seems that all knowledge is of one kind, and that the notion of perfection must be placed on the human plane; a long way off, perhaps, but still ultimately attainable, either by the individual or by the race. The very mention of the word 'religious' is likely to make the humanist feel uneasy: he begins to suspect charlatanry and hocus-pocus; for he has accommodated everything knowable on his single plane, and to speak of any other plane seems to be a piece of useless mystification. Hulme realizes that to people who think themselves emancipated the word 'religious' will at once suggest something exotic or mystical or sentimental. He therefore explains that he has none of the reverence for tradition, the desire to recapture the sentiment of Fra Angelico, that seems to animate some of the defenders of religion. 'All that seems to me to be bosh.'

When Hulme talks of religion, he is not arguing that spiritual truth requires a world of discourse of its own:

he is talking about facts of ordinary life, and there is
nothing mysterious in his approach to the notion of
absolute values. His distinction between human things
and divine seems to resemble the mathematical distinction between rational and irrational numbers: the
irrationals can be defined as the limits of series of ra-
tionals, but they are not themselves rational. In the same
way, the things of the divine world can only be apprehended through things human; but they are not themselves human. The important point is that man is essentially limited and that perfection is a concept not to be
placed on the human plane. Hulme identifies this belief
with the dogma of Original Sin, which he accepts as an
abstract statement of a possible and reasonable outlook.
'It is not, then, that I put up with the dogma for the
sake of the sentiment, but that I may possibly swallow
the sentiment for the sake of the dogma.'[1] He says that
the notions of God, Freedom, and Immortality are quite
secondary matters in comparison with this dogma, and
on it he bases his whole distinction between what he
calls the religious and the humanist attitudes.

In the religious view, the values of religion and ethics
are not personal, nor are they relative to ordinary human
desires and feelings; they are absolute and objective; and
in the light of these absolute values man himself is judged
to be essentially limited and imperfect. He can occasionally accomplish acts which partake of perfection, but he
can never himself *be* perfect: he is endowed with Original
Sin, and only by moral and political discipline can he

[1] *Speculations*, p. 71.

accomplish anything of value. Thus order is not merely
negative, but creative and liberating: institutions are
necessary.

In the humanist view, everything is justified by its
results, and the results are justified by *their* results, and
so on. The ultimate justification is either future happiness
or human survival. This is totally opposed to the outlook that Hulme sometimes calls religious, and sometimes classical. In that view, there are absolute goods,
which are not justified by anything that they may lead
to, but are simply good in themselves. Restraint, courage, self-sacrifice, truthfulness are qualities of this kind.
If people have no sense of the reality of these absolute
values, they have no standard by which they can perceive the radical imperfection of either man or nature,
and they begin to think that life is the source and measure of all values, and that man is fundamentally good.[1]
They begin to talk about 'natural justice' and 'natural
rights', and they begin to look upon all forms of truth as
relative. They blame kings and priests and institutions
for man's obvious short-comings, and in their politics
they emphasize rights rather than obligations. They
begin to look on qualities like truthfulness and courage
as means to an end; yet they are indignant when other
people abandon them, for they believe them to be innate.

Hulme claims that the religious attitude was characteristic of the Middle Ages from Augustine to the Renaissance, and that the humanist attitude has been widely

[1] *Speculations*, pp. 47, 116.

held from the Renaissance to the present day. 'The ideology of the first period is religious; of the second, humanist. The difference between them is fundamentally nothing but the difference between these two conceptions of man.'[1] It is not merely that the first period accepted beliefs such as the dogma of original sin, whereas the second did not. 'It is necessary to realise that *these beliefs were the centre of their whole civilisation, and that even the character of their economic life was regulated by them.*'[2] Hulme does not explain why those beliefs were abandoned, and he is inclined to ignore the influence of material conditions on the popularity of ideas; but he goes on to quote the opinion of the sociologist Max Weber, who saw in the spontaneous change in religious experience (at the Renaissance), and the corresponding new ethical ideals by which life was regulated, one of the strongest roots of the capitalist spirit.[3]

In the Renaissance, a new attitude to life appeared: an attitude of acceptance rather than renunciation, a new interest in 'man the measure of the universe', and a new emphasis on personality. No sooner had Copernicus shown that man was not the centre of the universe than philosophers like Pico della Mirandola began to assume that he was. The justification of man's existence was placed in this world—at a great distance in time perhaps, but not altogether outside of time. In these writers the idea of the sufficiency of the natural man appeared

[1] *Speculations*, p. 50.
[2] *Speculations*, p. 51.
[3] Max Weber (1864–1920): *The Protestant Ethic and the Spirit of Capitalism.* English translation by T. Parsons. (1930.)

for the first time, and this idea has been assumed by nearly all philosophers since. It may be expressed in very different languages and with very different degrees of profundity, but Hulme says that even Hegel and Condorcet are one, from this point of view. Humanism thus contains the germs of the disease that came to its full development in the romantic deification of Progress and the Natural Man.[1]

The changed conception of man appears in science, philosophy, and literature: 'In Machiavelli you get the conception of human nature as a natural power, as living energy. Mankind is not by nature bad, but subject to passions. The absolute standards in comparison with which man was sinful disappear, and life itself is *accepted* as the measure of all values. You get Lorenzo Valla (1407), in his *De Voluptate*, daring to assert for the first time that pleasure was the highest good. A secondary consequence of this acceptance of life is the development of the conception of personality. . . . So with the establishment of the new conception of man as good, with the conception of personality comes an increased interest in the actual characteristics of man. This is at first manifested indirectly in literature. You get autobiographies for the first time —those of Cellini and Cardan, for example. It leads later, however, to more direct study of man's emotions and character, of what we should call psychology. You get

---

1 Introduction to *Reflections on Violence*. (*Speculations*, p. 257n.). The point had already been made by Lasserre, who went further: 'Ces déités du romantisme s'appelèrent, l'une Nature, l'autre Progrès. Le Panthéisme en fut la synthèse.' *Le Romantisme français*, p. 537.

works like Vives, *De Anima*, and Telesio, *De Rerum
Natura.*'[1]

Hulme recognizes, of course, that no period is ever
completely coherent. There are always some people
whose outlook is opposed to that which is characteristic
of their own age. At the beginning of the Christian
period, for example, many of the Fathers retained the
Greek conception of man; and at the time of St. Augustine there was Pelagius, who in many ways resembled
Rousseau. Hobbes, whilst working out some of the
consequences of humanism, retained something of the
older outlook, and Pascal was another of these isolated
men whose attitude and range of ideas are opposed to
those of their own time. But in spite of these exceptions,
every age has its characteristic axioms, and these axioms
underlie nearly all its apparently diverse philosophies.

People under the influence of any particular outlook
always want to fix it, to make it seem to depend not on
assumptions, but on facts; and just as a barrister might
frame a leading question they consciously or unconsciously disguise their assumptions by building up a metaphysic based on conceptions that already take the assumptions for granted. The first attempts are always untidy
and unsystematic: thus the change of outlook at the
Renaissance produced a crop of unsystematic philosophers, who tried to find conceptual clothing for the
new interpretation of life. Bruno, Telesio, Montaigne,
and Francis Bacon were philosophers of this kind, and
the eager interest that was shown by the readers of their

[1] *Speculations*, pp. 59–60.

48

books, and by the men whom Bruno talked to on his travels, showed how widespread was the wish to see the new attitude erected into a system.

The new outlook emphasized material science, human personality, and the relativity of knowledge. Descartes, Hobbes, Berkeley, Hume and Hegel systematized and codified this outlook, and worked out its consequences in ethics and politics; sometimes with emphasis on one point, sometimes on another, but always keeping within the limits of the new outlook, and combining it with more and more of what was properly and strictly scientific philosophy. It thus follows that nearly all modern philosophies are amalgams of 'scientific philosophy' and humanism. By the nineteenth century people had become so used to this state of affairs that they did not notice the humanist assumptions at all, but looked on the humanist outlook as an inevitable way of thinking, and allowed it to colour all their art and politics, and even their religion.

Hulme noticed signs of the break-up of this period, both in art and in philosophy, and particularly in the work of Moore[1] and Husserl.[2] From Husserl, Hulme takes the distinction between scientific philosophy and *Weltanschauung*.[3] Philosophy in general, although it has an air of impersonality and precision, is not

[1] G. E. Moore (b. 1873): *Principia Ethica* (1903.)
[2] Edmund Husserl (b. 1859): *Logische Untersuchungen* (1900), *Ideen zu einer reinen Phänomenologie* (1913).
[3] The same distinction is made by Wilhelm Dilthey (1833–1911) in his *Weltanschauung und Analyse des Menschen seit Renaissance und Reformation* (Ges. Schr. Bd. II), and in his *Weltanschauungslehre* (Ges. Schr. Bd. VIII).

a science, or it would have the same steady growth as the sciences. Some philosophers try to escape from this difficulty by admitting it, and saying that philosophy is only the expression of an attitude to the world; but it is more correct, says Hulme, to regard it as a mixed subject: it is partly a critique of concepts, an impersonal study of the relations between certain abstract categories; and partly a *Weltanschauung*, a personal outlook on life.

Most philosophies are personal attitudes disguised in the armour and accoutrements of the critique of concepts: 'Something quite human but with inhumanly sharpened weapons.' The philosopher, having shown that the world is not what it seems to be, produces a picture of the world as he thinks it really is. In doing this he is influenced, more or less unconsciously, by his preference for one kind of picture, usually one that seems to offer a satisfying destiny to man.

This combination or compromise, says Hulme, must be rejected. The personal and unscientific element in philosophy should be subjected to a critique of satisfaction, and this critique of satisfaction should be clearly separated from the critique of concepts that forms the scientific part of philosophy. As philosophers like Bertrand Russell have pointed out, wisdom, which is the expression of an outlook, is not science; and a purely scientific philosophy has nothing to do with the expression of a particular attitude or faith. But whereas these philosophers want the personal attitude eliminated from philosophy because they think that it has often injured the scientific part of the subject, Hulme wants it separated because it forms part of a distinct subject, and it is with this subject that he is concerned. He approves of the description of purely scientific philosophy that is given by Russell and Husserl, but he is thoroughly dissatisfied with the way in which they propose to judge the 'wisdom' or 'faith' that is embodied in a *Weltanschauung*.

Husserl, for example, makes this distinction between the two parts of philosophy, but he brings the two together again by asserting that the *Weltanschauung* is an imperfect anticipation of the scientific part of philosophy; and he assumes that the humanist outlook is the only possible *Weltanschauung*: 'A *Weltanschauung* should be the highest possible exaltation of the life and culture of the period. The word "Wisdom" taken in its widest sense comes to mean the most perfect possible development of the idea of Humanity. Personality is to be developed to the greatest intensity in a many-sided activity—the result will be a *philosopher* in the original sense of the word. ... While science is impersonal ... a *Weltanschauung* can only spring from the highest possible development of personality.'

Hulme dislikes this statement because it lays all the emphasis on harmonious personality without giving any standard by which we can decide whether a personality is harmonious or highly developed. The possibility of an outlook in which there would be absolute truth and absolute moral standards quite apart from expediency or the development of personality is not even considered. Hulme believes that such underlying assumptions should be examined in the light of what he calls a critique of satisfaction. 'When you have recovered from the precision and refinement of the *method* in such philosophers, you will be able to recognise the frequent vulgarity of their *conclusions*. It is possible to combine extreme subtlety in the one, with exceeding commonplaceness in the other.'[1] It is in his last chapter, or in his popular handbook, that the philosopher is revealed. There he lays aside all his technical skill and perspicacity, and shows the quality of his mind and perceptions. It is with this quality that the critique of satisfaction is concerned.

The humanists, however, do not recognize the existence of such a critique: they unconsciously take as the only possible kind of satisfaction the consolation that they get from humanist idealism and its glorified view of man. In the same way, the scientific materialists of the last century refused to recognize metaphysical knowledge because they themselves were unconsciously under the influence of a metaphysic that took physical science as the only possible type of real knowledge.

The critique of satisfaction is concerned with values, and its subject matter is found in the sphere of religion, for the characteristic axiom of religion is the conservation of values. The weakness of all humanistic philosophy is that it fails in this conservation: it talks of vitality and the fulfilment of personality, and yet it ends by destroying vitality and making the fulfilment seem pointless. This is the inevitable result of trying to represent the whole of

1 *Speculations*, p. 20.

human experience on a single plane and setting the justification of all suffering and effort at some point in that
plane. Any serious discussion must start by admitting
the vanity of desire in this sense, as it is admitted in
Ecclesiastes, or as Pascal admits it in the section of his
Pensées that is concerned with the misery of man without God:

'The struggle alone pleases us, not the victory. . . .
We never seek things for themselves, but for the search.
. . . Hence it comes that play and the society of women,
war, and high posts, are so sought after. Not that there
is in fact any happiness in them, or that men imagine
true bliss to consist in money won at play, or in the hare
which they hunt; we would not take these as a gift. . . .
And those who philosophise on the matter, and who
think men unreasonable for spending a whole day in
chasing a hare which they would not have bought,
scarce know our nature. The hare in itself would not
screen us from the sight of death and calamities; but the
chase which turns away our attention from these, does
screen us. . . . And thus, when we take the exception
against them, that what they seek with such fervour cannot satisfy them, if they replied—as they should do if
they considered the matter thoroughly—that they sought
in it only a violent and impetuous occupation which
turned their thoughts from self, and that they therefore
chose an attractive object to charm and ardently attract
them, they would leave their opponents without a reply.'[1]
But this is not the end of the matter; for as long as men

[1] Pascal: *Pensées* (Everyman edition), Fragments 135 and 139.

have the humanist habit of mind and look to the ends to justify all activities, even this reply, once it is given, will ultimately make the activity seem pointless. There is a difference between Buddhism and Christianity at this point: the Buddhist like the Christian recognizes the vanity of desire, but the Christian recognizes also an absolute obligation laid on man, and this recognition restores value and meaning to activities that are empty and worthless judged solely as means to the fulfilment of natural desire.

There is nothing specially mysterious in this absolute obligation; it is a fact that we know through experience like any other: but it is not the kind of fact with which we deal in material science, nor is it recognized as an ultimate verity in the humanist philosophy of life. To express this, Pascal says that there are three regions of reality. In Hulme's discussion, these are called the regions of mechanical science, of life, and of religion. In the first and third of these regions, absolute knowledge is possible, but in the second region things can only be known relatively and under conditions.

This distinction is repugnant to the modern mind, because we have got into the habit, since the Renaissance, of thinking in terms of continuity: things merge into one another, and even into their opposites, by imperceptible gradations. At times this way of looking at things may be useful; but if we are concerned with the conservation of values, we must recognize that certain regions of reality differ not relatively but absolutely. There is a gap between the region of organic things and human things, and the region of the absolute values of ethics and religion. If we introduce into human things the concept of perfection that properly belongs only to the divine, we destroy the absolute obligation that is the only ultimate motive or driving force.

The third region is real and necessary; it cannot be described in terms of the other two. God is not the ultimate manifestation of 'life' and 'progress', although it is the concept of God that gives force and value to these concepts. Similarly the *divine* is not life at its intensest, although it gives intensity to life. Religion and religious art do not spring from a delight in life, but from a feeling for certain absolute values. If we try to interpret the middle zone (where knowledge is essentially relative) in terms of mathematical physics we arrive at the mechanistic view of the world; and if we try to explain the *absolute* of religious and ethical values in the terms appropriate to the middle zone we arrive at romanticism in literature, relativism in ethics, idealism in philosophy, modernism in religion and utopianism in politics. All these, according to Hulme, are demonstrably wrong: they rest on a mistaken reading of the facts, and they end by stultifying the purposes they are meant to serve.

To escape from the humanist attitude is not easy, for humanist ideas are not ideas that we have deliberately chosen to believe; they are embedded in our thought and speech, and they are rooted in our habitual metaphors. If we are conscious of them at all, we think of them as indubitable facts, or as necessities of thought; but more often we do not see them at all, but see other things through them. People are inclined to look on the past as an age that had to do without an important piece of knowledge, rather than an age that saw things in a different way. The emergence of the humanist conception of man and progress is regarded, so Hulme says, like the gradual development of the conception of gravitation, that is, as the gradual emergence of something that once established would always remain.

To examine ingrained ideas, we must first of all become conscious of them as a particular way of interpreting the world, and not as the only possible way. If we see how the ideas arose, we are less likely to accept them uncritically. 'Humanity ought therefore to carry with it a library of a thousand years as a balancing pole.' We need to appreciate Egyptian and Negro art before we can see that all European art since the Renaissance is one particular kind of art, with minor variations; and we cannot escape from the assumptions that underlie all the different philosophies of the last three hundred years, and recognize that they *are* assumptions, unless we study the older philosophies resting on a different basis.

By studying the history of the ideas of progress, human perfectibility, and the relativity of knowledge, it may be possible to persuade the humanist that his own attitude is not the inevitable attitude of the instructed and emancipated man. 'We may not be able to convince him that the religious attitude is the right one, but we can at least destroy the *naïveté* of his canons of *satisfaction*.'

Chapter Three

A NEW CLASSICISM?

'I do think that there is a certain general state of mind which has lasted from the Renaissance till now, with what is, in reality, very little variation. It is impossible to characterise it here, but it is perhaps enough to say that, taking at first the form of the "humanities", it has in its degeneracy taken the form of a belief in "Progress" and the rest of it. It was in its way a fairly consistent system, but is probably at the present moment breaking up. In this state of break-up, I think that it is quite natural for individuals here and there to hold a philosophy and to be moved by emotions which would have been unnatural in the period itself. To illustrate big things by small ones I feel, myself, a repugnance towards the *Weltanschauung* (as distinct from the technical part) of all philosophy since the Renaissance. In comparison with what I can vaguely call the religious attitude, it seems to me to be trivial. I am moved by Byzantine mosaic, not because it is quaint or exotic, but because it expresses an attitude I agree with. But the fate of the people who hold these views is to be found incomprehensible by the "progressives" and to be labelled reactionary; that is, while we arrive at such a *Weltanschauung* quite naturally, we are thought to be imitating the past.'—T. E. HULME, *The New Age*, 25. xii. 13.

The attention, as Dr. Johnson says, naturally retires from a new tale of Venus, Diana, and Minerva. Nothing is more boring than plaster casts of antiquity offered as new creations, and in so far as the modern spirit differs from that of Greece, it is impossible to produce new versions of old stories that will have the same profound significance as the old. Hulme maintains that art always expresses a view of the world; and when he pleads for a new classical art, he is not asking for imitations of an art of the past, but for one that will express the religious view of the world, and not the romantic or humanist view. His own interpretation of the history of art is based largely on the work of Wilhelm Worringer,[1] and he deserves the credit of being the first English critic to recognize the importance of Worringer's correlation of particular types of art with particular outlooks. But Hulme's essays on art contain something more than this: he not only prefers one particular kind of art to any other, he also prophesies that it will gradually replace the kind that is now most widely accepted; and he describes the kind of outlook in religion, philosophy, and politics that will find expression in the new 'classical' art.

Worringer uses the word 'classical' to describe Greek and Graeco-Roman art, but Hulme uses it to describe art that expresses a belief in objective ethical values. Classical man, in Hulme's sense, does not regard these values as a mere rationalization of his own instinctive wishes: he insists that there is an absolute separation between the world of religion and the world that we know through the senses; he does not regard himself as the centre and justification of the world-process. He sees

[1] Wilhelm Worringer: *Abstraktion und Einfühlung* (1907), *Formprobleme der Gotik* (1912) (English translation edited by Herbert Read: *Form in Gothic* (1927)).

himself as a limited, imperfect creature; and his art does not express delight in natural forms, but tries to express his own sense of limitation and imperfection by reducing these forms to hard, geometric lines and surfaces.

This bears some resemblance to Worringer's description of primitive man, but still more to his description of oriental man, whose art 'exhibits an absolute redemptive character' and has a 'sharply outlined, transcendentally abstract complexion' that divides it from all that Worringer calls classical. This oriental art 'expresses no joyful affirmation of sensuous vitality, but belongs rather entirely to the other domain, which through all the transitoriness and chances of life strives for a higher world, freed from all illusions of the senses, from all false impressions, a domain in which inevitableness and permanency reign and to which the great serenity of Oriental instinctive knowledge gives its consecration.'[1]

Hulme is compelled to take Egyptian, Indian, and Byzantine art to illustrate his conception of classicism; he regards Greek architecture and sculpture as humanist, not classical; and his description of the humanist is exactly parallel to Worringer's account of classical man:

'For him, the world is no longer something strange, inaccessible, and mystically great, but a living completion of his own Ego, and he sees in it, as Goethe says, the responsive counterparts of his own sensations. . . . The divine is stripped of its otherworldliness; it is made worldly, is absorbed into mundane actuality. For Classical man, the divine no longer exists as an exterior world,

[1] *Form in Gothic,* p. 37.

it is no longer a transcendental idea but exists for him in the world, is embodied in the world. . . . Religion gains in beauty what it loses in sovereign importance and power. Being supplanted by science, it becomes more a luxury of the spiritual life and of no immediate necessity. . . . At this Classical stage of human development, creative art consists in the ideal demonstration of conscious and chastened vitality; it becomes an objectified sense of one's enjoyment.'[1]

Worringer applies this description primarily to Greece, but Hulme is more interested in its application to the Renaissance. He admits that he is attracted by the spirit of free enquiry and the delight in discovery that he finds in Telesio, Bruno, Campanella, and their predecessor, Nicholas of Cusa, and he feels a strong sympathy for the art of Donatello, Michelangelo and Marlowe; but he maintains that their humanism contains the seeds of errors that culminated in Rousseau and the romanticism of the nineteenth century.

Rousseau, in his *Discours sur le Rétablissement des Sciences et des Arts*, was pleading for the natural man, and Hulme says that in Rousseau the last vestiges of religious truth that remained in humanism have been driven out by the romantic doctrine that treats man as the measure of the universe, naturally good and capable of perfection. Lamartine, Hugo, Coleridge, Byron and Shelley are romantics in this sense, and on the classical side Hulme puts Horace, most of the Elizabethans and the English Augustans, as well as Racine; and Shakespeare, whom he

[1] *Form in Gothic*, pp. 27–31.

calls a dynamic classic. The classical attitude is taken to be the opposite of the romantic: it recognizes that man is limited and sinful, that he cannot make any appreciable moral progress, and that although it is always his duty to work for justice and equality he can never build a utopia; nor can he ever tell what is just unless his morality is founded on religion.

This classical view Hulme believes to be 'absolutely identical with the normal religious attitude'; and for Hulme this attitude is not merely a possible one, it is the only right one. 'I regard the difference between the two attitudes as simply the difference between true and false.' He is not arguing that the religious attitude may be relatively as true as the humanist, he is not content merely to say that it is a tenable attitude, perfectly possible to-day. He holds 'quite coldly and intellectually as it were, that the way of thinking about the world and man, the conception of sin, and the categories which ultimately make up the religious attitude, are the *true* categories and the *right* way of thinking.'

Belief in the Deity is inevitable, he claims; it is like appetite, the instinct of sex, and all the other fixed qualities. We can no more avoid it than we can avoid believing in the existence of matter and the objective world, we can only distort it and hinder it. When the fixed instincts are repressed, whether by force or rhetoric, they burst out, says Hulme, in some abnormal direction.[1] If

[1] Lasserre makes the same point in *Le Romantisme français* when he quotes (p. 452) Renouvier's criticism of Hugo: 'Le dogmatisme optimiste de la philosophie de l'histoire qui a détourné des voies de l'expérience et du bon sens tous les penseurs influents du XIXᵉ siècle, et forcé

you are not allowed to believe in Heaven, you begin to believe in heaven on earth; if you don't believe in God, you begin to believe that man is a god. Concepts that are right and proper in their own sphere spread over and blur the clear outlines of human experience, like a pot of treacle poured over a dinner table. Romanticism is spilt religion.[1]

The classical poet never forgets human limitations: he may jump upwards, but he always returns to earth, deliberately, and as part of his design. The romantic poet, on the other hand, is always talking about the infinite, and is always flying off into space. Sorel, speaking of the romantic poets of the nineteenth century, described this process even more vividly than Hulme:

'Poets, who were not, as a matter of fact, much to be pitied, professed to be victims of fate, of human wickedness, and still more of the stupidity of a world which had not been able to distract them; they eagerly assumed the attitudes of a Prometheus called upon to dethrone jealous gods, and with a pride equal to that of the fierce Nimrod of Victor Hugo (whose arrows, hurled at the sky, fell back stained with blood), they imagined that their verses inflicted deadly wounds on the established powers who dared to refuse to bow down before them. The prophets of the Jews never dreamed of so much destruction to avenge their Jehovah as these

l'inaliénable sentiment de l'existence du mal à se porter tout entier sur le passé . . . ce dogmatisme imbécile, entré peu à peu dans toutes les têtes, a exercé sur les idées et les œuvres de Victor Hugo une influence déplorable.'

1 *Speculations,* p. 118.

literary people dreamed of to satisfy their vanity.'[1]

Romantic poetry moves at a pitch of rhetoric that is always a little highfalutin, and in a classical period that kind of thing is felt to be wrong and irritating. A modern romantic, says Hulme, would never have used the word 'lads' in

> Golden lads and girls all must,
> As chimney-sweepers, come to dust.

'He would have to write golden youth, and take up the thing at least a couple of notes in pitch.' The difference is the difference between Henley and Ben Jonson. Henley writes with romantic bombast, posing before the infinite and admiring his own heroism:

> Out of the night that covers me,
>   Black as the pit from pole to pole,
> I thank whatever gods may be
>   For my unconquerable soul.

Ben Jonson, in the poem that begins 'False world, good night!', speaks of the same situation, but with more humility:

> No, I do know that I was born
>   To age, misfortune, sickness, grief:
> But I will bear these with that scorn
>   As shall not need thy false relief.
>
> Nor for my peace will I go far,
>   As wanderers do, that still do roam;

[1] *Reflections on Violence,* p. 8.

A NEW CLASSICISM?

But make my strengths, such as they are,
Here in my bosom, and at home.

People who have grown up in the romantic tradition judge poetry by its sentiments, they ask that it should satisfy their own unsatisfied emotions. 'The essence of poetry to most people is that it must lead them to a beyond of some kind. Verse strictly confined to the earthly and the definite (Keats is full of it) might seem to them to be excellent writing, excellent craftsmanship, but not poetry. . . . In the classic it is always the light of ordinary day, never the light that never was on land or sea. It is always perfectly human and never exaggerated: man is always man and never a god. But the awful result of romanticism is that, accustomed to this strange light, you can never live without it. Its effect on you is that of a drug.'[1]

In so far as romantic poetry contains vivid and accurate sensuous description, it resembles all great poetry, but when it is yearning after the infinite and claiming attention and admiration for its own soulful sentiments, it is specifically romantic, and Hulme detests it: 'I object even to the best of the romantics. I object still more to the receptive attitude. I object to the sloppiness which doesn't consider that a poem is a poem unless it is moaning or whining about something or other. I always think in this connection of the last line of a poem of John Webster's which ends with a request I cordially endorse:

End your moan and come away.

[1] *Speculations*, p. 127.

'The thing has got so bad now that a poem which is all dry and hard, a properly classical poem, would not be considered poetry at all. How many people now can lay their hands on their hearts and say they like either Horace or Pope? They feel a kind of chill when they read them.

'The dry hardness which you get in the classics is absolutely repugnant to them. Poetry that isn't damp isn't poetry at all. They cannot see that accurate description is a legitimate object of verse. Verse to them always means a bringing in of some of the emotions that are grouped round the word infinite.'[1]

Hulme contends that this romantic taste is a natural consequence of the romantic outlook, and that the romantic view is wrong, both morally and as a statement of fact. To those who share Hulme's outlook romantic poetry, too, will seem aesthetically wrong; and Hulme believes that the romantic age is coming to an end: 'I want to maintain that after a hundred years of romanticism, we are in for a classical revival, and that the particular weapon of this new classical spirit, when it works in verse, will be fancy.'[2]

The older classical poets, Pope and Horace for example, held that the essence of poetry was conformity to certain fixed forms; and like the Egyptian and Byzantine artists, these poets cut and twisted their material to fit the forms. The romantic artist distorts and exaggerates his material in a different direction: he gives to human affairs the perfection and universality that belong to the divine and to abstract ideas. By good classical

[1] *Speculations*, p. 112.   [2] Ibid., p. 113.

verse, Hulme means verse that is primarily exact description of ordinary finite things. This accuracy cannot be attained by a mere careful use of prose; for poetry is a sensuous, concrete language that forces the reader to feel the thing described as if it were actually present, whereas prose is a language of counters that can be manipulated according to fixed rules without being visualized at all. It is a kind of algebra in which the x's and y's are not changed back into physical things till the end of the process. 'Verse is a pedestrian taking you over the ground, prose—a train which delivers you at a destination.'[1]

Ordinary plain prose is vague and unconvincing; but good poetry makes the reader feel the actual, physical state the poet was in when he was writing. The root of aesthetic pleasure is in this rare fact of exact and detailed communication. Wherever you get an extraordinary interest in a thing, a great zest in its contemplation that carries on the contemplator to accurate description, there, says Hulme, you have sufficient justification for poetry. Contemplation, in Hulme's sense, is a kind of detached interest unconnected with any conscious need or intention; and the merit of the poem depends not on the greatness of the subject or the nobility of the poet's emotions, but on the accuracy of the observation. 'It doesn't matter an atom that the emotion produced is not of dignified vagueness, but on the contrary amusing; the point is that exactly the same activity is at work as in the highest verse. That is the avoidance of conventional language in

1 *Speculations*, p. 135.

order to get the exact curve of the thing. . . . It isn't the scale or kind of emotion produced that decides, but this one fact: Is there any real zest in it? Did the poet have an actually realized visual object before him in which he delighted? It doesn't matter if it were a lady's shoe or the starry heavens.'[1]

Poetry must always use fresh epithets and fresh metaphors, not for the sake of novelty ('Art is not eggs') but because words and phrases that have become familiar cease to convey any physical sensation at all. The object of the poet is to prevent the reader from passing over the words as if they were abstract counters, and images and epithets are most likely to be vivid and exact if they are new and unexpected. Images are essential to intuitive language, for it is only by drawing attention to similarities and differences that the writer can make words stand up and startle the reader. Plain speech is essentially vague: it is not intended to arouse a vivid sensation in the reader, but only to give him practical instructions. Only by new metaphors, that is, by fancy, can it be made to evoke a particular definite sensation. It follows that fancy is not mere decoration added to plain speech, and conversely, that imagery that is merely decorative—a reminiscence of other poetry—is not really poetic at all. It is a kind of humbug and affectation that blurs the picture instead of clarifying it.

In his dislike of vagueness and obscurantism Hulme sometimes makes the whole business of poetry sound more mechanical and more conscious than it ever can be.

[1] *Speculations*, p. 137.

At times he recognizes this; but there are momentswhen he is inclined to think that his brisk talk about precision and accurate analogies is more business-like and more widely applicable than it really is. Sometimes, for example, he is inclined to speak of imagination as if its activity were less valuable than that of fancy; at other times he suggests that the operations of the imagination are merely complex operations of fancy. He obviously dislikes the word because of its romantic associations. He tries to show that imagination in the romantic sense is not a necessary part of poetry; but he admits that an operation, very like that of the imagination in Coleridge's sense, exists and must be recognized in aesthetics.

In Hulme's use, 'imagination' is an act of apprehending things in their essence and grasping all their implications and interrelations; and 'fancy' is the instrument through which the imagination expresses itself. The opposite of imagination is thus not fancy, but scientific measurement, which deliberately concentrates on a single chosen aspect of the thing observed. This distinction is based on Bergson's distinction between 'intensive' complexities, which are organic and vital, and 'extensive' complexities, which are merely mechanical. According to both Hulme and Bergson, a mechanical complexity is the sum of its parts, and if the parts are put side by side they form the whole. In a vital or organic complexity, on the other hand, the parts cannot be treated as isolated elements: each one is modified by the other's presence, and each one can only be understood in relation to the whole. This distinction is not scientific or exact, but it is a useful common-sense classification. 'The leg of a chair by itself is still a leg. My leg by itself wouldn't be.'

According to Bergson, the intellect can only think in terms of mechanical complexities.[1] It is compelled to use a kind of language that can only represent disjointed parts (the kind of thing that Bergson calls extensive multiplicity). It can only make diagrams, and diagrams are things whose parts are related mechanically and not organically. The intellect must therefore either restrict itself to mechanical complexities (if there are any things that are merely mechanical complexities), or else it must admit a certain amount of distortion. Its methods are analytical, not synthetic.

The intellect and its language cannot deal with intensive complexities: that is the business of intuition, and intuition always seems mysterious to our intellect. We can say some things about it that are true enough for some purposes, but it escapes analysis. In this, it is like reality itself: it cannot be defined in terms of more familiar notions. To call it 'mysterious' or 'magical', however, merely adds a confusing glamour to a familiar experience. The process cannot be described in finite intellectual terms because these are invented for quite different purposes; but it is nevertheless a common experience. In literary work, for example, one studies a subject, takes notes, works out the implications of

[1] By 'intellect' both Hulme and Bergson mean the mind in so far as it is a thinking-machine, using logic and logical language: they do not mean a faculty that co-ordinates conscience, imagination and empirical knowledge.

possible statements before beginning the work of composition itself. Then a moment comes at which all this material rearranges itself and takes on a new significance. The action at this moment, when the writer places himself at the heart of his subject and lets his scraps of knowledge fit themselves into an organized whole, is properly called an intuition. The fragments grow into a whole as chemical elements grow into a tree; to use Coleridge's phrase, they are fused together in the central heat of the imagination, and something new emerges that could not be predicted by a purely logical machine.

We may wonder at this imaginative intuition as we wonder at a rainbow or a blade of grass, but if we keep this wonder separate from the objective notion, we see that the intuition is not mysteriously higher and purer and nobler than fancy: it is merely more complex. Hulme therefore says that the poetry of which he was thinking would owe more to fancy than it would to imagination, if imagination is understood in the romantic, magical sense as something altogether transcending fancy: 'The particular verse we are going to get will be cheerful, dry and sophisticated, and here the necessary weapon of the positive quality must be fancy.'[1]

Hulme was not trying to describe the classical art of the past, but a new classical art that he believed to be on the way. 'I don't want to be killed with a bludgeon, and references to Dante, Milton and the rest of them.'[2] He noticed, in his own age, a growing impatience with ro-

[1] *Speculations,* p. 137.   [2] *Lecture on Modern Poetry.*

mantic poetry, and he believed that the impatience was more deeply rooted than the usual reaction of any age against the work of its immediate predecessors. The poetry of Swinburne, for example, was not merely going out of fashion among the people who gave most time and attention to poetry; it was arousing in them a vague dislike and uneasiness. They felt uncomfortable in the presence of romantic art, as if it were in some way indecent. They disliked the heroics of romantic poetry, its melodramatic attitudes, cosmic posturings, and wild pursuits of the impossible. They did not object to it on moral or intellectual grounds, but they felt that behind their instinctive dislike moral and intellectual objections could be found. This attitude was intensified by the coming of the war; and it is still more common to-day. It is sometimes called an attitude of disillusion, but it was not merely due to disillusion with current political claptrap. It was the result of a disillusion with the whole romantic outlook, and it brought with it new ideals in poetry, and a new metaphysics.

Hulme's criticism offered an intellectual basis for this change in taste. In ethics, in politics, and in metaphysics Hulme believed that the romantic attitude was coming to an end. Hedonism, utopian liberalism and pragmatism were all unsatisfactory; and the change in poetic taste was only a symptom of a much larger change that might have important effects on our attitude to politics, religion and philosophy. 'May not the change of sensibility, in a region like aesthetics, a by-path in which we are, as it were, off our guard, be some indication that the *humanist tradition is breaking up*—for individuals here and there, at any rate?'[1]

Since Hulme's time some 'neo-classical' poems have been written: the poems of the Imagists, for example, did not deal with 'important' subjects, they made no display of emotion, they said nothing about the grandeur of man. For most readers, visual accuracy alone could not make up for the lack of regular metrical form and romantic emotion; and imagist poetry of this kind has had no lasting popularity; but the imagist discipline has certainly influenced modern poetry, and more and more people have grown to dislike romantic rhetoric.

As Hulme expected, the change in taste has developed slowly, for we are seldom free to make our own judgments in accordance with our needs. Our opinion is nearly always determined by the literary history of the age that came just before us; and the things that we like in middle age are often the things that we learned to like in adolescence. Even if we become dissatisfied with romanticism, it is not easy to throw off the habit of mind that looks for romantic qualities in art. We may think that we can observe two attitudes and make a free choice, but in this we are like Spinoza's falling stone: if it had conscious mind, it would think that it was falling because it wanted to. 'That we are free on certain rare occasions, both my religion and the views I get from metaphysics convince me. But many acts which we habitually label free are in reality automatic. It is quite possible for a man

1 *Speculations*, p. 55.

to write a book almost automatically. I have read several such products.'[1] The forms of familiar beauty can be imitated by mere reflex action, as victims of dementia sometimes give intelligent answers to questions that they cannot possibly have understood. The grammatical and logical forms have become reflexes as automatic as the use of words. In the same way, we are inclined to condemn anything that is not a repetition of the forms we once admired, and we do not notice that we have stopped thinking; so that when something radically new is presented, we become angry. It thus happens that every receptive attitude is always apt to outlast the age to which it belongs.

Hulme claimed that in his own day the romantic tradition had already run dry, but that the attitude of mind that demands romantic qualities from verse still survived: 'If good classical verse were to be written tomorrow very few people would be able to stand it.'[2] A change in sensibility takes a long time to come to completion, for apart from the fact that there will always be some people whose outlook is opposed to the general outlook of the age, the change is hindered by the fact that very few people really try to make mature judgments for themselves. In a society in which the arts are held to be unworthy of the attention of an adult, the change will take two or three generations; people will form their opinions in childhood and the change will only filter through very slowly from those who continue to exercise their aesthetic judgment in middle age.

[1] *Speculations,* p. 123.   [2] Ibid., p. 126.

But a change more significant than a casual change in fashion has nevertheless taken place during the last thirty or forty years: it is now noticeable in poetry and architecture, but to Hulme it was most apparent in painting and sculpture. He was strongly impressed by the new geometrical art of Epstein, Gaudier-Brzeska, William Roberts and Wyndham Lewis; and his sympathy with Worringer's approach to art led him to read a metaphysical meaning into their work. He saw in their insistence on geometrical form and their disregard of all that the romantics mean by vitality a kind of parable or allegory: man must adapt himself to fit into the conditions of existence; he cannot alter those conditions at will; he is not a creature of infinite potentiality, but a limited being who can achieve decency only by conformity to some fixed pattern and tradition.

'What is really behind the main movement, what makes it important is the re-emergence of a sensibility akin to that behind geometrical arts of the past. At first, in its rather fumbling search for an appropriate means of expression, it naturally went back to these past arts. You thus got a period in which the work produced had a certain resemblance to Archaic, Byzantine and African art. But this state has already been left behind. The new sensibility is finding for itself a direct and modern means of expression, having very little resemblance to these past geometric arts. It is characterised, not by the simple geometric forms found in archaic art, but by the more complicated ones associated in our minds with machinery. . . . The beauty of banal forms like teapot-

74

handles, knuckledusters, saws, etc., seems to have been perceived for the first time. . . . It is not the emphasis on form which is the distinguishing characteristic of the new movement, then, but the emphasis on this particular kind of form.'[1]

Worringer's analysis of these changes is not identical with Hulme's, but it points in the same direction. Like Hulme he believes that the new movement expresses a new intellectual and spiritual attitude, and he associates it with a new interest in machinery and steel construction. The fact that for the first time since the Renaissance some people were beginning to appreciate the non-romantic, non-humanist art of earlier religious periods seemed to Hulme to be further evidence of the decline of the romantic sensibility. As long as people were unconsciously romantic, they could not appreciate Byzantine art; as long as they were unconsciously humanist, they could not see the point of scholastic philosophy. By getting rid of an unconscious prejudice they were taking the first step towards a new kind of classicism.

Hulme said that he did not imagine that humanism was breaking up merely to make room for a new medievalism, nor did he believe that men would change in their essential natures. But their categories and their way of thinking would change, and the new mode of thought would bring men of a different type to the top. Something would be carried forward from the humanistic period; its honesty in science and a certain conception of freedom of thought would remain. 'Compare a Byzan-

[1] *The New Age*, 26. iii. 14.

tine relief of the best period with the design on a Greek vase, and an Egyptian relief. The abstract geometrical character of the Byzantine relief makes it much nearer to the Egyptian than to the Greek work; yet a certain elegance in the line-ornament shows that it has developed out of the Greek.'[1]

The new classicism, with its rejection of romantic art, pragmatic philosophy, modernist religion, and utopian liberalism, may repel the orthodox believer in 'Progress', but it is not meant to be attractive to him; it is meant to be a recognition of true perceptions. To-day, most people recognize that there is no inevitable evolution in the direction of liberal democracy. If we want 'progress' in this direction, we must work for it, and we must seriously ask ourselves to what extent we can rely on 'economic forces' to do our work for us, or on 'innate goodness' in ourselves and other people.

It is now twenty-five years since Hulme wrote his essays in defence of Epstein, Gaudier-Brzeska, and Wyndham Lewis; and their work is still discussed. Some of Hulme's prophecies about art and poetry have been fulfilled, and it is worth while to ask ourselves whether Hulme is right in claiming that the work of the artists whom he defended is an intuitive expression of a new attitude. Both Hulme and Worringer exaggerate the geometrical element in Byzantine art and in religious art in general, and we may reasonably doubt whether the geometrical element in the modern paintings and drawings that Hulme admired does really express a

---

[1] *Speculations,* p. 57.

religious feeling. But there is no doubt that he is right in his main observation: a change in sensibility is taking place, and the changing sensibility corresponds to a changing attitude. The purpose of this book is to discuss the attitude that Hulme called religious or classical, and to throw some light on the apparent contradictions in his notes.

Chapter Four

THE INFLUENCE OF BERGSON

'One of the main reasons for the existence of philosophy is not that it enables you to find truth (it can never do that) but that it does provide you a refuge for definitions. . . . You start in the confusion of the fighting line, you retire from that just a little to the rear to recover, to get your weapons right. Quite plainly, without metaphor this—it provides you with an elaborate and precise language in which you really can explain definitely what you mean, but what you want to say is decided by other things. The ultimate reality is the hurly-burly, the struggle; the metaphysic is an adjunct to clear-headedness in it.'—T. E. HULME, *Speculations*, p. 130.

Hulme resembles the fervent philosophers of the Renaissance, Telesio, Campanella and Bruno, rather than systematic philosophers such as Aristotle, Descartes, Spinoza or Kant, and he resembles them not only in the untidiness of his ideas, but in the ideas themselves, and in the enthusiasm with which he presents them. He picks up from writers like Bergson and Sorel an assortment of ideas that seem to him to be true and necessary, and he tries to put them into some sort of logical order; not for the sake of order alone, but to reinforce the appeal of each notion by joining it to another.

It may seem curious that Hulme, who insisted so

strongly on the existence of intrinsic values and objective truths, should be indebted to Bergson, who is sometimes regarded as the chief exponent of the pragmatic and 'relativist' position that Hulme so vigorously denounced; but the important point in Bergson is that while he admits the relativity of all conceptual knowledge, he also insists that this is not the only kind of knowledge. All is flux and uncertainty, all our beliefs and enjoyments are tangled in a web of cause and effect; and it may seem to some people that nothing is worth while, because every enjoyment is merely the result of a conditioned reflex. But this is only one aspect of the truth: it is not *the* truth; and Hulme is interested in Bergson because his philosophy recognizes this limitation.

It is worth while to quote at some length from Hulme's translation of Bergson's *Introduction à la Métaphysique* (which has been out of print for some years); for nearly all the points properly called metaphysical that are contained in Hulme's notes are also found in Bergson's summary of his own position:

'I. *There is a reality that is external and yet given immediately to the mind.*

'II. This reality is mobility. . . . *All reality, therefore, is tendency, if we agree to mean by tendency an incipient change of direction.*

'III. Our mind, which seeks for solid points of support, has for its main function in the ordinary course of life that of representing *states* and *things*. . . . *Our intellect, when it follows its natural bent, proceeds on the one hand by solid perceptions, and on the other by stable conceptions.*

'IV. The inherent difficulties of metaphysic . . . are largely the result of our applying, to the disinterested knowledge of the real, processes which we generally employ for practical ends. . . . In other words, *it is clear that fixed concepts may be extracted by our thought from mobile reality; but there are no means of reconstructing the mobility of the real with fixed concepts.*

'V. But because we fail to reconstruct the living reality with stiff and ready-made concepts, it does not follow that we cannot grasp it in some other way. *The demonstrations which have been given of the relativity of our knowledge are therefore tainted with an original vice; they imply, like the dogmatism they attack, that all knowledge must necessarily start from concepts with fixed outlines, in order to clasp with them the reality which flows.*

'VI. But the truth is that our intelligence can follow the opposite method. It can place itself within the mobile reality, and adopt its ceaselessly changing direction; in short, can grasp it by means of that *intellectual sympathy* which we call intuition. . . . Only thus will a progressive philosophy be built up. . . . *To philosophise, therefore, is to invert the habitual direction of the work of thought.*

'VII. The most powerful of the methods of investigation at the disposal of the human mind, the infinitesimal calculus, originated from this very inversion. . . . *The object of metaphysics is to perform qualitative differentiations and integrations.*

'VIII. From the overlooking of this intuition proceeds all that has been said by philosophers and by men of science themselves about the "relativity" of scientific knowledge. *What is relative is the symbolic knowledge by pre-existing concepts, which proceeds from the fixed to the moving, and not the intuitive knowledge which installs itself in that which is moving and adopts the very life of things.* This intuition attains the absolute.

'IX. That there are not two different ways of knowing things fundamentally, that the various sciences have their root in metaphysics, is what the ancient philosophers generally thought. Their error did not lie there. It consisted in their being always dominated by the belief, so natural to the human mind, that a variation can only be the expression and development of what is invariable.... Now it is the contrary which is true.... While science needs symbols for its analytical development, the main object of metaphysics is to do away with symbols.'[1]

Like Bruno, Bergson insists that reality cannot be represented by the fixed and limited signs of logical language, and like Campanella he emphasizes the importance of the *image* rather than the abstract sign or symbol. The image, he says, has this advantage, that it keeps us in the concrete. 'No image can replace the intuition of duration, but many diverse images, borrowed from very different orders of things, may, by the convergence of their action, direct consciousness to the precise point where there is a certain intuition to be seized. By choosing images as dissimilar as possible, we shall prevent any one of them from usurping the place of the intuition it is

[1] *Introduction to Metaphysics,* pp. 55–67.

intended to call up, since it would be driven away at once by its rivals.'[1]

Hulme's conception of logical language as something essentially limited and inaccurate is taken from Bergson: 'Both empiricists and rationalists are victims of the same fallacy. Both of them mistake partial notations for real parts, thus confusing the point of view of analysis and of intuition, of science and metaphysics.'[2] In Bergson's view, the proper business of metaphysics is to express an intuition of the flux of experience, an apprehension of the whole situation, without any conscious directing purpose. He says that there is nothing mysterious in this process, and he takes as an example one that we have already discussed—the imaginative intuition that some-times comes to a writer in the course of his work, and sets his mind on a path where it rediscovers all the infor-mation that has been collected, and gives it a new order and a new significance. This sort of experience is quite common, says Bergson, and many other examples might be found; but his own choice of illustration is significant. When Hulme talks of intuition, he makes it the basis of poetry, whereas Bergson makes it the chief aim of meta-physics: 'Metaphysical intuition seems to be something of the same kind. . . . We do not obtain an intuition from reality—that is an intellectual sympathy with the most intimate part of it—unless we have won its confidence by a long fellowship with its superficial manifestations. . . . But metaphysical intuition, although it can only be obtained through material knowledge, is quite other

[1] *Introduction*, p. 14.   [2] Ibid., p. 26.

than the mere summary or synthesis of that knowledge.
. . . In this sense metaphysics has nothing in common
with a generalization of facts: and nevertheless it might
be defined as *integral experience*.'[1]

Bergson differs from most of the philosophers of the
post-Renaissance tradition, both in his description of the
aim of metaphysics, and in his account of the language
that metaphysics must use. Modern metaphysics has
usually been limited to abstract concepts, but these Bergson rejects as inadequate for an evocation of reality:
'The concept can only symbolize a particular property
by making it common to an infinity of things. It therefore always more or less deforms the property by the
extension it gives to it.'[2] The normal work of the intellect, he says, is far from disinterested. We do not usually
aim at knowledge for its own sake, but in order to take
sides, to draw profit, to satisfy an interest. We ask to
what known class an object belongs, up to what point
it is *this* or *that*, and what kind of action, bearing or attitude it should suggest to us. Most of our concepts are
invented in the first place to serve these practical purposes, and it follows either that no philosophy is possible,
and all knowledge of things is aimed at some kind of profit
to be drawn from them, or else that philosophy consists
in expressing an intuition by means of diverse images.

It is certainly true that philosophers have very often
tried to give an intuitive apprehension of the world:[3]

[1] *Introduction*, pp. 77–9.   [2] Ibid., p. 16.
[3] The notion of the philosophical activity as an intuition attained by
freeing the mind from all conscious preconceptions is found in most of
the philosophers in whom Hulme was interested. For example, it is found

but Bergson's insistence on the need for images is unusual, and here we can apply the distinction between the
scientific part of philosophy, which uses abstract concepts and the operations of logic, and the personal part
which expresses a particular outlook. If Bergson's definition of metaphysics is right, then the scientific part
does not exist; and the part that does exist is indistin-
guishable from poetry. True, Bergson makes no mention of rhythm and verbal music; but this omission
appears to be accidental, for all his arguments about
the limitations of abstract speech could easily be turned
against any speech that has a sound that is not appropriate
to its intended meaning.

According to Bergson, reality cannot be represented
in abstract terms without being distorted and falsified,
because reality is always changing, whereas analytical
concepts and diagrams always have to be treated as if
they remained stationary while being considered; but
he claims that in the act of intuition, the philosopher (or,
we might say, the poet) passes beyond particular needs
and arrives at an apprehension of reality. That intuition
must be expressed in a language that other people can
understand; and if what Bergson is writing is metaphy-

in Heidegger and Scheler, who derive it from Husserl's somewhat for-
bidding statement of what he calls the principle of all principles: 'that
every primordial dator Intuition is a source of authority for knowledge, that
whatever presents itself in "intuition" in primordial form (as it were in its
bodily reality) *is simply to be accepted as it gives itself out to be,* though *only
within the limits in which it then presents itself.*' *Ideen zu einer reinen Phänomenologie und phänomenologischen Philosophie* (1913), I, ii, 24. (English
translation by W. R. Boyce Gibson: *Ideas: General Introduction to Pure
Phenomenology* (1931), p. 92.)

sics, then in so far as he writes in abstract terms, he might seem to have succeeded in doing what he has proved to be impossible. What has happened, of course, is that he has overstated his case: it is true that no abstract scheme ever gives a representation of the world that is valid for all purposes, but it is equally true that the 'exact' sciences are accurate enough for working purposes. They are never wholly free from the distortions and limitations of bias and intention, but they can be *relatively* disinterested; that is to say, they may serve a wide range of purposes. A still more disinterested critique of the concepts used in these sciences is possible, and this study, which has always been considered a major part of metaphysics, deserves a name. Metaphysics, in the ordinary sense, is concerned with analysis and representation rather than with synthesis and evocation; and although abstract concepts are not wholly satisfactory even for this purpose, they are not wholly inadequate. No abstract metaphysical description can ever be complete,[1] but some descriptions are better than others. The business of the metaphysician is to improve the precision and

[1] It is not so much between abstract concepts and concrete names or images that Hulme and Bergson wish to distinguish, as between words regarded as having a definite, limited, meaning, independent of their context, and words as they are envisaged in a 'context' theory of meaning, with all their wealth of association and suggestion. But neither the 'context' theory nor the 'intrinsic meaning' theory is satisfactory by itself. The meaning of words owes something to the contexts in which they are used, but unless some words had a core of intrinsic meaning (a more or less definite significance) the context itself would be a meaningless fog. In that case, we would be compelled to go beyond Hulme's statement that something is always lost in expression ('All expression is vulgar') and say (or not say) that all expression is impossible.

scope of his language, not to abandon the attempt and take to poetry. A case can be made out for hybrid writing (like that of Bergson) that uses some of the resources of poetry, but it need not be turned into a case against the pursuit of traditional metaphysics.

Something like this criticism of Bergson appears to have been implicit in Hulme, but he did not actually state it. He uses these ideas as the basis of a theory of aesthetics: but he also makes notes on metaphysics, and these notes continually restate and elaborate Bergson's position. It is from Bergson that he derives his conception of reality as a general cindery chaos into which some sort of order is introduced by the conscious mind. 'The apparent scientific unity of the world may be due to the fact that man is a kind of sorting machine.'[1] This sorting, as Bergson says, is governed by our need of action. 'There is no inevitable order into which ideas must be shifted.'[2] Hulme combines this doctrine with something of the materialist interpretation of history; and says that all a writer's generalizations and truths can be traced to his personal circumstances or to the prejudices of his class. 'There is no average or real truth to be discerned among the different fronts of prejudice. Each is a truth in so far as it satisfies the writer.'[3]

This is one of Hulme's overstatements, and he modifies it when he discusses his 'Critique of Satisfaction', but even in this extreme form it does not contradict the assumption he often makes elsewhere, that ideas must sometimes be regarded as being among the causes of

[1] *Speculations*, p. 228.　　[2] Ibid., p. 226.　　[3] Ibid., p. 229.

material events. There is an interaction of matter and thought; and material history cannot be understood without taking into account the ideas in people's minds. Furthermore, there is no general background of agreement against which competing systems of ideas can be compared and measured; and therefore, the last resort, violence is the only medium of debate. It is at this point that Hulme makes the jump from Bergson to Sorel, whose *Réflexions sur la violence* he translated. The springboard is Bergson's insistence on the relation of purpose and idea.

Although Hulme is intrigued by the argument that different systems of ideas cannot be compared, because they are based on different needs and prejudices, he does not go the whole way with the materialist who claims that all history can be interpreted and understood as the outcome of material conditions and material appetites: he insists that ideas are real historical forces; but he also insists that ideas and aspirations are nearly always determined by material conditions. 'The soul is a spirit certainly, but undifferentiated and without personality. The personality is given by the bodily frame which receives and shapes it.'[1] Thus Hulme's outlook is neither idealist nor materialist: there is an objective material world, partly organized, and there is also a world of people. Whether we say that there are really two worlds, distinguishable and yet inseparable, or whether we say that our experience and our language compel us to talk as if there were, is to Hulme a matter of indifference.

This avoidance of the familiar categories of philosophy

[1] *Speculations*, p. 240.

is not the accidental result of a jackdaw eclecticism. If the world is cindery, it cannot be adequately represented by neat, clearly defined abstractions. All clear-cut ideas turn out to be wrong, says Hulme, and all large, pretentious attempts to build up an abstract philosophy are founded on the illusion that the real, cindery world can be exactly represented by the abstract counters. These abstract words give the illusion of impersonality and detachment, and the metaphysician imagines that he surveys the world with an eagle's eye. But this analogy is false: he is *in* the world, always, and complete detachment is impossible: 'Philosophical syntheses and ethical systems are only possible in arm-chair moments. They are seen to be meaningless as soon as we get into a bus with a dirty baby and a crowd.'[1] We must not be taken in by the arm-chair moments. The real level-headedness is found in the ability to disregard the pretentious clothing of philosophy, and to imagine it at first sight without the glitter and stiffness of its terminology, as we might imagine a pretty girl dipped in water.

When we look at metaphysical systems in this way we see that their pretended discoveries about the world are often no more than discoveries about language. What they have discovered is not the way in which the world is built up, but the way in which we have taken it apart to give it labels: there are no ultimate principles on which the whole of knowledge can be built once and for ever as upon a rock. Knowledge is interrelated, and no one part is fundamental; it is like the surface of a sphere, not

---

[1] *Speculations,* p. 228.

like a pyramid: and similarly all the divergent purposes in the world are related, but they do not converge into one Grand Purpose. 'The absolute is invented to reconcile conflicting purposes. But these purposes are necessarily conflicting, even in the nature of Truth itself.'[1] No magnificent, over-riding purpose is made manifest by human history, and no finality appears in any scientific knowledge: 'That great secret which all men find out for themselves, and none reveal—or if they do, like Cassandra, are not believed—that the world is round. The young man refuses to believe it.'[2]

When we realize the futility of pursuing the perfect absolute, the zest goes out of the search. 'The *absolute* is to be described not as perfect, but if existent as essentially imperfect, chaotic, and cinder-like.' This is the end of all humanistic knowledge and philosophy: even the heroic virtues can be reduced to the simple laws of egoism. There is no bridge from the finite to the infinite: the world is finite, and we cannot escape from its surface. The infinities of grandeur and perfection, the idea of history as a grand march to Utopia, all these are illusions.

Up to this point, it might be said that Hulme's philosophy is almost completely sceptical. Although when he distinguishes between scientific metaphysics and *Weltanschauung* he regards the former as certain and the latter as personal, at other times he makes plain his belief that all metaphysical speculation in abstract terms is tentative and relative—authoritative, perhaps, but never absolute. When he puts forward his own outlook he

---

[1] *Speculations*, p. 228. [2] Ibid., p. 233.

does not call it a scientific metaphysic but *A Sketch of a New Weltanschauung*:

'I. In spite of pretensions to absolute truth, the results of philosophy are always tested by the effects, and by the judgments of other philosophers. There is always an appeal to a circle of people. The same is true of values in art, in morals. A man cannot stand alone on absolute ground, but always appeals to his fellows.

'II. Therefore it is suggested that there is no such thing as an absolute truth to be discovered. All general statements about truth, etc., are in the end only amplifications of man's appetites.

'The ultimate reality is a circle of persons, *i.e.* animals who communicate.

'There is a kind of gossamer web, woven between the real things, and by this means the animals communicate. For purposes of communication they invent a symbolic language. Afterwards this language, used to excess, becomes a disease, and we get the curious phenomena of men explaining themselves by means of the gossamer web that connects them. Language becomes a disease in the hands of the counter-word mongers. It must constantly be remembered that it is an invention for the convenience of men; and in the midst of Hegelians who triumphantly explain the world as a mixture of "good" and "beauty" and "truth", this should be remembered. What would an intelligent animal (without the language disease), or a carter in the road, think of it all?

'Symbols are picked out and believed to be realities. People imagine that all the complicated structure of the world can be woven out of "good" and "beauty". These words are merely counters representing vague groups of things, to be moved about on a board for the convenience of the players.

'III. Objection might be taken that this makes man the measure of the world, and that after all he is only an animal, who came late, and the world must be supposed to have existed before he evolved at all. The reply to this is as follows:

'(i) Analogy of courage and capacity. Courage in the Wild West requires capacities different from those it requires in the city. But the phenomena are the same: A non-muscular man is inevitably physically a coward.

'(ii) The mental qualities of men and animals are common, though they are realised by different means.

'(iii) These qualities—e.g. the common return to egoism, the roundness of the world, the absence of all infinitude, the denial of all Utopias—are extended to the ultimate nature of the world.

'(iv) These qualities extend to the amoeba and the inorganic world.

'(v) It is these qualities with which the world is measured in § I.

'(vi) Hence in a sense "Man is the measure of all things" and Man (egoism) *has always existed and always will exist.*

'IV. Just as no common purpose can be aimed at for the conflicting purposes of real people, *so* there is no common purpose in the world.

'The world is a plurality.

'A unity arrived at by stripping off essentials is not a unity. Compound is not an inner reality.

'V. This plurality consists in the nature of an ash-heap. In this ash-pit of cinders, certain ordered routes have been made, thus constituting whatever unity there may be—a kind of manufactured chess-board laid on a cinder-heap. Not a real chess-board impressed on the cinders, but the gossamer world of symbolic communication already spoken of.'[1]

Hulme draws a distinction between the vague philosophic statement that 'reality always escapes a system' and the real intuition of the world as cinders, 'felt in a religious way' and used as a criterion of nearly all philosophic and aesthetic judgment. Unlike Bergson, he does not always insist that his own intuition is an objective metaphysical truth, but he feels that it is important and he wants to show it to other people. 'I must tell someone' is, he says, the final criterion of philosophy, and he claims that there is a critique of satisfaction by which the value of an outlook can be tested. By means of this critique of satisfaction Hulme passes beyond the sceptical position to positive assertions.

There are moments when Hulme seems to lapse into the most hopeless scepticism, and there are others when he roundly asserts the existence of intrinsic values and objective truths. This apparent confusion is the source of his importance: most of his assertions are true in their proper field; the problem is to restate them in a way that will make their limitations clear. Hulme can see that in

1 *Speculations*, pp. 217–19.

one way the humanist is right, and that all knowledge that can be expressed in logical counters is relative and limited; but in spite of this he does not give way to the feeling that there is no objective truth, beauty, and virtue in the world. He argues that this kind of scepticism is inevitable if we think clearly enough within the humanist limitations; but he goes on to argue that humanist thought is not pushed far enough: it is neither using adequate terms nor taking all the evidence into account. In substance, both Hulme and Bergson are trying to restore to 'reason' the meaning that it had for Coleridge and the Cambridge Platonists. The reason, in this sense, is not merely the mind regarded as a machine manipulating logical counters; it is a power that controls and co-ordinates not only science and scientific philosophy, but also the intuitions of music, poetry and art: it takes into account not only the empirical evidence of the senses, but also the sense of absolute obligation and of the absolute *value* of existence that is the foundation of all religion and all vitality.

Chapter Five

DEMOCRACY AND VIOLENCE

'When vulgar thought of to-day is pacifist, rationalist, and hedonist, and in being so believes itself to be expressing the inevitable convictions of the instructed and emancipated man, it has all the pathos of marionettes in a play, dead things gesticulating as though they were alive.'—T. E. HULME, Introduction to Sorel's *Reflections on Violence* (*Speculations*, pp. 254-5).

In the Middle Ages, the belief that we are children in the hand of God, that all our blessings come from His bounty, and that we are imperfect creatures who bring sorrow and suffering upon ourselves through our own evil ways, was accepted as axiomatic. Men believed that all our misfortunes are trials through which God's glory may shine the brighter, that it behoves us to give due respect to those who are set above us in this world, and to accept the station of life to which His providence has called us. If they looked for a reward for virtue, they did not expect to find it in this world. There was no need of a Milton to justify God's ways to man until men had begun to doubt; but in spite of Milton and all the other apologists, belief in the ultimate wisdom and justice of incomprehensible Providence slowly gave way to a new belief in progress and the rights of man. The Divine

Right of Kings was replaced by the Natural Rights of Man, the 'dispensation of providence' was replaced by the 'inevitable march of progress'. People no longer expected a reward beyond the grave to justify their present misery: they began to look forward to the happiness of posterity.

During the seventeenth and eighteenth centuries this new philosophy grew from speculation into theory, and from theory into axiom. The doctrine that virtue, skill, and wealth were gifts of Providence was replaced by the doctrine that all men were equal and had the same potentialities: they differed, said the eighteenth-century philosophers, only in opportunity and training. 'Is' and 'ought to be' were confused, and the doctrine that all men were equal, not only as souls, but also in the affairs of the political and material world, grew into a demand for equal privilege for all. By the end of the eighteenth century this democratic ideal was regarded as a moral principle, and in the early nineteenth century it became ingrained as deeply as an unconscious habit of the mind.

Tocqueville, in his *Démocratie en Amérique* (1835), put the case for democratic progress with the surprise and awe of one who discovers a new and wholly unsuspected law of physics.[1] Providence had come to mean 'progress', and progress meant progress towards demo-

---

[1] 'Le livre tout entier qu'on va lire a été écrit sous l'impression d'une sorte de *terreur religieuse* produite dans l'âme de l'auteur par la vue de cette révolution irrésistible qui marche, depuis tant de siècles, à travers tous les obstacles et qu'on voit encore aujourd'hui s'avancer au milieu des ruines qu'elle a faites. . . . Si de longues observations et des méditations sincères amenaient les hommes de nos jours à reconnaître que le *dévelop-*

cracy; progress was good, therefore democracy was right, and the good man would work to establish democracy. In exactly the same way, the nineteenth-century writers who believed in the ideal of economic equality, though they believed that the only real progress was progress towards communal ownership of the means of production, again assumed that 'progress' was an inevitable and permanent fact; and like the political democrats, they argued that the good man would work for this inevitable end.

The insistence that it is right to work for an inevitable end is usually justified either by the argument that progress is right, and therefore opposition or indifference to progress is bad and reactionary; or else by the argument that progress is inevitable, and therefore the man whose wishes accord with it will get his wishes fulfilled and be happy, and the man who opposes it will fail and be unhappy. In either case the old standards of absolute right and wrong are abandoned, and virtue is measured by the happiness it gives or is likely to give to the individual, or the race, or the whole world present and future. In particular, anything that can be justified as contributing to the happiness of posterity is taken to be noble and admirable. This worship of progress, democracy and posterity has been responsible for many actions that are good, judged by any reasonable standards, and the same

pement, graduel et progressif de l'égalité est à la fois *le passé et l'avenir de leur histoire,* cette seule découverte donnerait à ce développement le caractère sacré de la volonté du souverain maître. Vouloir arrêter la démocratie paraîtrait alors lutter contre Dieu même et il ne resterait aux nations qu'à *s'accommoder a l'état social* que leur impose la Providence.'

faith may produce many more good actions in the future. It remains to ask whether the beliefs that it implies are really justified by facts, or whether they are assumptions. If they are assumptions, they may not be the only possible assumptions for enlightened and unselfish people.

In physics and astronomy, inaccurate theories have often been taken for fact, and for a time they have served a useful purpose; in the same way, the theories of romanticism in literature and utopianism in politics may be false although they have sometimes been useful. A change, a revolution for example, may spring from material causes: it may be necessary and desirable. But in the course of its development it naturally encourages all those ideas and prejudices that seem to favour it, and some of those ideas may be false. Thus the romanticism of Rousseau favoured the French Revolution. The fact that one opposes those ideas does not mean that one opposes the material changes that they helped to produce. Opposition to ideas that have served or are likely to serve a revolutionary purpose is not necessarily reactionary: it may simply be a matter of longsightedness.

Many people have questioned the belief that happiness or human survival can be made tests of morality, but with very little popular success. Kant's arguments still go unheeded, whereas Rousseau's have been the basis of popular literature and democratic politics. Hulme's whole attitude obviously leads him to oppose the utopian democratic view, and he finds the clearest statement of many of his own beliefs in the French Syndicalist, Georges Sorel.[1]

Hulme did not always distinguish between the doctrine that humanity is prospering and the doctrine that it ought to be; and this confusion sometimes makes it difficult to understand his position. Hulme attacked the belief that man is inevitably progressing morally and intellectually at an appreciable pace; and he attacked the view that morality could be based on the single axiom that man *ought* to progress, for such a view justifies the morality by the progress and measures the progress by the morality: but he certainly did not deny that people ought to try to make moral and intellectual progress. He argued that moral effort is the concern of individuals; it cannot be replaced by a belief in inevitable progress, and it can only be based on a conception of absolute values. With the working-class demand for more equitable economic conditions Hulme had the deepest sympathy, but he believed that the ideas of peaceful progress and the innate goodness of the natural man were not only an unnecessary appendage of the movement, but a hindrance to it: at one stage they had served a useful purpose, but they sprang from a confusion of thought. The only real progress is progress in machinery and industrial methods; no real moral progress accompanies that development, and any doctrine that assumes such a moral progress is bound to lead to disaster.

[1] Georges Sorel (1846–1928): *Réflexions sur la violence* (1906); *Les Illusions du progrès* (1908); *De l'utilité du Pragmatisme* (1917); *Matériaux d'une théorie du prolétariat* (1914, published 1918), etc.

In this, Hulme agrees with Sorel: 'The optimist in politics is an inconstant and even dangerous man, because he takes no account of the great difficulties presented by his projects; these projects seem to him to possess a force of their own, which tends to bring about their realisation all the more easily as they are, in his opinion, destined to produce the happiest results. He frequently thinks that small reforms in the political constitution, and, above all, in the personnel of the government, will be sufficient to direct social development in such a way as to mitigate those evils of the contemporary world which seem so harsh to the sensitive mind. As soon as his friends come into power, he declares that it is necessary to let things alone for a little, not to hurry too much, and to learn how to be content with whatever their own benevolent intentions prompt them to do. It is not always self-interest that suggests these expressions of satisfaction, as people have often believed; self-interest is strongly aided by vanity and by the illusions of philosophy. The optimist passes with remarkable facility from revolutionary anger to the most ridiculous social pacifism.'[1]

Sorel insists that liberal ideas and methods are useless in the struggle against capitalist ideas, morality and economy. He regards the modern state as thoroughly corrupt: it is the creation of capitalism, and is designed to protect capitalism. Where two groups of people differ on the fundamental conceptions of morality, there can be no common conception of justice. Capitalist justice

---

[1] *Reflections on Violence* (second edition, 1925), p. 9.

is designed to protect the capitalist state: if the capitalist state is to be overthrown, it is useless to look to capitalist justice for help: the issue cannot be settled except by violence. A morality is secure and powerful only when it is grounded in the industrial organization and methods of production of the community: to establish such a harmony, violence will be necessary; and that violence will take the form of a general strike. All opposition to violence is based on self-interest or illusion: the parliamentary socialist has a vested interest in parliamentary methods, he lives on the margin of production like the capitalist, the soldier and the intellectual, and he will not risk any action that will jeopardize that margin.

Sorel believes that if revolutionary violence is made the aim of the working classes, this aim will encourage the heroic virtues, and so lead to the re-establishment of absolute ethical values. The revolutionary objective will thus serve the purpose of a myth, and a myth of violence will always lead to effort, whereas utopian myths lead to day-dreaming and idleness. According to Sorel, liberal democracy is essentially utopian: it offers a kind of day-dream satisfaction without facing the fact that the real morality of existing society, the motive force of history to-day, is totally different from the ideals that prevail in the dream. The arguments for social pacifism therefore spring from selfishness or from misunderstanding.

'Neither do I attach any importance to the objections made to the general strike based on considerations of a practical order. The attempt to construct hypotheses about the nature of the struggles of the future and the means of suppressing capitalism, on the model furnished by history, is a return to the old methods of the Utopists. There is no process by which the future can be predicted scientifically, nor even one which enables us to discuss whether one hypothesis about it is better than another; it has been proved by too many memorable examples that the greatest men have committed prodigious errors in thus desiring to make predictions about even the least distant future.

'And yet without leaving the present, without reasoning about this future, which seems for ever condemned to escape our reason, we should be unable to act at all. Experience shows that the *framing of a future, in some indeterminate time*, may, when it is done in a certain way, be very effective, and have very few inconveniences; this happens when the anticipations of the future take the form of those myths, which enclose with them all the strongest inclinations of a people, of a party or of a class, inclinations which recur to the mind with the insistence of instincts in all the circumstances of life; and which give an aspect of complete reality to the hopes of immediate action by which, more easily than by any other method, men can reform their desires, passions, and mental activity.'[1]

All that Sorel says here might be used to justify any imperialist ambition, or any kind of revolutionary movement that is not utopian; and like the reaction against romanticism in literature, this rejection of utopian libera-

[1] *Reflections*, p. 133.

lism is common to many different schools. The similarity between the outlook of Sorel and that of the royalists of *L'Action française* was eagerly seized on by those who were anxious to discredit him. But the utopian theory may be opposed by different people for different reasons. There is the objection of Hulme and Sorel that the theory is based on error and sooner or later must lead to failure; there is also the objection that, in practice, the liberal theory often leads to corruption, spinelessness, and stupidity; and there is a third and very different objection, that the theory has already helped the working class to gain some concessions from the employers and is likely to help them to gain more. In practice, most fascist movements are based on an uneasy combination of the second and third objections. The leaders of the French neo-royalist movement put forward the first and second, but they draw much of their support from people whose aim is the defence of property and privilege against the encroachments of the working class. Hulme and Sorel are in agreement with the *ideas* of the neo-royalists, but they have no sympathy with the aims of their supporters. Sorel shares most of the royalist ideology, but finds a different application for it. He expects a return of the classical spirit through the struggle of the classes.

The belief that man is inevitably progressing intellectually and morally (not merely adding to his store of available knowledge), and that democratic institutions are the necessary and inevitable expression of this progress, leads to a pacifist ethic. Violent resistance to other nations and classes is unnecessary, for time will work out their salvation;[1] material force is the weapon of the past, the weapons of the future are persuasion, argument, and example. On this view, the use of violence is bad because it is reactionary, and pacifism is good because it belongs to the future.

Here again we have the double use of 'progress'; it is held up as an ideal justifying a line of conduct, and it is also put forward as a necessary fact. *Why* one should work for what is inevitable is not explained: this is the mystical element concealed in the rationalist-democratic outlook. In every philosophy there is an ultimate mystery of acceptance, and this is an anti-religious form of it.

On a less optimistic view of human nature, it would appear that non-resistance to admitted evil might lead to a state of affairs that would be bad and lasting. Killing, on such a view, may be an evil, but neither the only nor the worst of evils. Furthermore, given that we want to make progress towards a peaceful world, with a fair share of material goods for everybody (and Hulme, like Sorel, believes in progress in this sense), it is still true that such a world will not come about without effort and self-sacrifice, and this effort and self-sacrifice will not be forthcoming except in a society that regards these qualities as good in themselves, independently of any ulterior end. The 'mystery' of sacrificing yourself to hasten an inevitable progress may sometimes work, but

[1] This position differs, of course, from that of the absolute pacifist, whose objection to direct personal violence is not derived from any belief about progress, but is an ultimate moral principle, considered as superior to all other principles and commandments.

not often enough accomplish anything of value, and it will certainly not regenerate society.

'From the pessimistic conception of man comes naturally the view that the transformation of society is an heroic task requiring heroic qualities . . . virtues which are not likely to flourish on the soil of a rational and sceptical ethic. This regeneration can, on the contrary, only be brought about and only be maintained by actions springing from an ethic which from the narrow rationalist standpoint is irrational, being not *relative*, but absolute. The transformation of society is not likely to be achieved as a result of peaceful and intelligent *readjustment* on the part of literary men and politicians.'[1]

For this reason, said Sorel, the working classes must reject the myth of progress, and replace it by the myth of the general strike. Hulme does not discuss this matter, but he explains his own views on pacifist democracy and on the heroic virtues in the articles that he contributed to *The Cambridge Magazine* in 1916. He believed that England ought to fight until Germany was beaten, because a German victory would establish German dominion from the North Sea to the Mediterranean. The pacifists at that time were prepared to face that possibility, but they denied that it involved any permanent danger to liberty. They maintained that 'no free self-governing State could long be ruled, if it quietly held out for freedom', and that to fear the results of a German victory was to 'assume that Germany lacks the power of

[1] T. E. Hulme: Introduction to *Reflections on Violence* (*Speculations*, pp. 257–8).

development . . . her *natural* line of development towards a tolerant liberalism'.

Hulme denied that Germany had 'a natural line of development towards a tolerant liberalism', and he denied that a defeated State could 'quietly hold out for freedom'. A German victory would not only change the map; it would kill much that was valuable in the world. Ideas, morals, standards of value are not indestructible; they do not spring inevitably out of the natural goodness of man; they can be altered by education, prestige and propaganda if these are backed by military and financial strength. This possibility of a radical change in the world and its outlook was overlooked by the pacifists:

'They tend to look on war as of the same nature, and probably as caused by the same childish motives, as the struggles of a number of boys in a room. Some may get more damaged than others, but the framework of the struggle is not changed—in the end, as at the beginning, you have a number of boys in a room.'[1]

Some wars have left the participants stronger or weaker, but unchanged in their national character. It does not follow that all wars will do so. Hulme quotes the German philosopher Max Scheler[2] to show that Germany was not fighting for a limited objective, but for absolute dominion. Scheler says that the main object

[1] *Cambridge Magazine,* 29. i. 16.
[2] Max Scheler (1875–1928): *Zur Phänomenologie und Theorie der Sympathiegefühle und von Liebe und Hass* (1912); *Der Genius des Krieges und der deutsche Krieg* (1915); *Krieg und Aufbau* (1913); *Vom Ewigen im Menschen* (1921); *Philosophische Weltanschauung* (1929), etc.

of war is the destruction of the balance of power, and the creation of a new Mediterranean culture founded on the military power of Germany. To attain this end, Russia must be finally driven out of Europe, and France completely crushed. He goes on to attack those Germans who were surprised and shocked at the entry of England into the war. 'It was inevitable that England should come in. Her whole existence as an empire was threatened by the building of the German Fleet.' He reproves those who, 'with an imitation of English cant', have pretended that the fleet was built for defensive purposes. 'The only possible aim in the building of the German Fleet was directed against England.... Our first object must always be the destruction of the English naval supremacy, for this stands between us and the fair division of the earth. If this object is not attained now further struggles must and will follow.'

This argument of Scheler's was the more significant in that it came from one of the younger philosophers who were already beginning to have great influence on the new generation of students. To Hulme, the prospect of a German Europe was intolerable because it meant the extinction of ideals of liberty and democracy; and though he was opposed to the *ideas* with which the democratic movement was associated, he was willing to fight for democracy as an ideal. In its *ideas*, the German outlook resembled his own (Hulme had himself been strongly influenced by Scheler); but his *ideals* remained the same as those of English democrats.

In answer to Hulme, Bertrand Russell maintained

that ethical values were objective: some actions were right and others wrong, whatever their consequences. Hulme agreed with this conception, but he did not believe that non-resistance could be made a supreme value over-riding all others: 'I do not disagree then, with Mr. Russell in his conception of ethical values as *objective*. But I do disagree most profoundly as to the scale or order in which particular "values" should be placed.'

Russell did not at that time base his arguments for pacifism solely on this absolute moral ground, and Hulme claimed to find in Russell an appeal to values such as 'personality' and 'natural growth' that were not objective at all, but came from an uncritical acceptance of the romantic tradition. That is to say, they sprang from a false conception of human nature. They were not morally wrong, because they were not objective at all: even if the romantic conception of human nature was tenable, it was only one of many possible conceptions, and therefore any ideals based upon it could not be objective. The ideal of democracy was not dependent on this conception, and the pacifists were therefore not entitled to talk as though they were the only true supporters of democracy.

'The values. . . . there is nothing *inevitable* about them. They form part of one *ideology* amongst other possible ones. Above all, it is necessary to notice that there is no *necessary* connection between this ideology and the democratic movement. As a rule the two things are never even thought of as separate. Arguments are based alternatively on the one and on the other. . . . It is this innocence—the source of so much pacificist complacency—that must be destroyed. Your ideals may be right or wrong; but they are not to be identified with democracy.'[1]

Hulme thus maintains that the democratic movement in history must not be confused with the belief in the perfectibility of man and the inevitability of progress, nor with the conceptions that spring from that belief. When Hulme attacks 'democracy', in his *Speculations*, he is careful to italicize the word, and he explains clearly that he is using it to denote the ideas usually associated with the democratic movement, and not the movement itself.

Any attack on democratic notions, however, was liable to be mistaken for an attack on the democratic ideal, and Hulme found it necessary to say: 'I have no disguised reactionary motives. I am not in favour of the war because I think all wars favour reaction.[2] I am, on the contrary, inclined to think that this war will hasten the disappearance of the rich.'[3] He readily admits that the arguments against pacifism are often a screen for motives that are entirely different, but he is convinced that his own actions really do spring from the considerations he has put forward. The scepticism with which the pacifist greets all arguments in favour of the war is often justified:

1 *Cambridge Magazine*, 5. ii. 6.
2 As printed in *The Cambridge Magazine* (and in *The New Age*, 3. ii. 16), this sentence has a comma after the word 'war' which wholly alters its sense, and gives it a meaning obviously foreign to Hulme's intention.
3 *Cambridge Magazine*, 12. ii. 16.

'Many people are moved not only by the impulses mentioned above, but by a certain instinct which makes men want life at a higher pitch and intensity (the instinct that makes a man seek the excitement to be got from gambling)—and they imagine that war will provide them with this. Under these circumstances we might deceive ourselves. . . . I do not say that I was not moved by such impulses at the beginning of the war; but I am writing now at a period when any such bellicose impulses in us, any exuberance in this direction, have been cured by experience; I don't think I have an ounce of belli-cosity left. I probably have quite as intense a *desire* for peace as any pacifist.'[1]

To those who argue that the war is pointless, and say that they would fight for some great cause, such as the abolition of capitalism, but will not fight in a war that has no definite objective, Hulme replies that this posi-tion, too, is based on the false conception of inevitable progress. There is no guarantee that the degree of demo-cratic liberty that we have gained will last. It can be maintained only by constant effort, and the German threat to it is all the more dangerous because it is based on ideas that are sounder, and more likely to be effec-tive, than the ideas of pacifist democracy:

'So it comes about that we are unable to name any great *positive* "good" for which we can be said to be fighting. But it is not necessary that we should; there is no harmony in the nature of things, so that from time to time great and useless sacrifices become necessary,

[1] *Cambridge Magazine*, 12. ii. 16.

merely that whatever precarious "good" the world has achieved may just be preserved. These sacrifices are as negative, barren, and as *necessary* as the work of those who repair sea-walls.'[1]

Hulme's position rests on his belief that some values are objective and absolute: they are not justified by any appeal to the fulfilment of personality or the ultimate preservation of the human race. They are the values that make humanity worth preserving, and they are themselves the measure of the fulfilment of a personality.

Any system of ethics that depends on 'progress' or 'personality' is involved in serious difficulties; for we have no means of judging whether a change is really progressive except by asking what further effects it produces, and so on. The plain way of escape from this difficulty is to say that some actions and experiences are good in themselves, and do not need to be justified by their effects. A thing can be good because it is intrinsically good, or because it contributes to the intrinsic value of some whole of which it forms a part, or because it has effects that are good. Thus an action may be good because it favours life, and perhaps most good actions do have effects of this kind. But life itself is good only in virtue of the intrinsically good things.

It is, however, very hard to persuade other people that a thing is intrinsically good or that it enhances an intrinsic good, and this difficulty often tempts people to try to justify the things they consider good by proving that they lead to a remoter good. That is to say,

[1] *Cambridge Magazine*, 12. ii. 16.

people do not like to make the bold claim that such-and-such a thing is good in itself. True, we all feel that some things are good in themselves, but we always like to justify ourselves by showing that these things have effects that are recognized as good by people we respect.

There is some justification for this view: there are no *purely* intrinsic goods, and things that are intrinsically good usually do have good effects as well. In judging a thing, we have to take into account its intrinsic merit, its contribution to other intrinsic goods, and its effects; and one of the most difficult problems of criticism is to decide what relative importance we are to attach to all these. But we cannot assume that *all* intrinsic goods do have good effects as well, unless we use the word 'effects' in a very wide sense. We might reasonably say that a liking for Bach is good because the whole outlook and sensibility that is likely to go with it, and is encouraged by it, is good in other ways; and we can justify our argument by pointing to specific examples. But we are still compelled to count the liking for Bach as an intrinsic good. The attempt to justify the liking is not irrelevant, but it can never be wholly successful.

The 'rational' argument, which tries to do this, proves nothing in the end, and therefore those who share Hulme's outlook are quite willing to put up with being called 'irrational', because they know that they are no more irrational than anyone else. The difference between them and the rationalists is that they consciously make assumptions based on authority or revelation or personal intuition, whereas the rationalists choose their moral values unconsciously and delude themselves into the belief that somehow these values are 'proved' by their reasoning.

'The principal feature about this ethic is the "irrationality" of certain values, i.e. the assertion that certain actions, though good, may involve sacrifice of life and personality; *a sacrifice which it may be impossible to rationalize, by showing that it furthers life in remoter ways.* We can conveniently refer to such values as the *Heroic* values.'

The rationalist admits that men do feel these values, and feel that they are superior to the more 'useful' values; but he explains this feeling by calling it an atavism. Thus he says that the admiration of useless courage is a survival from the early stages of history, when a disposition to ferocity was a biological advantage. Hulme thinks that such an explanation of the heroic values is quite untrue:

'When a man, after much weighing of motives, suddenly brushing calculations on one side . . . sees clearly that this is an *absolute* value, and must be accepted as absolute, above calculation, and superior to values based on *life* and *personality* . . . then, I think it wrong to say that he has been moved by some underlying atavistic impulse which has suddenly come to the surface. On the contrary, I should say that he was understanding the nature of ethics for the first time.'[1]

In all systems, whether of ethics or aesthetics or metaphysics, there comes a point at which something gratuitous and undemonstrable must be introduced, something taking a place in the system like that which life takes in the world. The rationalist introduces this mys-

[1] *Cambridge Magazine*, 4. iii. 16.

tery or singularity in his talk of 'personality' and 'progress': Hulme introduces it when he deals with 'heroic values' and claims that these values are essential to 'the true (as opposed to the rationalist) ethic'. The rationalists, he says, 'seem to have known *instinctively* that this conception of heroism was the central *nerve* of the ethic they opposed; and have consequently always tried to disintegrate it by ridicule. The author of *Arms and the Man* thus reminds one of the wasps described by Fabre, who sting their prey in the central ganglia in order to paralyse it, in this way acting as if they were expert entomologists, though in reality they can have no conscious knowledge of what they are doing.'[1]

In what way these 'heroic values' can be made the basis of a civilization, Hulme does not say. Perhaps he would have claimed that most of what we call civilization does not depend on ethics at all, but on expediency and enlightened self-interest. He is tantalizingly vague about the nature of the true intrinsic values, and his articles stopped just at the point at which he seemed to be about to make it all plain:

'There are two senses in which the heroic values may be regarded as the key to a proper understanding of ethics.

'(a) It is most probably only through a realization of these values that the sceptic about ethics comes to see what there is that is *objective* and *absolute* in the subject.

'(b) Any system of ethics establishes a hierarchy of values, the lower terms of which are founded upon the higher. In this sense it may be said that most of the com-

[1] *Cambridge Magazine*, 4. iii. 16.

moner virtues presuppose and rest upon the heroic values; just as these rest (not as a matter of individual psychology, but essentially) on the values given in religion.'[1]

In these War Notes, Hulme does not always maintain the distinction between (a) the romantic ideas associated with democracy, (b) certain historical changes, the collapse of the landowning aristocracy, for example, that were brought about by those ideals and by technical and industrial changes, but would be irreversible even if the ideas that hastened them were reversed, and (c) something positively valuable in 'liberalism'. Neither Hulme nor Sorel speaks plainly about this last quality. To call it 'the democratic ideal' was journalistically tactful, but it was needlessly confusing. What they really admired was first of all the responsibility that democracy lays on the individual, secondly the liberal conception of intellectual freedom, and thirdly the idea of a society whose economic arrangements would conform to the morality and ideology that it publicly professed. On this point, Scheler agrees with Sorel and Hulme: he says that it is impossible to maintain a religious belief in absolute values, except in a society whose economy is based upon such values.[2]

Hulme had been very deeply impressed by the ethical writings of Moore and by Husserl's philosophy; and presumably Scheler, who was also a follower of Husserl, would have agreed with most of Hulme's arguments. Scheler, indeed, resembled Hulme both in temperament and outlook. Husserl claimed that the only certainties

[1] *Cambridge Magazine*, 4. iii. 16.   [2] See quotation, p. 168.

were those given directly in intuition, and Scheler, in his earlier work, applied Husserl's methods to the study of ethics. But his analysis is less rigorous than Husserl's, and lacks the patient submission to facts and the resolute preliminary suspension of judgment that were an essential part of Husserl's method. In Scheler, as in Hulme, we see the influence of Nietzsche, not only in the doctrine that science and abstract thought have a limited significance, but also in the view that humanist culture, together with the values of religion and morality, is in decline. Nietzsche believed that civilization could not be saved from nihilism except by a philosophy deliberately based on 'the will to power'. Scheler[1] wavers between the view that Nietzsche rejected—that behind the empirical world there is another which is 'absolute' or 'divine'—and the view that all virtues and all values are the outcome of the instincts. *Vom Ewigen im Menschen*, which Scheler published in 1921, was deeply sympathetic to the Catholic Church: it seemed to him, that beyond the relative 'humanist' values, there were 'pleasure-values', 'life-values', and 'holiness', set in a universe whose essence is love. In this view, the divine is not wholly separate from the human; the two are united in the mystical body of Christ, as they are in the doctrine of Nicholas of Cusa. But Scheler could not rest here, nor could he long accept the authority of the Church, and in a later period of his work the sceptical element and the emphasis on instinct became so marked that he was accused of the 'atheism' and 'nihilism' with which he was trying to deal.

[1] *Der Formalismus in der Ethik und die materiale Wertethik* (1913–16).

Much of this description applies as well to Hulme as to Scheler, and yet Scheler's arguments in favour of the war were based on principles very like those that actuated Hulme. Two variants of one philosophy, acting on two men of like temperament, incite them to help to kill each other. The fact does not disprove the philosophy, but it points to a weakness. The evasive attitude to the Church may seem to be the crucial point. There must be some authoritative way in which the absolute values can be tested and established: they cannot be established by each man for himself, on his personal intuition. The Church in practice does not always rise above national quarrels, nor can it prevent them, but it can do something towards establishing absolute values without glorifying war. The absolute values may include the 'heroic virtues', and the person who believes in them may believe that violence is sometimes the right and necessary way to defend ideals, but the values must not of themselves incite those who accept them to fight each other. That which is intrinsically valuable is the willingness to fight, not the actual fighting; the value of the fighting depends on the purpose behind it. Hulme's doctrine and the doctrine that Scheler professed in 1915 had no common basis by which such purposes could be judged. It is this fact, and not Russell's argument, that reveals the inadequacy of Hulme's position.

Chapter Six

AN ANALYSIS OF HULME'S POSITION

'We live in a room, of course, but the great question for philosophy is: how far have we decorated the room, and how far was it made before we came? Did we merely decorate the room, or did we make it from chaos? The laws of nature that we certainly do find —what are they?'—T. E. HULME, *Speculations*, p. 226.

There is scarcely a single statement in Hulme that is not borrowed: his distinction between scientific philosophy and *Weltanschauung* comes from Husserl and Dilthey, his 'classical' conception of man and his notion of the three worlds come from Pascal, his view of the world as flux from Bergson, his doctrine of intrinsic moral values from G. E. Moore, his talk about geometrical and vital art comes from Worringer, his interpretation of romanticism from Lasserre, his defence of violence from Sorel, and his conception of poetry as a logic of images might have been taken from any one of half a dozen French or German writers.[1] Hulme's merits are seldom those of originality, but originality is more often a vice than a virtue, and Hulme, though he added little to the European

[1] Hulme's essay on *Romanticism and Classicism*, his *Lecture on Modern Poetry*, and his *Notes on Language and Style*, owe a great deal to Rémy de Gourmont's *Dissociations* and *Le Problème du Style*.

tradition, did something to preserve it. He writes with a brilliant metaphysical style, very different from Husserl's abominable sludge, he seizes important points and puts them pungently, he knows more of philosophy than most art critics do, and his judgments in art are worth more than those of most philosophers. He writes more vividly and more coherently than Sorel, but like his master he does not pause to answer an objection. He has the enthusiasm and the naïveté of the amateur, and rushes on with the same dogmatic and incisive style and the same air of excitement and exploration, whether he is discussing the familiar quaysides of New York or the wilds of an unexplored Kamchatka.

In Hulme's philosophy, there is little that can properly be called scientific, and much that is personal. He admires systematic philosophers like Moore and Husserl, who try to doubt every statement they are tempted to make, and do not pass over a possibility until it has been shown to lead to a contradiction or other absurdity; but his own method is to assert impetuously his views, and only when those views contradict common beliefs does he set to work to make an ingenious, and often useful, distinction. He echoes Dilthey's plea for a critique of historical reason, but he seldom uses the historical approach to test his own ideas. He uses suitably chosen historical examples to show other people that the set of terms they use in speaking of the world is not the only possible one, but he does not use the method in order to transcend particular interpretations.

The unity of Hulme's work is temperamental rather

than logical, and one important point about him is that men of Hulme's temperament seldom write philosophy at all. He was active and restless, rather than sedentary and contemplative; he was a man of exceptionally wide interests and not only knew something of the arts and sciences, but enjoyed them and showed ability and taste in their pursuit; there was a touch of personal arrogance in his attitude to humanity in general, and some reverence for tradition when the tradition was old enough and could be used against his own contemporaries. Like Sorel, he seemed to hate followers quite as bitterly as he hated his opponents. An audience, yes, but not followers, because followers would corrupt and vulgarize all that he had said. He even speaks, in his notebooks, of the danger 'that when all these notes are arranged, the order will kill them in commonplace'.

It would be absurd to claim that Hulme was a very original thinker or that his motives were always philosophically 'pure', but it would be equally absurd to dismiss his writing as a mere scrap-book of favourite quotations. Hulme has three great merits. First of all, the ideas that he borrowed are important and not as widely known in England as they ought to be. Secondly, he expressed those ideas with great vigour and clarity. Thirdly, though Hulme was temperamental and unsystematic, his ideas are far less contradictory and incoherent than they appear to be.

The action of European thought on English criticism is intermittent: for the most part, the English critic goes his own way, and accepts his language 'as God and his

English people made it'. What Mill said of our philosophical insularity in 1835 is still true of our position in
politics and in literary criticism to-day. Even if Hulme
had no other merit, he would still deserve thanks for his
labour in carrying ideas across the Channel. It is work
of the kind that was done by Sidney, Dryden, Coleridge
and Arnold, and it is always useful and never easy. Even
if the ideas, once stated, seem obvious and familiar, it
needs a special kind of ability to detect that it was exactly
those weapons that were lacking, or lying idle, in the
armoury of English criticism. If Hulme's work is an
anthology, it is at any rate an anthology of the most
active thought of his time; and its apparent contradictions and incoherences point to something more than a
personal failure. For our purposes, it may be worth
while to tabulate some of Hulme's assertions:

1. *a.* There is an objective external world.

   b. The apparent order in the external world is not
   objective: the world is really cinders.

   c. Other people exist.

   d. The apparent order in the world is the result of our
   habits of thought; our minds pick out the bits that
   seem more or less ordered.

2. *a.* There are three worlds, the mechanical, the vital,
   and the religious.

   b. These are absolutely distinct.

   c. In the first and third, absolute knowledge is possible.

   d. We cannot know anything of the second or natural
   world except relatively and under conditions.

3. *a.* In the mechanical and religious world, it is possible

to isolate entities whose relations can be discussed by rules of logic.

b. In the natural or vital world it is not possible to detach fragments and discuss them in this way, but fragments exist and can be apprehended by an act of intuition.

c. Anything that expresses and communicates such an intuition is a work of art.

d. This is the only test of a work of art.

4. *a.* Every philosophy contains two parts.

b. One of these parts is scientific and objective; it is a critique of the concepts used in the special sciences.

c. The other part is personal: it is the outcome of the philosopher's wish to regard the world as satisfactory and to justify himself in it.

d. In discussing this personal part, a critique of satisfaction is needed.

5. *a.* Ideas are sometimes accepted because of their coherence and correspondence with the facts.

b. Material conditions sometimes decide whether ideas are to become widespread or not.

c. Ideas, if they are widely accepted, can influence the course of history.

6. All men are equal.

7. *a.* Man is not fundamentally good.

b. Humanism makes man and man's desires the measure of all things.

8. Tradition and discipline are necessary if anything good is to be got out of man.

9. *a.* Man is not naturally progressive in a moral sense.

b. Nor is he capable of attaining perfection.

c. Liberal democracy assumes that man is both perfectible and naturally progressive.

10. *a.* There is no natural standard of justice.

b. It is possible to define absolute standards of ethics.

c. It is necessary to define these standards.

d. These standards ultimately rest on values derived from religion.

e. There is a hierarchy of these values.

f. Non-violence is not one of the highest values.

g. The use of violence in defence of the highest values may sometimes be necessary.

h. The willingness to use violence in this way is itself one of the objective values.

As a scientific philosophy, this would be heartbreaking; it blandly ignores some of the most difficult problems of philosophy; it includes some assumptions, such as (6), that are never made clear, and some that are unnecessary. Hulme's *Sketch for a New Weltanschauung* is a mixture of moral principles, definitions, assertions about history, and assumptions that belong to systematic philosophy. It is not an orthodox philosophy, but it resembles the Thomist philosophy in not recognizing any distinction between moral and aesthetic values. Hulme says that a work of art is an intuition of reality, and the standards by which he condemns romantic art and commends classical art are always moral and intellectual. This, perhaps, is what one might expect from a follower of Worringer, who is more interested in works of art regarded as parables or allegories expressing intellectual and moral beliefs than in art simply as a thing in itself, valuable quite apart from its ascertainable meaning.

The metaphysical assertions are derived from Bergson, but are modified by Hulme's tendency to describe everything in spatial metaphors, even when he is talking about time. Further, these metaphysical assumptions imply others that are never explicitly stated. No doubt the position is tenable, but it is a description of the raw material of a metaphysics, rather than a metaphysics itself: it offers a framework for Hulme's assertion of his personal creed, but the creed could be expressed just as well within quite a different framework.

Hulme sometimes allows his metaphor about cinders to run away with his judgment: he then says that the world is wholly chaotic. In more sober moments, he seems to believe that the whole of our experience is a featured continuum like a landscape: some patches of that continuum resemble others, as one hill resembles another, and so we can divide the continuum up into features, such as hills, rivers, towns, counties, that are arbitrary but yet objective. Different maps of the continuum can be drawn (like rainfall maps, population maps, and so on); and these are related to each other, but often in a very complex way. And though experience is partly ordered, we cannot accurately represent it by sharply defined symbols, because the things we try to represent merge into each other as hills merge into valleys, and rivers into glaciers and seas.

This description of experience leaves unanswered all the old problems about the nature of knowledge and the relation of language to reality; but there seems to be no devastating objection to it; and it has one great merit: it keeps the attention firmly directed to the existence of *people*. Hulme did not base an argument on it—it was the vehicle of his thought and not the thought itself— and his other assumptions and arguments might have been stated in other terms without losing their force. In any case, if we are going to say that there is no means of knowing whether a particular perception of order is really a perception of external reality, or an impression common to all reasonable people, it does not matter whether we describe the order as external or not; it is objective; that is to say, it can be shown to anyone and does not vary from one person to another. If we go on to say that in addition to these objective perceptions of order, there are others, which are not common to everybody, but only to people in one place, or living at one time, or educated in one special way, or speaking one special language, and if we add that these perceptions common to one group of people cannot readily be distinguished from perceptions of truly objective truth, then we admit all that is needed for the development of the rest of Hulme's outlook.

As we have seen, Hulme does not set up aesthetic judgment as something distinct from moral and intellectual judgment; furthermore, he does not separate moral and intellectual judgment. He does not assert that there are two kinds of truth or that there is a realm of values distinct from the realm of things. In place of the humanist's absolute distinction between things and their value, Hulme sets his distinction between three orders of reality.

This he derives from Pascal: 'The infinite distance between body and mind is a symbol of the infinitely more infinite distance between mind and charity; for charity is supernatural. . . . Great geniuses have their power, their glory, their greatness, their victory, their lustre, and have no need of worldly greatness, with which they are not in keeping. They are seen, not by the eye, but by the mind; this is sufficient. The saints have their power, their glory, their victory, their lustre, and need no worldly or intellectual greatness, with which they have no affinity; for these neither add anything to them, nor take away anything from them. They are seen of God and the angels, and not of the body, nor of the curious mind. God is enough for them. . . . All bodies, the firmament, the stars, the earth and its kingdoms, are not equal to the lowest mind; for mind knows all these and itself; and these bodies nothing. All bodies together, and all minds together, and all their products, are not equal to the least feeling of charity. This is of an order infinitely more exalted. From all bodies together, we cannot obtain one little thought; this is impossible, and of another order. From all bodies and minds, we cannot produce a feeling of true charity; this is impossible and of another and supernatural order.'[1]

Hulme's distinction, however, is not quite the same as Pascal's: in Hulme's description the three regions are not those of body, mind, and charity,[2] but those of inor-

[1] Fragment 792.

[2] 'Charity', as Pascal uses the word, seems to mean the divine gift of grace, the love of God. The 'region of charity', as he describes it, is wider than the 'realm of moral values' as the positivist or the ethical

ganic matter, the organic world, and the world of religious values. Pascal's distinction between mind and body raises one of the perennial problems of philosophy, but Hulme confuses the problem instead of clarifying it when he replaces it by the distinction between the vital and the mechanical worlds, which he tries to make clear by an example. 'A mechanical complexity is the sum of its parts. Put them side by side and you get the whole. Now vital or organic is merely a convenient metaphor for a complexity of a different kind, that in which the parts cannot be said to be elements as each one is modified by the other's presence, and each one to a certain extent is the whole. The leg of a chair by itself is still a leg. My leg by itself wouldn't be.'[1]

This useful common-sense distinction works fairly well as long as we are talking about bricks and tables on the one hand, and eels and rabbits on the other; but when the scientist begins to study things that are neither seen nor felt directly, he becomes less confident. The 'atom' of theoretical chemistry is assumed to be 'mechanical' in Hulme's sense, but in atomic physics it shows nasty signs of being something more than the sum of its parts. 'Vital events are not completely *determined* and mechanical', says Hulme.[2] But neither are physical events: they cannot be foreseen in detail. There is always a margin of uncertainty, and the smaller the system the bigger the uncertainty. The only world that completely satisfies

atheist uses the phrase. On this point, Hulme is at one with Pascal; and when he speaks of the world of religion or religious values it seems that he means to include 'grace'.

[1] *Speculations*, p. 138.   [2] Ibid., p. 7.

Hulme's conditions is the ideal world of theoretical reasoning: theoretical mechanics may indeed be mechanical, but the real world that is partially and more or less accurately represented by the theory is not 'mechanical' in the same sense. We cannot detach portions of reality either physically or mentally without altering or misrepresenting reality itself. A hill is a hill *in situ* not *in vacuo*.

Again, not only is the mechanical world ('the leg of a chair') quite as organic as Hulme's own leg, but also the world of theoretical biology is quite as mechanical as the world of theoretical physics. The scientist always tries to find a formula, that is to say, to find concepts that when manipulated according to fixed rules will represent the behaviour of the empirical world. The arguments for and against vitalism in biology therefore have nothing to do with this discussion. If a special concept such as 'organism' is ultimately found to be necessary in the biological sciences, it will be like any other scientific concept: it will be a new concept modifying all the others, as the notion of an electron modifies the notion of an atom. It will not belong to a world apart, but will take a place in a definite technique for describing and forecasting the behaviour of some aspects of the world.

When we talk in this way, we are in danger of confusing the literal and the figurative senses of the word 'mechanical': there is a plain sense in which it is ridiculous to say that a human leg is mechanical. Hulme himself does confuse these two senses, and he adds to the difficulty by combining a figurative meaning of 'mech-

anical' with one, or perhaps two, of the meanings of
'determined'. This combination must be rejected, and
unless Hulme's distinction between the 'vital' and the
'mechanical' worlds is nothing more than the usual rough
and ready division between the vegetable and mineral
kingdoms, it must be taken as a distinction between the
real world of the senses and an ideal world that more or
less represents one part of it. The one is an objective
reality (the real cinders), the other is a world of discourse (the built-up picture of the cinders). This possible interpretation leads us to ask whether the world of
ethical and religious values is also a world of discourse,
a symbolic picture of a natural cindery world.

The question is this: can we distinguish between a
'natural' world (the vital and mechanical worlds) and
some other world? In what sense can we say that there
is no 'natural' objective justice, if we nevertheless believe
that there is a world of religious values that is objective
and accessible to everybody? Furthermore, if something
good can be got out of man by tradition and discipline,
and the tradition and discipline are supplied by other
men, how can you say that 'man is not naturally good'?
The only way out seems to be to say that there are two
kinds of knowledge, the one 'natural' and the other 'revealed', and that the tradition and discipline come from
this 'revealed' knowledge. But how can revealed knowledge be established, and how can true 'revealed' knowledge be distinguished from false?

It is here that Hulme invokes his 'Critique of Satisfaction'. It seems (though Hulme never makes this clear)

that in one sense the critique is as 'natural' as the special sciences: the ordinary process of reasoning, if it is applied to our natural knowledge, and if it is pursued long enough, shows the vanity of desire; but by an intuition, as certain as any knowledge that we have, we know that this conclusion cannot be final. This intuition marks the boundary between 'natural' knowledge and the knowledge of what Hulme would call the world of religion: it leads us to recognize the existence of an absolute moral imperative, and once this is admitted a new development of our knowledge becomes possible. By appealing to history and authority we can guard against personal errors in the application of this intuition, and thus our knowledge in the new region is as reliable as our scientific knowledge. Interpreted in this way, it seems that the distinction between the three worlds does not imply that there are two kinds of knowledge: the knowledge of the world of religion is as 'natural' as any other, though it rests on a process of criticism that seems unusual to the humanist, and on an intuition that he does not question but is reluctant to use.

Hulme's assertion that we can have absolute and certain knowledge of the mechanical and religious worlds, and that this knowledge can be exactly reflected in logical terms, seems to rest on a misunderstanding of the nature of mechanics, and on a confusion of knowledge about the structure of ethics with knowledge of ethical values. The scientist himself does not claim that he arrives at absolute knowledge even in mechanics: 'A scientific belief is a policy, not a creed.' Of course, the fact that the ideal world of mechanics does more or less represent one part of our experience may be taken to show that there is some kind of order in that part; although we can only know that order more or less roughly, partly because our language does not really fit it, and partly because our own observation always alters it to an unknowable extent.

That is the position of the Thomist, who accepts the nominalist argument that all science is only an approximate representation, but insists that there must be some underlying order that produces the approximate correspondence with human logic. In the same way, it may be said that there is an underlying moral order, whose form is approximately represented by theoretical ethics, and the Thomist can go on to say that there are some ethical concepts that are as useful and 'accurate' as mathematical numbers. But it does not follow that we have any certain knowledge that one thing is right and another wrong; or that such knowledge, if we have it, can ever be expressed in logical terms. Even if we accept Moore's ethical system, either we must test an ethic by experience, as we test a particular geometry when we propose to apply it to the real world, or we must find some basis for it outside our ordinary experience. We can still believe in a morality, as we believe in a geometry, but we do so on the strength of experience and authority.

Hulme is confused at this point: he has tried to combine Bergson's distinction between what can be said in logical language and what cannot, with Pascal's distinction between the material, intellectual and spiritual worlds. Pascal's distinction is valid and useful; but there is no reason whatever for saying that the first and third are mechanical, and the second organic, or that absolute knowledge is possible in the first and third and only relative knowledge in the second. Each of these three 'worlds' can be discussed, more or less adequately, in logical language and in poetic language: the difficulties and the advantages vary only in degree.

Part of Hulme's difficulty comes from the fact that he never properly distinguishes between 'intrinsic values', 'objective values', and 'absolute values'. If for some people something is good in itself, he at once assumes that it can be treated as a detached inorganic entity, that its existence and value can be demonstrated to other people, and that it can be given a definite place in a hierarchy of values. This is the outcome of his passion for geometrical images, and combined with his limited knowledge of physical and biological science it leads him to say that the 'mechanical' and 'religious' worlds share some quality which they do not share with the 'vital' world.

All that is really essential to Hulme's position seems to be this: all our reasoning about empirical knowledge does nothing more than show the structure of experience; it does not strengthen our motives or set them in order, but rather weakens them and destroys their order. All is vanity and uncertainty, if reasoning and empirical knowledge are the only sources of truth. 'All bodies together, and all minds together, and all their products, are not equal to the least feeling of charity.' The confidence that gives reality to courage and love, and all the things we value, cannot be known solely through the description of mind and body, though our language nearly always forces us to speak in terms of mind and body. To represent the relations of this source of value to the world of mind and body, which is the field of 'natural' knowledge, we must use metaphors; we can talk, for example, of a 'world' of values or a 'sphere' or 'plane' of values distinct from the material and intellectual regions, but this is always, and only, a metaphor.

When Hulme says that the world of religion is like the world of theoretical mechanics, he is needlessly adding to his own difficulties. It might equally well be argued that religious values cannot be described in logical terms, and must always be expressed in parable or poetic metaphor; and this view would in no sense weaken Hulme's essential doctrine that these values are objective and absolute. Pascal's statement is more judicious than Hulme's; he keeps closer to the fundamental contention that all is vanity unless the values of religion are objective. The assertion that there is a world of religious values, distinct from the world of mind and body, presents difficulties, like any other fundamental distinction; but these difficulties need not be confused with those that follow from the assertion that the distinction between logical and poetic language is the same as the distinction between inorganic and organic matter.

The doctrine of the three worlds certainly enables Hulme to state very clearly his view that man is neither fundamentally good nor naturally progressive; it has a metaphorical value, and it points the way by which we can pass beyond the conclusion that all is vanity. If we believe not only that there is only one kind of knowledge, and one kind of reality, but also that everything of value must be justified by its consequences, we are led to this conclusion of vanity, for a morality of this kind becomes nothing but a matter of prudence unless we back it up with a belief in the desirability of human survival, and human survival hardly seems worth while unless we can point to some intrinsic goods that are incidental to it.

In order to make it clear that the value of any action or experience depends, not on its consequences in the world that is of a piece with the world of matter and thought, but on itself alone, Hulme says that the value is a manifestation of another, quite different, world; and by saying that this other world is disparate, he denies the relevance of the consequences altogether. He speaks as if 'intrinsic' values were necessarily 'isolated'—as if the Weisshorn, being beautiful, existed by itself, apart from the Dent Blanche and the Rothorn and the earth and sky. But there is no need to chose between the one assertion, that the object or its value exists utterly alone, and the other, that the object or its value exists only as a wholly undetachable feature of the whole universe. It is better to say that as we can *focus* on the Weisshorn, so we can focus on an 'intrinsic' value; we need not ignore completely the relations between it and the rest of the world. In this matter there is a sort of law of inverse squares ('charity begins at home' expresses the notion) and in practice we all recognize this law and act upon it.

When Hulme attacks an error he is always inclined to assume that its opposite must be true; he seldom asks whether it is based on a false antithesis. Thus in dealing with the view that man is naturally good he does not examine the word 'naturally', but goes to the other extreme and says that man is naturally bad. This doctrine he identifies with the dogma of original sin; but in Christianity the dogma of original sin is inseparable from the doctrine of redemption, and this last involves the possibility that man may recognize and accept redemption. Pascal insists on this: 'It is equally dangerous for man to know God without knowing his own wretchedness, and to know his own wretchedness without knowing the Redeemer who can free him from it.'[1]

Hulme, in spite of his Bergsonian ideas, has a passion for making those distinctions that are the basis of all logical thought; and having made his distinctions, he has a quite un-Bergsonian belief that they are universal and unalterable. This belief he reinforces by running two or three distinctions into one: he speaks as if the distinction between the spiritual and the natural world were the same as the distinction between logic and poetry or between physics and biology. Hulme's combination of different antitheses often does more to confuse issues than to clarify them. To this point we must return; but we must first ask whether the Bergsonian element in Hulme's thought—the philosophy of *Cinders*—really contradicts his assertions that some values are objective and absolute.

[1] Fragment 555.

Chapter Seven

A CONTRADICTION?

'There is no such thing as an absolute truth to be discovered. All general statements about truth, etc., are in the end only amplifications of man's appetites.'—T. E. HULME, *Speculations*, p. 217.
'I hold the religious conception of ultimate values to be right, the humanist wrong. From the nature of things, these categories are not inevitable, like the categories of time and space, but are *equally objective*. In speaking of religion, it is to this level of abstraction that I wish to refer.'—T. E. HULME, *Speculations*, p. 70.

There are two elements in Hulme's work: the one nominalist and agnostic, the other realist and religious; the first derived from Bergson, the second, from Pascal, Husserl, and Moore; and at first sight these two seem to be contradictory. In the fragments he calls *Cinders*, Hulme says that there is no such thing as absolute truth to be discovered, and his outlook is thoroughly nominalist and pragmatic. 'Language becomes a disease in the hands of the counter-word mongers. It must constantly be remembered that it is an invention for the convenience of men. . . . Symbols are picked out and believed to be realities. People imagine that all the complicated structure of the world can be woven out of "good" and "beauty". These words are merely counters representing vague groups of

135

things, to be moved about on a board for the convenience of the players.'

In the essays on *Humanism and the Religious Attitude* and *Romanticism and Classicism*, on the other hand, his outlook is realist. 'Logic, then, does *not* deal with the laws of human thought but with these quite *objective* sentences. In this way the anthropomorphism which underlies certain views of logic is got rid of. Similarly, ethics can be exhibited as an objective science, and is also purified from anthropomorphism.'[1]

No doubt there is a discrepancy between the two doctrines that Hulme is echoing: Hulme was an impressionable man, and sympathized first with one current of thought and then another. In this he resembled his contemporary, Max Scheler, and Hulme's notebooks show that he felt a good deal of sympathy with Scheler's published work. Both Hulme and Scheler showed judgment and discrimination in seizing on just those elements of contemporary thought that were most significant, and both of them tried to reconcile the resulting contradictions in their outlook. Scheler was deeply impressed by the psycho-analyst's argument that the instincts are the driving-forces of life, and that consciousness has no power of its own; but as a disciple of Husserl he believed that objective knowledge was not wholly impossible. In the last of his completed books,[2] he came to the conclusion that 'Man's essence, and what we may call his peculiar position, consists in something far beyond what is meant by intelligence and the power of choice.' The essential

[1] *Speculations*, p. 44.　　[2] *Die Stellung des Menschen im Kosmos* (1928).

quality of man Scheler calls *Geist*, or 'spiritual intelligence'. This 'spiritual intelligence' is powerless from the beginning; it owes its strength and efficiency to the energy that comes from suppressed impulses, but it does not arise out of sublimation. It draws its sustenance from the forms of life, as the forms of life draw theirs from the inorganic world.

To many people, it seems that the conclusion to which Scheler comes is sceptical and incoherent: they are not convinced that he has reconciled the two apparently conflicting attitudes with which he started. *Die Stellung des Menschen im Kosmos* did not appear until long after Hulme's death, but already in *Cinders* Hulme faces the same problem. If all belief can be traced to the circumstances of the writer's class, experience, capacity, and body, there is no average or real truth to be discovered anywhere; the whole structure of logic is seen to be something imposed upon the world of experience. 'World is indescribable, that is, not reducible to counters; and particularly it is impossible to include it all under one large counter such as "God" or "Truth" and the other verbalisms, or the disease of the symbolic language.'[1] 'The absolute is invented to reconcile conflicting purposes. But these purposes are necessarily conflicting, even in the nature of Truth itself. It is so absurd to construct an absolute which shall at each moment just manage by artificial gymnastics to reconcile these purposes.'[2]

It is easy to see the temptation to jump from this into complete scepticism, but there is another element

[1] *Speculations*, p. 221.   [2] Ibid., p. 228.

in Hulme that points in a different direction. Hulme knew that there might seem to be a difficulty in combining a metaphysic like Bergson's with a belief in objective ethics—it was this point that he discussed with Lasserre in Paris—but he believed that the two views were consistent and that both were necessary. The statements that we can make in the special sciences are good enough for particular purposes, but they are only relatively valid; we can discover no absolute universal truth that is valid for every purpose and in every context. Within its proper field, we cannot escape from the doctrine that 'All is flux. . . . Truth is what helps a particular sect in the general flow.' But there is another task for the philosopher. 'To take frankly that fluid basis and elaborate it into a solidity, that the gods do not exist horizontally in space but somehow vertically in the isolated fragment of the tribe. There is another form of space where gods, etc., do exist concretely.'[1]

It is with that aspect of the philosopher's work that Hulme is most deeply concerned. His conception of *Cinders* is not put forward as the final truth, for there is no finality; as long as we are thinking of arm-chair philosophy, knowledge has no absolute foundations. It is like the surface of a sphere, and the only absolute truths in that surface are tautologies and rules of grammar. But the moment we leave this uncertain world of empirical knowledge and abstract reasoning we are compelled to ask, what is the reality that underlies this partial and relative knowledge? In trying to answer this question

[1] *Speculations*, p. 244.

we become aware of something outside the surface, and it is 'at this level of abstraction' that Hulme finds his objective truths.

As a workshop habit of mind for the theoretical scientist, some kind of nominalism or pragmatism is necessary: it offers him a matrix and solvent of ideas that enables him to develop his theory in a way that fits the facts. He does not expect to arrive at final truths, nor does he wish to. He uses a scientific belief as a policy and not a creed. His aim is to think of more and more experiments and to fit more and more observations into a calculus. Some of the philosophers who take their cue from the scientists go further. They say that we can arrive at theories that work fairly well by consciously false assumptions. We know that these fictions do not reflect reality, but we handle them *as if* they did. Among such fictions are God, freedom, the average man, empty space, matter, points, rays, the atom, infinity, the absolute. All general ideas, all abstract comparisons and classifications, and all the sciences and arts, are built on fictions.

To say this, however, is to go beyond the nominalism that is needed in science. The general concepts by means of which we describe our empirical knowledge must certainly be regarded as 'fictions' if we are to preserve that flexibility that will enable us to modify and develop our science. Husserl, upon whose work Hulme bases his attitude, does not dispute the legitimate scientific notion that all abstract concepts are 'fictions'; but he maintains that quite apart from all the rules of grammar and the conventions of language, beyond the partial and relative 'facts' on which our fictions are based, there are essential features that cannot be doubted. Thus we can doubt whether a particular sheet of paper is red or orange, but we cannot doubt that orange is a colour between red and yellow, or that colour is a property that belongs to extended surfaces. Husserl's 'phenomenology' is a study of these essential features, which are known intuitively even when we refrain from all conscious presuppositions about the 'reality' of our conscious experiences and judgments.

Husserl's method, though it may reveal some 'essential' features of ethics, hardly leads to an objective code of morals. Hulme does not follow Husserl very closely: he assumes that Husserl establishes the existence of some kind of objective knowledge in ethics; and he goes on to assume the existence of an objective hierarchy of moral values behind the appearances that make up our experience. Our personal knowledge of these absolute truths and absolute values is limited and relative, and we approach them only through authoritative knowledge. In the same way we say that there is an outside material world, though we do not know this world directly, but only through authoritative science. The common-sense view of metaphysics suggests that there *is* a material world independent of human wishes and perceptions; and in the same way the common-sense view of ethics suggests that there are absolute ethical values, independent of our wishes and perceptions. Hulme believes in a world of absolute ethical values as we believe in other kinds of external reality; but when it comes to the discussion of our actual *knowledge* of these values, then he says that our knowledge is always limited and relative.

In arriving at this position, Hulme was influenced by *Principia Ethica* of G. E. Moore. Like all English amateurs in philosophy, Hulme was by nature empiric and nominalist, and when he first read Russell's logic and Moore's ethics the whole discussion seemed to him almost entirely verbal. But in the work of Husserl and his followers Hulme found the same methods applied to things that already interested him. He began to believe that in some kinds of knowledge the same type of non-empirical reasoning is possible as in geometry. Logic, in such a view, does not deal with the laws of human thought, but with objective sentences; and ethics, too, is an objective science. 'The entities which form the subject-matter of these sciences are neither physical nor mental, they "subsist". They are dealt with by an investigation that is *not* empirical. Statements can be made about them whose truth does not depend on experience. When the empirical prejudice has been got rid of, it becomes possible to think of certain "higher" concepts, those of the good, of love, etc., as, at the same time, *simple*, and not necessarily to be analysed into more *elementary* (generally sensual) elements.'[1]

The realist position, as Hulme states it, is open to severe nominalist criticism: it is very doubtful, for example, whether geometry deals with entities that 'subsist' in a world beneath the world of appearance. The nominalist might claim that a geometry is not an objec-

[1] *Speculations*, p. 45.

tive science, but a game played in accordance with rules invented as an approximation to empirical facts, and that the whole of language, with its vocabulary, syntax and logic, is another human invention to reflect the empirical world. A geometry, he might say, leads to unforeseen conclusions, and so does language: often those conclusions are demonstrably false if we apply them to the empirical world, and no good purpose is served by postulating a purely verbal world in which they are true.

To this, the realist replies that he is not identifying a particular geometry or physics with the real subsistent world (that would be a form of materialism) any more than he is identifying one particular moral code with the world of absolute ethics: he is merely saying that the essential features of our studies of geometry, physics and ethics are more economically explained by assuming that there is some underlying structure than by assuming a degree of uniformity in all human minds.

This, however, will not satisfy the nominalist, who will maintain that even this level of abstraction merely produces another special science that has resulted from the rules of language, etc., and has no claim to be considered to apply to any sort of 'real' world at all, because all that will be discovered 'about' that world will be the latent consequences of the rules of language.

It is not our business, nor was it Hulme's, to stop this merry-go-round of rejoinder and reply at any particular moment. Our business is to show that there is no contradiction in Hulme's work that vitiates his main contentions about man's limitations and the reality of intrinsic values. The question is whether his statement that no empirical knowledge leads to certainty contradicts any of the conclusions that he wishes to draw from Husserl and Moore.

The main difficulty seems to be this: Hulme wants to maintain that there are intrinsic values, which are good in themselves and do not need to be justified by any reward or good results. At the same time, he recognizes that no region of reality is completely detachable from the rest: 'Nothing is what it is, alone.' But to speak of 'intrinsic' values is to postulate just that kind of isolation; and therefore the second belief contradicts the first.

Suppose, however, that we grant that the world cannot be considered as separate fragments without destroying the nature of the fragments themselves. It then follows that all our distinctions, as between space and time, wishes and perceptions, mind and matter, are illegitimate. In such a view, articulate thought is impossible, whether in poetry or prose; for all our words represent *partitions* of experience and we cannot think without such partitions.[1] For practical purposes, therefore, we must make these partitions, and at once we create a contradiction like that which we seem to find in Hulme. Whether we regard this as a necessary limitation of thought, or as a consequence of the limitations of language, is immaterial for our purpose. We can, if we like, postulate a 'subsistent' world that does contain parts that can be considered in isolation, or we can say that

[1] Bergson's 'intuitions', Moore's 'organic wholes' (*Principia Ethica*, p. 36), and Husserl's 'essential features' are partitions in this sense.

it is necessary to talk *as if* there were such a world. The first attitude is the realist, the second nominalist.

Stated in this way, the difference seems to be merely a difference in emphasis, but the two outlooks do produce different results.[1] Realism in the past has often tempted people into fundamentalism and materialism; nominalism prevents this mistake, but sometimes seems to undermine the foundations of ethics altogether, and in the extreme case it leads people to feel that knowledge is not worth while since it never leads to the discovery of absolute truth. It is significant that Husserl and Moore, like Hulme himself, are mainly concerned with ethics, whereas none of the modern nominalists or logical positivists have produced a book that deals with that subject: the nominalist attitude does not seem to lend itself easily to the treatment of ethical problems. Both realism and nominalism, then, can lead to a restriction of human activity and sensibility. These consequences may not be the logical results of the philosophies, but they have often been the practical results; and if we dislike this kind of

---

[1] In politics, for example, a strict scholastic realist is likely to think that 'the State' is as real as the individuals of which it is composed, and he may even be tempted to go further and say that 'the State' is in some way more important than the individual citizens. A nominalist is more likely to say that the individuals are real and that 'the State' is merely an abstract concept or classification of individuals: 'There are subjects in which Realism is perhaps the true doctrine,' says Hulme, 'but the greatest gift that the Heavens ever allotted to this country was our endowment of an all-prevailing *Nominalism*. It will always save us from belief in the bastard phenomena of the "organic" State. . . . There are some absolute things about the individual, but the State is not one of them.' (*The New Age*, 30. xii. 15.)

restriction and atrophy, we must try to phrase our philosophy in a way that guards against both errors.

This Hulme claims to do by regarding *both* philosophies with detachment: *Cinders* is not wholly nominalist or pragmatist; it includes nominalism and pragmatism only as partial truths, valid in so far as we are not concerned with action. But when we are concerned with action, then a realist view is appropriate. The two quotations at the head of this chapter can thus be reconciled. The first is a statement about 'arm-chair philosophy': it deals with the conditions of human thought when detached from the need for practical action; but it provides no basis for action, and therefore needs to be supplemented by the second. If we try to make one of these two attitudes superior to the other, a critical question arises; and at this point Scheler came near to nihilism, whereas Hulme seems to have been determined to hold fast to authoritative ethics.

As we saw in the last chapter, Hulme makes two quite separate assertions: first, that empirical knowledge is not the whole of knowledge, and second, that everything that is said in logical language can only be true relatively and under conditions. These two assertions leave him free to maintain, like Pascal, that on the one hand there is a world of organic wholes whose intrinsic value cannot be revealed by analysis and explanation; and on the other that there is no 'natural' justice, and in 'natural' science no absolute truth.[1] The assertion that, in dealing

---

1 'Three degrees of latitude nearer the Pole reverse all jurisprudence, a meridian decides what is truth; fundamental laws change after a few years

with intrinsic values, we can use the same kind of reasoning as we use in geometry, has nothing to do with this belief: the mistake arises only because Hulme confuses Moore's 'organic wholes' with Husserl's 'essential features' of ethical theory.

In considering Hulme's work, we must always allow for the over-emphasis and distortion that resulted from his propagandist intentions. We must remember, too, that his notes often represent stages in his development, quotations from books that he was reading, and points that he thought ought to be taken into account. If we want to form some notion of the 'great unities which I am at any rate at present quite unable to carry out', we must turn to the writers whom he so often quotes with approval—Pascal, Cusanus, and the earlier philosophers of the Renaissance. The philosophy of St. Thomas seems to contain more of Hulme's doctrines than Hulme realized; but the new outlook, Hulme said, was not to be a return to scholasticism, whether of Ockham or St. Thomas, and it was to be different from all post-Renaissance philosophy. It seems that he is willing to go some distance with the Humanists, and especially with Cusanus.[1]

of possession, right has its epochs, the entry of Saturn into the constellation of the Lion marks to us the origin of such and such a crime. . . . We must, it is said, get back to the natural and fundamental laws of the State, which an unjust custom has abolished. This is a game certain to result in the loss of all; nothing will be just on the balance.' (Pascal: Fragment 294. The passage is quoted by Sorel: *Reflections on Violence*, p. 17.)

[1] Nicolaus Chrypffs of Cusa (1401–64): *De Docta Ignorantia*. For a discussion of the influence of Cusanus on modern German philosophy, see A. Metzger: *Phänomenologie und Metaphysik* (1933).

The apparent contradiction that we have been discussing is one that finds expression in many philosophies. Hulme and Pascal solve it by postulating more than one world of knowledge; and Cusanus deals with the same problem in a way that has many affinities with Hulme's treatment. He regards thought as an activity that combines and assimilates the scattered impressions given by the senses. By means of higher syntheses that give a background and a scale for the differences, the intellect reduces all differences of kind to differences of degree. In this way it tends to reduce everything to absolute unity, but our thought can know nothing without plurality and difference, and therefore at its zenith thought also reaches its limit. It can approach the absolute unity only by means of a mystical intuition that brings thought itself to an end. Thought has reached the state of *docta ignorantia* when it is aware of its own limit and yet knows that all that is perfect lies beyond this limit. God, therefore, cannot be described in finite terms at all, and nothing can be predicted of Him. But in religion, the *docta ignorantia* is succeeded by *Sacra ignorantia*, and names and predicates are attributed to God. But none of these are to be taken in their primary sense: God is Light, but when we say that God is Light we do not mean that God is the light that is the opposite of darkness. We mean that God comprehends the infinite scale of Light that includes all degrees of light, and in which darkness itself is included.

God is thus approached through a continual comprehending of opposites, whereas Nature is a continual evolution; and thought is the mediary between the two.

Hence there is a profound difference between the knowledge of God and the knowledge of Nature; and if Cusanus had been logically consistent, he might have regarded all purely religious ideas as symbols of something beyond reason. For him, however, the limit of natural science is the limit of logic, but not of experience; and the experience that lies beyond logic is as true as the experience that can be defined by natural science. The range of the intellect is not limited to the field of logic (the field that Hulme calls the world of counter language): nominalism is true, but it is not the whole truth.

In Cusanus we see the beginnings of Renaissance philosophy: he is foremost among the philosophers who pushed God out of the world of theoretical physics, and at the same time showed that the universe was not as limited and inert as men thought. His recognition of the world of nature as an unfolding, or evolution, paves the way for a new outlook. He assumes that natural law is uniform throughout the whole of space, and he argues that the world can have neither centre nor circumference, because it could only have these in relation to something external, which would be part of the world. In this he prepares the way for Copernicus; but in his metaphysics he sees further than the scientists of the Renaissance, and in his contention that all our concepts hold good only in certain relations, and have no validity in others, he recognizes the relativity of all conceptual knowledge.

It is easy to see how much Hulme derived from Cusanus, either directly or through Scheler. Hulme's talk about reasoning in terms of images, his conception of the fancy (*phantasia*) as a faculty that compares and equates sense-impressions, his conviction that a limit must be set to natural knowledge somewhere this side of the knowledge of God or the attainment of perfect thought, all these are found in Cusanus; and even idea of the world as cinders, with the mind as a kind of sorting machine, is implied in *De Docta Ignorantia*.

It may be less easy to see how Hulme could accept so much and yet avoid the conclusions to which the successors of Cusanus—Telesio, Bruno, Descartes—were driven as they became more systematic, more keenly interested in the natural world, and less interested in God; but it must be remembered that the historical consequences of a doctrine are not always its logical consequences. Bruno and Descartes were driven to defend material science against the theologians, and therefore developed their own doctrine in a lopsided way.

Like Cusanus, Hulme certainly accepts premises that lead to the ejection of God from the sphere of 'scientific' knowledge, but he does not go on to say, as some of the philosophers of the Renaissance did, that there are two kinds of truth, for that statement always leads, in the end, to the denial of one of the kinds of truth. Hulme says that God does not exist in the empirical plane, but he qualifies this statement, as Pascal would qualify it, by pointing out that it is no more than a convenient figure of speech. If we disregard Hulme's attempt to identify the inorganic world with the world of theoretical physics, and the world of religion with Husserl's world of essential truths about ethics, we see that the relation in which he sets the inorganic, organic, and spiritual worlds is very similar to Scheler's. The statement that they are 'absolutely distinct' is no more than a way of saying that the concepts by means of which we describe the 'higher' worlds cannot be deduced from those of the 'lower'. The statement then implies a criticism of the concepts used in dealing with the 'lower' worlds; but it does not imply the existence of two or three kinds of truth. What Hulme calls the abstract counter language is never wholly adequate for the expression of truth. Poetic language, too, is an imperfect instrument, but in some ways it is more accurate and wider in scope.

It is not merely that words in poetry have a sensuous effect, though this is the feature on which Hulme most frequently comments. In poetry, words are not used as counters corresponding to the pieces of a mosaic; they are used with their full meanings, and these are rich with all the past experience of the race, and spread out into all experience, as events themselves do. Within the limits of logical language, pragmatism and nominalism are true, but those limits are not the limits of knowledge. The 'intuitions' of Bergson, and Moore's 'organic wholes' whose intrinsic value 'is different from the sum of the values of their parts',[1] these can sometimes be reflected more adequately in poetry than in logical prose, and in dealing with such expressions, the nominalist criticisms lose their force. It is not that poetry is necessarily illogical, but that it implies and communicates more than its

1 *Principia Ethica*, p. 29.

explicit logical meaning. Good poetry is often as logical as Spinoza.

There are not two faculties of the mind, nor two kinds of truth, but two ways of using words. The test of truth, as far as it concerns correspondence with external reality (*i.e.* increased power over outer reality) and correspondence with internal needs (*i.e.* increased power over inner reality), is the same. The emphasis may vary, and it is in deciding which aspect of this test to emphasize that the human being *judges*, and becomes concerned with the inter-relations of metaphysics, aesthetics, and ethics. Neither aspect is ever wholly irrelevant; but there is another test, which is that of coherence, and in this there may seem to be a discrepancy between logical and poetic coherence. We may be inclined to say with Coleridge 'that poetry has a logic of its own as severe as that of science, and more difficult, because more subtle, more complex, and dependent upon more fugitive causes'. But the activity of the intellect in judging coherence is *one*, as the faculty used in playing draughts is the same as that used in chess. It is a mistake to assume that we know the rules and precepts in the one case and not in the other: our minds can grasp a bigger fraction of the rules and precepts of draughts and logic, but not all; and the rules and precepts of poetry and chess are not wholly unknown. The error comes from the common fallacy of considering only the *deductive* side of scientific logic and only the *inductive* side of poetic logic. Both logics have these two aspects, and each aspect has its own difficulties, but there is no absolute difference of kind.

A CONTRADICTION?

It may be said that this position is anti-rationalist; it is, but only in the popular atheistic sense of the word 'rationalist'. If rationalism is a belief that the whole of experience can be reflected in logical counter language, and that human conduct can be adequately directed by deductions from observed facts and the principle of 'the greatest good of the greatest number', then Hulme is opposed to rationalism. If, on the other hand, to be rational is to believe in the widest possible use of reasoning and the most accurate possible reflections of experience in words, then Hulme is more rational than the rationalist. Hulme believes that philosophy must provide motives and justification for action as well as an account of the external world, and he thinks that poetry, like ethics, is concerned with action. The apparent contradiction in his work is not a flaw: it springs from a recognition of the limits of logical language, from a determination not to sacrifice *any* part of reality, and from a conviction that poetry and art are neither meaningless nor unimportant.

Chapter Eight

TWO ALTERNATIVES?

'Si les sentiments, les passions, les idées, les mobiles, les actions et les situations, familiers à l'imagination du poète romantique étaient des sentiments, des passions, des idées, des mobiles, des actions et des situations humainement possibles, si, à les supposer séparément possibles, il était possible qu'ils se combinassent comme il les combine dans une même âme ou une même destinée, la conclusion n'est pas douteuse: la Civilisation, l'État, la Patrie, la Loi, la Religion, la Tradition, la Famille, auraient tort, seraient absurdes dans toutes les bornes qu'ils opposent et les exigences qu'ils imposent à la Liberté sacrée de l'Individu.'—P. LASSERRE, *Le Romantisme français*, p. 198.

For over half a century English critics have been fond of offering definitions of romanticism and then attacking or defending the thing they have defined; but the romanticism that one critic defends is never quite the romanticism that another attacks. The game is a combination of amateur psychology and blind man's buff rather than literary criticism, and in France and Germany it has been even more popular than in England. Continental critics usually start with Lamartine and Victor Hugo or Bürger and Schiller as their examples. When their conclusions have been transplanted into English criticism, they have caused a good deal of confusion, for what is true of Victor Hugo is not necessarily true of Coleridge or Byron.

The dictionary does not help us: it records half a dozen meanings of the word 'romantic' before 1700; and if we trace the history of the word back through the Gothic romances and the *Romaunt de la Rose* the confusion becomes even greater. The sense in which Hulme uses the word seems to be that which was intended by Byron when he wrote to Goethe in October 1820: 'I perceive that in Germany as well as in Italy, there is a great struggle about what they call *Classical and Romantic*.' Hulme sometimes talks as if all the writers of the nineteenth century were romantic; but a definition of romanticism that included Baudelaire, Nietzsche, Flaubert, Dostoievsky, and Tolstoy would be useless. Hulme, like the French critics, is thinking mainly of the romanticism of Byron, Lamartine, and Hugo; but it is not easy to define the common quality of these poets without doing violence to the English habit by which Coleridge, Wordsworth, and Shelley are called romantic. The qualities that are most prominent in Byron are seldom found in Shelley; and, moreover, the 'romanticism' of Wordsworth's sonnet to Toussaint L'Ouverture:

> There's not a breathing of the common wind
> That will forget thee; thou hast great allies;
> Thy friends are exultations, agonies,
> And love, and man's unconquerable mind.

is very different from that of the *Ancient Mariner* or *Kubla Khan*.

Systems of psychology that try to describe all men as

compounds of three or four fundamental 'humours' are rightly suspected of over-simplification. A system that divides all poets into two humours is still more unsatisfactory, and yet in a rough-and-ready way the division can be useful. Poets are people, not chemical atoms: no two are exactly alike, nor are they made up of various proportions of two elements. But it is quite plain that in a great deal of nineteenth-century literature there was a common quality or group of qualities that deserves a name. Enthusiasm for political liberty, and for the free expression of emotion, was not wholly new, but it was carried to a point that made it characteristic of the age, and throughout the first half of the century this emphasis became more and more pronounced.

The division between Classic and Romantic can be traced back to the quarrel of the Ancients and the Moderns in the seventeenth century. In that early quarrel, it was plain that all writers had to fall into one class or the other; or at any rate could be regarded as made up of a blend of the two, and nothing else. In the same way, it is often assumed that the words 'classic' and 'romantic' are opposites, and, taken together, cover the whole field of literature.

This is true as long as we do not try to define the words except by making lists of the writers in each class; but if we try to define them by writing down their specific qualities a possibility of error creeps in. For example, we can take two qualities to define romanticism, and their opposites to define classicism, and if the two qualities are not inseparable there will be four possible combinations and not two, and some awkward hybrids will turn up. This is exactly what happens when Hulme tries to make a definition: 'Here is the root of all romanticism: that man, the individual, is an infinite reservoir of possibilities; and if you can so rearrange society by the destruction of oppressive order then these possibilities will have a chance and you will get Progress. One can define the classical quite clearly as the exact opposite to this. Man is an extraordinarily fixed and limited animal whose nature is absolutely constant. It is only by tradition and organization that anything decent can be got out of him.'[1]

The two qualities that Hulme uses to define romanticism are faith in man's infinite capacity for improvement, and faith in liberty. These are not inseparable: it is possible to believe that man can improve while also believing that discipline and tradition are valuable. Similarly, it is possible to believe in freedom without believing that it will lead to progress in a moral sense.

Even if we recognize the possibilities that Hulme ignores, we do not cover the whole field. The word 'infinite' in Hulme's definition conceals a second fallacy: there is no inevitable choice between 'infinite possibilities' and 'no possibilities at all'. Without believing in man's perfectibility one can quite easily believe that people make more effort to do good to-day than their ancestors did 10,000 years ago; and one can even say that this real moral progress involves an increasing recognition of man's essential imperfection. Hulme makes two

1 *Speculations*, p. 116.

other mistakes in his analysis: in practice, he confuses romanticism with sentimentality, and he explicitly identifies what he calls classicism with something he calls religion. The first of these two errors arises because he takes his examples from Lasserre, who was writing about the romanticism of 1830, with its emphasis on personality and its emotion for emotion's sake, and then applies the word to writers who were romantic in quite a different sense.

Although sentimentality and *sensiblerie* are often associated with the utopian liberalism that Hulme calls romantic, they are not identical with it. Early in the nineteenth century, the rebellion against political and poetic discipline split into two quite different movements. Rousseau may have been the father both of modern utopianism and of the sentimental exaltation of the personality that culminated in Villiers de l'Isle-Adam; but there is, after all, a difference between Lamartine and John Stuart Mill. Similarly, the revolt against formalism in religion cannot be identified with the revolt against formalism in poetry. The two are closely related, but they are not the same.

Hulme, however, identifies the romantic attitude with the utopian, and the classical attitude with the religious, because in so doing he can emphasize the aspect of religion that seems to him to be most likely to be overlooked. This emphasis is salutary, but once it has produced its proper effect it becomes misleading. The doctrine that man is radically imperfect is not the whole of Christianity, and a belief in the reality of original sin, and in the need for tradition and discipline, does not itself constitute an attitude that can reasonably be called religious. Even Kant went further than this when he pointed out that the fact of original sin is inscrutable: the individual is born imperfect, and cannot escape his imperfection, and yet is responsible for it. But even this is not Christianity: it is deism; and as Pascal said, deism is almost as far removed from Christianity as atheism. Hulme's classicism resembles eighteenth-century deism more than it resembles the Christianity described by Pascal: 'The Christian religion, then, teaches men these two truths; that there is a God whom men can know, and that there is a corruption in their nature which renders them unworthy of Him. It is equally important to men to know both these points; and it is equally dangerous for man to know God without knowing his own wretchedness, and to know his own wretchedness without knowing the Redeemer who can free him from it.'[1]

This is the essence of Pascal's teaching: *Console-toi, tu ne me chercherais pas si tu ne m'avais trouvé—tu ne me chercherais pas si tu ne me possédais: t'enquiète donc pas.* Here, as elsewhere, Hulme is following Pascal, but deliberately overlooking one half of Pascal's doctrine. This does not prove that Hulme rejected the half that he chose to ignore. He said plainly that everything he had written was to be regarded as a prolegomenon to a reading of Pascal, and when he spoke of man as 'a wretched creature' he nearly always added 'who can yet apprehend perfection'. But if we put Pascal's description of Christianity in place

1 Fragment 555.

of Hulme's, then it becomes absurd to identify religion and classicism. Something like the doctrine of original sin may be an essential part of a classical attitude, but the doctrine of redemption certainly is not.

Hulme is, in fact, using the word 'religion' to describe, not a state of faith, but a state that may lead to faith. It can be called pessimism, or deism, or stoicism, but it is not Christianity: Hobbes, in Hulme's sense of the word, is religious; he believes in the radical imperfection of man, and in the absolute necessity of discipline and tradition. This attitude, if it is to become Christian, needs to be completed by the act of the intellect that is called faith.

If we remember this, we can elucidate the decline of classicism in the seventeenth and eighteenth centuries and the subsequent growth of romanticism. When, in the seventeenth and eighteenth centuries, religious faith lost its strength, the classical attitude remained, but unconfirmed by faith it was intolerable. Pope's view of man was unbearable without Pope's faith in God; and in Swift, who was more certain of man's evil nature than of God's saving grace, we feel the bitterness of that outlook. Either the old faith had to be reinstated, or a new faith in the perfectibility of man had to replace the belief that mankind was essentially sinful and imperfect.

In England, both of these things happened. The humanistic outlook, which Hulme calls romantic, gained ground among the intellectuals, and at the same time there was a remarkable popular revival in the Christian faith. The Methodist movement supplied that confident knowledge of redemption without which religion is only dry bones. Some people do not feel an overpowering need for that kind of faith: for them, the abstract philosophic deity is enough, but for the Methodists, as for Pascal, deism was not enough: 'Though a man should be convinced that numerical proportions are immaterial truths, eternal and dependent on a first truth, in which they subsist, and which is called God, I should not think him far advanced towards his own salvation. The God of Christians is not a God who is simply the author of mathematical truths, or of the order of the elements; that is the view of heathens and Epicureans. . . . The God of Abraham, the God of Isaac, the God of Jacob, the God of Christians, is a God of love and of comfort, a God who fills the soul and heart of those whom He possesses, a God who makes them conscious of their inward wretchedness, and His infinite mercy.'[1]

Religion as Hulme defines it is different from religion as Pascal knew it—'*Dieu d'Abraham, Dieu d'Isaac, Dieu de Jacob, non des philosophes et des savants*'—and the experience of religion in Pascal's sense has some of the qualities of romanticism. And as the Methodist conception of religion had some relation to Pascal's, their outlook, too, had something in common with romanticism. The Methodists brought revelation from theory and dogma into personal experience: the realization of religion which they sought was still possible within the institutions and formularies of the Church, for the Christian philosophy has always recognized the need for faith as

1 Fragment 555.

well as understanding; but there are times when the members of the Church become more careful of its fabric than of its mission, and expound its doctrine in a way that makes the doctrine seem inadequate as the vehicle of a personal revelation. Rational theology is of little service at such times: '*Le cœur a ses raisons que la raison ne connaît pas,*' as Pascal said. The Methodist movement and the Romantic Revival sprang from the same causes, and each found relief and joy by escaping from a sterile formalism:

'My heart glowed within me, while the fields broke into singing, and the trees clapped their hands. . . . Whether I looked on man or beast, I saw the wisdom, power, and goodness of God shine conspicuously. I was filled with wonder, and felt the greatest tenderness and love for every creature God had made.'

So said the Methodist preacher, William Black,[1] and so said the Ancient Mariner. The excitement, the outburst of joy, the new keen delight in all God's creatures, have been the marks of many religious revivals, and not all of those revivals have been good. The joy, and the sense of deeper communion with the world and with something beyond the world, prove nothing. The sense of freedom and of sudden release from conscious and subconscious tension can follow a conversion to the most horrible and perverted doctrines, or to no doctrines at all. It seems to be a necessary stage of any great moral change that alters the believer's whole outlook and way

[1] Quoted by F. C. Gill: *The Romantic Movement and Methodism* (Epworth Press, 1937).

of life; but it does not prove that the new outlook is better than the old.

People in eighteenth-century England were ready for some kind of revivalism; Methodism and romanticism both resolved this tension, but they did it through very different beliefs. The one turned to Christianity in Pascal's sense; the other, in the hands of Shelley and Byron, became a faith based on premisses totally opposed to those of Christianity. The romanticism of Shelley offered the ecstasy of religion without the content, the flesh without the bones; it gave the feeling of release and of infinite communion without asserting the doctrine of man's limitation. Only in this sense can we understand Hulme's statement that 'Romanticism is spilt religion'. Romanticism, in the sense in which Coleridge and Wordsworth were romantics, is a permanent element in all poetry and all religion. Belief in progress and the innate goodness of man is not. The real choice that Hulme sets before us is not concerned with poetry or art at all; it is a choice between two opposing views of human nature. In the tragedy that André Gide portrays in *La Symphonie pastorale*, Hulme would sympathize more deeply with the son who stands for Christian discipline, than with the father who preaches the love of Christ. In Gide's story, both are heretics, whose over-emphasis brings disaster on themselves and those they love. Both insist on truths, but these truths are partial and complementary: they cannot stand alone. The strength of religion lies in the fact that it includes these complementary truths within itself.

Hulme felt that it was more necessary to speak of the discipline that is emphasized in the Epistles than of the Christian message of the Gospels. Hulme's underlying belief, though he never made it clear, seems to have been that the religious ecstasy is a part of religion, but that without the recognition of man's limitations the ecstasy is dangerous and misleading. There is a similar position in poetry; poetry can express and satisfy desires and motives that are not fully conscious, but this expression and satisfaction is dangerous if it is not based on a sound philosophy. For Hulme a sound philosophy is one that recognizes the non-perfectibility of man.

When Hulme tries to set up religion and romanticism as opposites he is involved in contradiction and confusion, not only because he uses more than one criterion to distinguish the two, but also because he states his definitions solely in terms of conscious philosophical beliefs. He is not content to say, with Worringer, that all art implies beliefs; he goes further, and tries to define a kind of art by means of the conscious beliefs that go with it. What he defines is not romanticism, but the utopian liberalism that very often went with romanticism. The characteristic of romanticism that he ignores is its deliberate appeal to something below the conscious level: when Shelley spoke of poetry as something not subject to the control of the active powers of the mind, he was only asserting the old theory of inspiration; but he was giving it a new importance. Such an emphasis implies a belief in the essential goodness of man's inner nature: 'Look in thy heart and write'; it ignores the dangers of a blind faith in the outpouring of the uncontrolled subconscious. Yet there can be no poetry that does not make some appeal to these powers beneath the conscious mind; it need not worship them, it need not accept their every prompting, but it cannot dispense with them. The poet is always concerned with achieving a balance between the inner and the outer world; it is his business 'to hold in a single thought reality and justice'. Whenever poetry becomes mere ingenuity or fixes its attention solely on material things, or when religion becomes merely stoical and formal, some outburst corresponding to the *Lyrical Ballads* or the Methodist movement will appear.

A revivalist movement is apt to fall into exaggeration and distortion: it deals with the transition from a sense of alienation from God and his universe to a sense of communication with both. It may exaggerate the first stage; it may blur the second into a state of confusion; it may over-emphasize the importance of personal revelation and lay too great a stress on its own inner experience; it may undervalue discipline, authority and tradition; it may fail to recognize the real nature of the experience it describes: but the experience itself, the experience that it sometimes overvalues and prolongs, is the source from which religion draws its strength, and without which it becomes an empty formula.

In the same way, the romantic is always apt to make an immodest fuss about his own affairs and to speak too stridently of 'man's unconquerable soul'. But these excesses are not an essential part of the romanticism of Coleridge and Wordsworth: they are mere vanity and sensationalism. The romantic experience is a normal part of youthful development, but that fact does not, by itself, justify one in saying either that it is good, or that it is bad. People will grow out of it, as a boy grows out of his trousers, but that is no reason for throwing away the trousers while they fit. A boy does not become a man through wearing long trousers, and when he does become a man, there is no need for him to denounce and hate his own outgrown habits. But the vice of refusing to grow up, and hanging on to Boy Scout shorts in middle age, is far more common, and Hulme's denunciation of that kind of romantic taste is at any rate understandable: one can only regret that he did not speak with the sober moderation of Pope's *Essay on Criticism*.

'Tis more to guide, than spur the Muse's steed;
Restrain his fury, than provoke his speed:
The winged courser, like a generous horse,
Shows most true mettle when you check his course.

Imagination, as Coleridge understood it, is an essential part of poetry, whether classic or romantic. It is something like the act of intuition of which Bergson speaks, except that Bergson is thinking only of intuitions of organic elements in the outer world. When Hulme insists on the importance of this intuition in poetry he, too, is thinking only of the outer and visible world. It seems to him that the poet is saving something from the flux of experience: our sudden intuitions are felt to be valuable, but they are carried away by time and cannot be recalled unless words give them life and liberate them from their place in space and time.

> O! how shall summer's honey breath hold out
> Against the wrackful siege of battering days,
> When rocks impregnable are not so stout,
> Nor gates of steel so strong, but Time decays?

In the midst of impermanence and change, something is rescued and given lasting shape; but it is not only the perceptions of the outer senses that we wish to save in this way (it is doubtful whether any act of intuition can really be called a sense-perception and nothing more). There is the experience of the inner world, and this Hulme distrusts. He is, to put it his own way, for the fancy against the imagination. Here he is at one with Pope, and in this sense he is classical; but he is more desperately anxious to keep the whole business of poetry on the level of conscious thought and sensuous observation than any 'classical' poet has ever been. If the evidence of the poets themselves is worth anything, Hulme is in error at this point, just as he is in error when he stresses the fact of original sin more than the fact of redemption; though it is only fair to add that in his *Notes on Language and Style* he seems to recognize the error and recant.

His antithesis of religion and romanticism is false and confusing, and he is guilty of wild exaggeration when he says that the whole of post-Renaissance art and philosophy is essentially romantic. Pascal did not stand alone, and the philosophies of Kant, Kierkegaard, and Schopenhauer show little sign of the optimist and utopian features that Hulme attacked. The music of Bach, Haydn and Mozart is classical in the sense in which Racine and Pope were classical. Many of Coleridge's arguments resemble those which Hulme calls 'classical', and in the nineteenth century there were many writers who were not romantic in Hulme's sense: Hulme's defence of an attitude based not on personality and progress but on absolute values is in an excellent tradition; it deserves to be heard, but no good purpose is served by identifying those absolute values with classicism; and his plea for poetry that is not concerned with the supremely good or the beautiful, or the startling, sounds very like some passages in Wordsworth's *Preface*.

The words 'romantic' and 'classical', however we define them, are vague and misleading: two terms are not enough to describe all the kinds of poetry, or even all the political and philosophical beliefs that are expressed in poetry. The words 'introvert' and 'extrovert' do one part of the work better, the words 'organic' and 'geometrical' make another useful distinction, and 'utopian' and 'non-utopian' yet another. It is not true to say that all extroverts like geometrical forms in art and dislike the utopian views of politics and human nature, nor is it necessary to use the word 'romantic' to describe people who exaggerate and display their emotions or the word 'classical' to describe those who inhibit and conceal them.

Chapter Nine

RELIGION AND THE CRITIQUE OF SATISFACTION

'Certainly, however, a unifying bond connects the two [the world of religious ideas and the economic structure]. Religion becomes dead tradition when this connection is broken, when it is no longer, in its social structure, flooded with *living* streams which have their source in the integrated and combined life of mankind. No longer then does it unite men as all living approaches to the transcendent and holy, in their very essence, must do; rather does it separate and divide. Then, and then only, does it become what Marx erroneously thought in its innermost being it was—a mere expression of unspiritual interests of every variety and an ideology for crystallizing outworn conditions of society for the benefit of a privileged class. Mere critical knowledge, however, will never be able to act as a substitute for it or to dislodge it.'—MAX SCHELER, *Future of Man.*[1]

Curiosity, whether about animals or other people or about inert things or the symbols in which we do our thinking, is a characteristic of human beings: sometimes the curiosity has a specific purpose, sometimes it seems to have none. But there are two kinds of curiosity: there is the kind that asks how specific things are related to other things, and there is another kind that asks what is the nature of things as a whole. Questions of the first

[1] *The Monthly Criterion*, February 1928.

sort can be answered more or less satisfactorily: we can always find some analogy, some symbolic representation, that will serve as a working hypothesis and lead us on to new experiments. But questions of the second kind cannot be answered, though they are often asked; for you cannot explain the whole in terms of a part. Questions of this kind express an overweening desire to know everything, but they stultify that desire by killing the impulse to acquire specific knowledge. Even in the sciences, people do not like the bother of deciding which piece of relative knowledge is reasonably reliable in particular circumstances; they want to find absolute and universal certainty. In morality and aesthetics, we find the same desire for final, absolute certainty, the same wish to give up the burden of judgment and responsibility altogether, and relegate the whole business to the operations of a calculating machine.

It is always right and healthy to try to see the uniformities of life, to recognize the recurrence of new examples of a familiar pattern, and to form rules that will reduce decisions in such instances to a mechanical calculation; but to expect to find explicit rules that will deal with all instances, even those that are radically new, is to throw up the whole burden of human responsibility and to sacrifice everything that make life conscious and valuable. The Christian religion is sometimes accused of being nothing more than an expression of this desire for death and negation, and certainly many hymns and prayers express weariness and exhaustion; they not only confess that the human being is weak and sinful, they

try to cast *all* their burdens on the Lord. The same purpose is served by some political philosophies: the individual is absolved from the responsibility of decision,
and has nothing to do but obey.

The desire for such a final solution of our difficulties is
very strong in most of us, and perhaps it grows stronger
as we **grow** older. It is a desire of which any serious religion or political philosophy must take account; but we
must also take into account our desire to live, to think,
to be active, and to make judgments and decisions.
The problem is to reconcile these two: to point toward
a general solution, and at the same time to enable the
individual to deal with his specific problems without
being overshadowed by a sense of general uncertainty
and futility. Religion is not concerned with fixing a
ratio between the impulses toward death and toward
life, but with giving the believer enough energy and
insight to make his own decision; and it must give pro-
portionately to his needs.

Christianity meets these difficulties by offering parables
that have to be elucidated, and these are supplemented
and expanded through the doctrines of the Church; it
does not offer downright moral precepts with an obvious
and single application. It is not a deterministic system
that gives a plain answer to all the questions: it leaves
fundamental decisions to the believer; it gives him some
of the data, and the energy to make the choice; and it
offers a priesthood and spiritual hierarchy that put the
issue before people and help them to make that choice.
When Hulme talks of 'A Critique of Satisfaction' it

might seem that he is asking for something beyond religion and beyond philosophy. If he wants a criterion that will enable him to judge Christianity itself, he is asking more than Christianity offers, for no comprehensive philosophy would be so silly as to profess to include within itself a test by which its own truth could be known. The appeal is always to tests that are recognized apart from the particular philosophy, and these tests are coherence, range of application, and effect on the believer. These tests in turn rest on axioms whose value cannot be proved by reasoning, for reasoning must always have foundations.

'Axioms in philosophy', as Keats said, 'are not axioms until they are proved upon our senses', but the fact that an axiom seems to be proved upon our senses does not prove that it is indispensable; often the beliefs that some people accept as axioms seem palpably false to other people. Hulme's critique of satisfaction is not meant to prove that one particular set of axioms is indispensable, but that some axioms are unnecessary or unsatisfactory. If it can be shown that some beliefs fail in the objects they are supposed to serve, or that it is possible to dispense with these beliefs and still lead a life that the believer would recognize as sincere, good, and sensitive, then the beliefs can no longer be accepted as axioms.

There are moments when Hulme seems to claim that this critique is a science with definite fixed tests and an unambiguous answer to every question. This only happens, however, when his personal enthusiasm for the 'religious' view outruns his discretion. The real object of his critique is not to establish a final, universal truth, but to show that the 'humanist' canons of satisfaction are unsatisfactory even by humanist standards. You cannot prove that a view is right by examining it in the light of its own standards, but you can sometimes prove that it is wrong.

When we judge any outlook, or build up one for ourselves, we are not always conscious of our canons of satisfaction, and the first business of a critique of satisfaction is to reveal these canons. It is therefore primarily a method, not a scale of values. Hulme comes nearest to describing this method when he refers to the passage in which Pascal shows that virtue and satisfaction are found not in attainment but in pursuit. Whether we write books or hew coal, whether we play cards or climb mountains, we can do nothing solely for the sake of the end we seem to have in view; the virtue and satisfaction are more often in the doing. 'Our nature consists in motion,' says Pascal, 'complete rest is death.'[1]

If we try to believe that every action is solely a means to an end, then all value vanishes from the action itself. This is the main thesis of the critique of satisfaction; and all humanistic studies that claim to show us the springs of action or the aims of our desire end by showing us its truth. Introspection, pushed far enough, leads to despair unless we are supported by faith in absolute moral values. If we try to 'explain' these moral values in terms of purposes that have no direct sense of moral impulsion for us, then their value seems to evaporate and

1 Fragment 129.

172

we are left with no aim in life. It is for that reason, says Pascal, that men distract themselves from thoughts of death and of their own nature by setting themselves to struggle against difficulties: when they have leisure from the immediate demands of life, they seek distraction in war, in games, in dancing, or making verses.[1] If they pause to ask themselves why they do these things, and if they persist until they find an answer, they find that all the satisfaction is gone.

All the secular religions that are based solely on a belief in the value of racial survival or personal fulfilment fail if we consider them in the light of this critique. The more we reason about these 'religions' the less convincing they seem. Why should we work for human survival or even for 'personal fulfilment'? If we are consistent humanists we must push our enquiries as far as possible, but we cannot in this way arrive at any ultimate and convincing foundation for faith. As long as we base our reasoning solely on the facts of empirical science, we tend to destroy our sense of value rather than reinforce it, and for that reason it might seem that it would be better not to think at all. That solution is sometimes offered: it is said that the instincts are deeper and more valuable than the power of thought, and that thought, when it no longer serves the instincts, tends to destroy them, and so destroys the vitality of a person or a nation. Therefore, it is argued, thought must be repressed.

This may be the doctrine of some religions, and some political philosophies, but it is not Pascal's. With Pascal

[1] Fragment 146.

it is axiomatic that 'man is made to think'; the word 'over-intellectual' would have no meaning for him; the problem is to think rightly and to ignore none of the materials of thought. If thought seems to prove the vanity of desire, and if that conclusion is nevertheless felt to be unacceptable, it is because some fact or axiom has been left out of account, and not because thought itself is evil.

Hulme calls this missing axiom 'the conservation of values'. If it is axiomatic that we must think, and think not only of things that serve immediate ends but also of the nature of our own wishes and our own thought, then it is also axiomatic that we must preserve our sense of value; and this can be done by recognizing absolute intrinsic values that are beyond our own tastes and wishes, and that can neither be justified by their effects nor reduced to psychological causes or atavistic habits. This doctrine differs from the irrationalism that tries to limit thought: it does not say that the instincts are necessarily good or that it is as honourable to appeal to the emotions as to the reason. It recognizes the difficulty of deciding what is good, and it does not claim to offer any simple criterion of value, such as the personal taste of a given individual, or the power of the state, or conformity to a fixed, unalterable code.

It is plain that there must be a hierarchy of values, but it is not argued that this hierarchy can be known plainly and without effort. The critique of satisfaction shows that there must be intrinsic values, and that the intrinsic values assumed in humanism are unsatisfactory because they are remote and illusory, and can be nullified by the methods of humanism itself; but it does not show what those values are. Though it demonstrates the necessity of religion, it is not a substitute for religion.

In Hulme's view, as we have seen, religion rests on the recognition of original sin, but Hulme is no more concerned with proving the existence of original sin than the biologist is concerned with demonstrating the existence of cats. He claims that we can recognize our own tendencies to evil, whatever we may call them, just as we can all recognize cats. The belief that man is sinful does not rest on any particular scale of values by which he is judged and found to be sinful. It is a sensation discovered by the inspection of our own minds, and it precedes the statement of a scale of values.

It is obvious that we are often deceived by such sensations: we often feel that some notion is inconceivable, or that some action is disgusting or some picture ugly; and then later we find that these sensations were due to accident or prejudice. An adequate critique of values must take account of such errors and correct them, and in that critique, psychological analysis of our own minds has a place. It makes no moral or aesthetic judgments, but sometimes it brings concealed motives to light, and sometimes it reveals the unreliability of the sense of compulsion that we call conscience. Psycho-analysis, although it may explain, and by explaining remove, some specific feelings of sinfulness, neither explains nor removes the *general* sense of being liable to sin and error. The sensations that it removes are morbid and accidental: the moral sensations remain; if they did not, the analysis would have converted a man into an idiot.

The successful use of psycho-analysis thus involves the use of some criterion of health and sanity: it shows how one state of mind can be converted into another, it releases the mind from forces that have hindered it from developing normally; but it does not itself say what is normal. As an instrument for the study of axioms and theories it is a form of the critique of satisfaction, and it may serve to show the reality of what Hulme calls the 'fixed desires' of man; but it does not say what form those desires ought to take, it merely points out their consequences and their interconnections, and when it is applied to people themselves it must be supplemented by some criterion of health.

If we use psycho-analysis as an instrument of the critique, we must remember that although it can be applied to our own thought, and to that of other people, it can only point to the motives that have made us think of certain ideas and arguments, it does not tell us whether the ideas are right or wrong. In criticizing ideas, our business is to ask whether they are coherent and fit the facts, and what effect they have on the believer. In studying the cause of those ideas we learn very little about their value, and this kind of study is seldom valuable unless we are trying to escape from the tyranny of the ideas. It is sometimes useful to ask why we think more acutely in some directions than in others (it is a question that Hulme might well have asked himself), and it is sometimes useful to examine the dictates of conscience itself, but we must not look to this kind of introspection for any final certainty.

In the play by W. H. Auden and Christopher Isherwood, *The Ascent of F 6*, the hero questions his own motives; he asks whether he is really disinterested and noble, or whether at the bottom of his determination there is a love of power, or an impulse to mortify himself, or humble somebody else, or some more heavily disguised desire dating from his childhood. This personal examination is different from the examination of standards of satisfaction in general; and if we have no durable standards it makes everything appear doubtful, and everything corrupt. That is to say, it paralyses the normal impulse by anxiety and bewilderment, as surely as some forms of pseudo-mysticism drug it into hypnotic sleep.

There remains a standard of health and sanity apart from individual prejudice and instinct, and it is by this standard that we have the right to use such words as 'drugged' and 'paralysed'. We cannot know the absolute values of this standard any more than we can know the final truths that underlie the relative and partial truths of science; yet we can make some approach to them in the same way as we approach the truths of science. We are under an absolute obligation to make this approach and this obligation involves not only personal effort but also personal humility. That is to say, in religion as in science, we must give due weight to tradition and authority. There may be some 'quite objective values', but the individual never knows them for certain: he is always liable to illusion and error, and it is only when he considers his own sentiments and intuitions in the light of tradition and competent authority that he can come anywhere near to a reliable knowledge of the objective standards. Nor is the human race at any time entitled to erect its own prejudices into standards, for these prejudices often spring from its immediate material needs. We must criticize any outlook in the light of historical authority as well as of psychological knowledge. A belief cannot be taken as an axiom if some ages have dispensed with it without producing results that are obviously bad, nor can anything be taken as an intrinsic value on the authority of one person or one age. It is not enough to recognize original sin, and responsibility, and the existence of values that are good in themselves. If the individual is to make sure that his judgments are not wholly personal, either he must accept some revelation as final (and in practice this leads to extreme individualism) or he must find some authoritative road to the absolute values or revealed doctrines. Reason is not complete unless it includes humility, and humility involves the recognition of tradition and authority.

If this solution is to be accepted, it is difficult to see how, for a Western European, the authority could be any other than that of the Christian Church. Soon after Hulme's death one of his closest friends, Ramiro de Maeztu, wrote: 'I believe that in essentials he was already a Catholic, although not in the ritualistic sense, but in the spiritual.' Hulme himself says nothing on this subject. Both Hulme and Scheler, in their published writings, imply that authority is necessary; they look towards the Church as the only possible authority; but even if they nominally become members of the Church, they do not face its problems from inside.

In this, they are like many other people, who hold back partly from their own intellectual pride, and partly because they quite honestly believe that the Church has very often been the instrument of repression and injustice, and very often still is. They fear that if they accept the authority of the Church their own influence will be used against the causes that they hold most worthy; and they are convinced that any human organization is liable to become more concerned with the retention of its own power than with the proper use of that power. Scheler's criticism goes deeper than this: he believes that when the connection between religious ideas and the economic structure is broken, religion becomes nothing more than a device for preserving outworn conditions of society for the benefit of a privileged class.

This criticism is just, if by religion we mean the form given to Christian doctrine by the Church in particular times and places. A Church that is tied to an economic system that is not based on Christian principles necessarily becomes infected, and a Church that exists in the midst of a non-Christian social order is liable to be influenced, through assimilation or reaction, by the false ideas of the age. The problem is to cast out the infection and to do this in proper humility. To stand aloof is no remedy, but a form of pride. We have no right to ask for a perfect Church at work in a perfect society; and we have no right to ask that the Church at any one time shall be infallible. No human ingenuity can build up a system that will fulfil the functions of such a hierarchy for an indefinite time. The priesthood of the Church has often been far from fulfilling all its functions, but the Church has time after time been saved and rejuvenated by the appearance of new Orders. Its strength has lain in the fact that it provided a model for such Orders, so that when they became necessary their organization was relatively easy and immediately effective.

The attitude of the utopian reformer, who tries to find a plan that will keep humanity right for ever, is very different from that of the Gospels: the first apostles were given no rules for choosing their successors. Good men have good successors, and there is no need of rules and examinations to detect them. To lay down rules for the future would be to deny the goodness of future genera-tions, and it is presumptuous to ask for sufficient unto the last day. The impulse towards faith is reborn in each generation: it cannot be handed on by an organization or an official Church; but a Bible, a liturgy and a creed can be handed on by such an organization, and these serve to strengthen faith in the minds of men who are the true successors. Ordained clergy are therefore necessary: but ordination is not a ceremony that confers sainthood or detects saints; that is not its function. Its business is to make sure that the deposit of faith is preserved. The clergy are the ministers of the Word and the Sacraments; they may not always succeed in revealing the significance of these to each person according to his capacity, but in preserving the deposit of faith they preserve something that will set men—perhaps men who have no liking for the clergy—on the road to re-living faith.

The critics who say that the clergy are often obscurantists and defenders of an un-Christian social order may be right, but as long as such people stand aside from the Church, the Church is not likely to show a very different spirit. Moreover, the Church has been for many centuries the main channel through which have been transmitted the moral standards by which they judge it. Any organization may become corrupt in the course of time, but that is no reason for refusing to help in its regeneration. The problems of politics are urgent, and to many people, who do not feel that they can 'put humanity right for ever' or even for a short time, it may seem that the Church is more likely to hinder them than to help them in their attempt to throw their weight against repression and injustice at the point where it seems at the moment most useful to do so. Hulme's argument is that such an attitude is untenable in the long run, because it does not provide for the conservation of the values on which it is based. But if we accept his argument, and if his use of the word 'religious' and his profession of faith in social justice and freedom of thought are to be taken seriously, we must go further than Hulme himself did; we must work to regenerate the Church from within, and at the same time we must work to abolish the outer sources of its shortcomings.

Chapter Ten

THE POLITICAL IMPLICATIONS

'No theory that is not fully moved by the conception of justice asserting the equality of men, and which cannot offer something to all men, deserves or is likely to have any future.'—T. E. HULME, Introduction to Sorel's *Reflections on Violence* (*Speculations*, p. 259).

Most of us agree that there are many features of our society that flatly contradict the morality that we profess. Successful greed is made a virtue, and money-makers are allowed to buy titles and honours whether they merit them or not. Great inequalities of wealth and opportunity are officially condoned, and people of wealth are given a power to influence legislation and public opinion that is disproportionate to their intellectual and moral worth. The organization of our economic structure is such that many people, in other ways kindly and intelligent, make themselves felt in some fields solely as a demand for the highest possible dividend, and the possession of great financial claims on the services of one's fellow creatures is treated as a privilege, not a responsibility. The ordinary worker is sometimes compelled to do work that he knows to be useless or shoddy or destructive, and at such times he is bound to feel less conscious of working for the public good than of making money for an employer whom perhaps he does not know, and against whom he has to struggle to get what he can for himself.

Not all of this is the result of ineradicable features of human nature. Some of it is the result of forms of organization that could be changed, and ought to be changed, if we really believe in the morality that we profess. No system is good if it confuses selfishness, prudence and 'service', or places a strain on men's honesty greater than it will stand, or absolves men from their proper responsibilities. Furthermore, a social structure built on two systems of morals, one practical and the other theoretical, is unstable as well as bad. People cannot go on deceiving themselves all the time, and one morality or the other must ultimately give way. The change may be brought about partly by moral pressure, but in practice it will also be influenced by considerations of expediency and the limitations of average human nature. It may be a change for the better; that is to say, the action of making the change may itself be good, but it will not result in any great and irreversible change in human nature.

Economic and political changes may diminish specific forms of injustice, they may serve to discourage the kind of morality that makes successful greed a virtue; but they will not eliminate evil from human nature, and new problems of the same kind will arise. By restricting the power of wealth, or changing the means by which wealth can be accumulated, we do not abolish the power of one human being over another, for that power springs from men's willingness to accept authority and leadership. If power is to be taken from its present holders, we must make sure it is not being placed in hands that are still less qualified to use it. The fundamental thing that needs to be altered is the kind of authority that people recognize and accept.

Often the argument that human nature is fixed and unalterable is made an excuse for resisting all changes. If we unreservedly accept the doctrine that there is no progress at all, it is quite easy to deduce that no form of society is better than any other, and that medieval Russia is neither better nor worse than Denmark or Tierra del Fuego, now or ten thousand years ago. Furthermore, it follows from such a view that there is not merely an inevitable tension, but an absolute and fatal impasse between the values of Christianity and those of any State whatever. This is the view to which Hulme sometimes seems to be committed. But it is nonsense to talk of the religious view and then ignore the principles of Christian sociology, or treat them as wildly impracticable advice. A little moral progress is possible, and some forms of society are more Christian than others, even though the progress can never lead to perfection; and the driving force behind comes from the religious sense of absolute obligation, and of the nature of man, that is expressed in the Gospels. The mistake of the liberal democrats, according to Hulme, was to assume that these principles were innate in human nature and did not need the backing of religious belief. Hulme's own mistake was to state the objection to utopianism in a way that implied that all effort was futile as a means to an end and could not be justified except by its intrinsic value.

In this, Hulme resembles both Pascal and Sorel. Pascal, in his famous passage on the huntsman and the hare, forgets that the huntsman would not pursue the hare if he could never catch it. The activity is valuable partly for its own sake, and partly as a means to an end. To-day, in the face of utopian moralities and pragmatic philosophies it is useful to insist that truthfulness, honesty, courage, and unselfishness are good for their own sake, and not merely for the sake of any 'progress' to which they may ultimately lead; there is no reason to assume that these qualities increase automatically with the mere passage of time, but there is also no reason to assume that people cannot become more keenly aware of their value and so spur themselves on to greater moral effort. It is in this sense that a little moral progress is possible, and if we deny this kind of progress altogether, then we return to the stoical pessimism of Hobbes.

Such a pessimism is wrong, first of all because its view of man is incomplete and therefore in a sense false, and secondly because it confuses fixed appetites with fixed forms of satisfaction. The desire for human leadership, for example, is ineradicable; but we need not pander to it in its evil and enervating forms. The human being wants leadership, and if he is not offered good leadership he will accept bad. Indeed, he has a strong bias in favour of bad leadership—the comfortable doctrines of the sentimentalist, the quack remedies of the amateur economist, the flattery of the literary humbug, all these commend themselves to the ordinary man, for he cannot see as far as the point where they break down. For that reason, the liberal optimist is inclined to wish that the desire for leadership could be abolished, and to talk as if it could. The social pessimist, on the other hand, not only recognizes the desire for leadership, but also believes in giving way, or pretending to give way, to the public weakness for leaders who are shortsighted and sentimental: he relies on hard fact to drive a bit of sense into people's heads at the last moment. Both optimist and pessimist are wrong, for a good system of government must not be based on any illusion about the omniscience and inevitable rightness of the average man, but neither must it discourage him from using his intelligence, honesty, and courage. It must itself be an incitement to him to observe, think, and judge to the best of his abilities, and it must make the fullest use of his capacity to recognize the real quality of those who set up to be his leaders.

Liberal democracy, tainted with the utopian doctrine of *laisser faire*, has often failed to fulfil these conditions, and to attack the doctrines of liberal democracy on such grounds as these is certainly less daring than it was when Sorel and Hulme were writing a quarter of a century ago. The decline of European liberalism; the problems raised by nature of modern war and by the attempt to make pacifism an article of faith; and the diversity of effects that have followed, in different countries, from the same economic causes; all these have turned people who are interested in politics to a new examination of their own premisses. Blind confidence in the inevitability of democratic progress is being replaced by a more wary attitude. It is recognized that utopian liberalism is sick, and that it is based on ideas about history and about human personality that are inadequate or false. Democracy may be the best form of government, at any rate for some countries, but even its most enthusiastic supporters no longer find it a self-sufficient panacea for all evils. It is one method among many: it is not necessarily good in itself, and its ultimate triumph is no longer taken for granted.

Sorel and Hulme did not believe that peaceful evolution in the direction of greater tolerance, understanding, and kindness was inevitable, or that economic pressure would naturally work out the salvation of man in a democratic State. Sorel claimed to show that utopianism was futile, and he argued that only a myth of violence could restore a proper faith in absolute values. Sorel, though he quotes Christian writers to support his case against romantic liberalism, is not a Christian. Hulme is fundamentally a Christian, though not always ortho-dox, and he recognizes a real moral element in the ideals of liberal democracy. He tries to distinguish between these ideals and an adventitious set of ideas that he called romanticism. If these ideas are adventitious, and if they are false, it remains to ask whether they are responsible for the decline of political liberalism in Europe, and what form of democracy is a possible ideal within a better framework of ideas.

If we state the question in this way, it is at once clear that we are not choosing between progressives and conservatives, for this simple division into two parties regarded as the horse and the cart is possible only if we assume that there is a single unquestionable line of progress to be followed. This is the usual liberal view, common to democratic tories, whigs, and radicals, and it is the view that has failed in practice and is now being called in question.

The liberal usually claims that the failure is due to lack of education. He says that people cannot be expected to fulfil their democratic responsibilities unless they are given enough knowledge and insight to recognize and accept responsible disinterested leadership. He points out that those who grudgingly gave the people a vote never gave them the means to make good use of it, and that instead of fitting the people for political responsibility they preferred to control them by cajolery, misrepresentation and false rhetoric. If liberalism is failing, it is failing because our democracy is not genuine: it is a veiled plutocracy, maintained through ignorance and prejudice.

The socialist agrees that more education is needed, but he also believes that liberal democracy is only the political counterpart of capitalism, and that it is absurd to expect a proper education and an honest Press under capitalism. Democracy is being maintained in the interests of the wealthy, and if some of our statesmen talk loudly of its virtues it is because they know that any other form of government, whether of the right or left, would curb the powers of the financial classes that they represent. Democracy will remain a sham until the economic system behind it is changed, and its apparent failure in so many countries is due to the desperate effort of the wealthier classes to keep their power even when the system of trade that gave them that power is breaking down.

Liberals after the style of H. G. Wells are often inclined to assume that more education will make much wiser and better citizens, and that this by itself will ensure good government. Yet it is very doubtful whether the opinions of university graduates are more far-sighted and unselfish than those of less well-educated people. We may agree that everything possible should be done to improve secular education, but still maintain that there is a limit, and a not very distant limit, to what can be done in this way. However highly developed an educational system may be, it will fail if people are not taught to recognize their own limitations and to admit their responsibilities as well as their rights, and moral training will fail if it is based on nothing more than an enlightened self-interest, or an illusory belief in progress and 'the palpable and obvious love of man for man'. One merit of democracy is that it makes high demands of the individual; but education will not help people to meet those demands unless it is based on a proper understanding of the nature of man. The liberal is willing enough to say that the fascist is wicked, but he will not admit the flaw in his own analysis of man in general.

The socialist diagnosis suffers from the same weakness as the liberal: it does not openly face the fact that events have not happened as expected. It is not enough to say that democracy has been a sham: it has been real enough in so far as the desire to catch votes influences politicians of all parties quite as strongly as their wish to further the material interests of their own class. We must go further than this, and admit that Sorel and Hulme were right in saying that there is no 'natural tendency to evolve in the direction of a sane liberal democracy', and that economic pressure does not automatically produce the kind of political change that the utopian liberal expects. Any political programme that assumes the innate goodness and wisdom of the natural man is bound to fail. Any sound policy must recognize that politics is largely a matter of expediency and the adjustment of conflicting interests; that the individual man is limited; and that there must be, somewhere, an authoritative scale of values that is not merely a matter of individual judgment. Neither liberalism nor socialism satisfy these conditions. In theory, both base themselves on a naturalistic morality; in practice, they fall back on the conventional mixed morality of the society around them; and therefore they have no real moral force that enables them to attack the conditions they dislike.[1] They represent only one group of interests fighting against another.

[1] 'La partie faible du socialisme est la partie morale: ce n'est pas que bien des auteurs socialistes n'aient écrit sur ce sujet des pages éloquentes; mais les amplifications oratoires sont faciles quand il s'agit de morale; ce sont toujours à peu près les mêmes choses qui se répètent; et toutes les homélies ont eu, jusqu'ici, peu d'influence sur les hommes.

'Il serait criminel de pousser à une révolution sociale qui aurait pour résultat de mettre en péril le peu de moralité existant. Dans un discours prononcé à Montigny-sur-Sambre, qui a été très souvent cité par les journaux français, E. Vandervelde disait: "Si les travailleurs triomphaient

The fascists' objection to the democratic state is not that it has no absolute moral basis, but that it is weak and vacillating. They not only argue that the machinery of democratic government is slow and cumbersome, they say that democracy gives too much responsibility and power to intellectuals, and that sensibility and intelligence diminish the capacity for action and decision. This argument finds some support in the common view that associates sensibility with ineffectiveness, and contemplation with inaction. The intellectual virtues probably do diminish the capacity for quick and unconsidered action, but they lead to ineffectiveness only when intellection and sensibility are combined with an absence of faith in any absolute values. The weakness of liberal democracy has been that its exponents have believed in it not as something that had to be justified and worked for, but as something self-evident and inevitable.

It has been said that Sorel's most famous pupils were Lenin and Mussolini; Mussolini at least has admitted

sans avoir accompli les évolutions morales qui sont indispensables, leur règne serait abominable et le monde serait replongé dans des souffrances, des brutalités et des injustices aussi grandes que celles du présent."

"Sans doute il est inexact de dire que la question sociale est une question morale, quand on entend cette formule dans le sens que lui donnent certains philosophes. Mais, d'autre part, il faut dire aussi que les transformations économiques ne peuvent se réaliser si les travailleurs n'ont pas acquis un degré supérieur de culture morale. La notion même de l'interdépendance des phénomènes, qui fait le fond du matérialisme historique, rend la chose évidente: cependant, on voit souvent les disciples de Marx montrer une insouciance étonnante dès qu'il est question de morale; cela tient à ce qu'ils ont reconnu que les principaux remèdes proposés par les philosophes sont d'une faible efficacité.' Sorel: *Matériaux d'une théorie du prolétariat*, pp. 124-5.

the debt, and it is easy to see how much there is in Hulme's position, and in Sorel's, that appeals to people who for other reasons are fascists. Sorel was an impassioned socialist, but his most enthusiastic readers were the neo-royalists, who were bitterly opposed to socialism. This curious position followed from Sorel's origins: he took ideas from Marx and Nietzsche, both of whom denied the existence of a natural, disinterested justice and morality, but were none the less shocked and horrified at the 'capitalist' morality of the moneyed classes. Both fascism and communism oppose this morality by violence; liberalism professes to oppose it, but in practice rests on a vague optimistic hope that people will grow out of it. Liberalism is often the doctrine of the capitalist who wants to go on reckoning everything in terms of profit, but to pay lip-service to a 'nobler' morality.

It may be argued that liberal democrats in different countries are more likely to live in peace with one another than socialists with fascists. Sorel would say that this, if true, is due to the fact that the liberals are guided by optimism tempered with expediency rather than by real moral principles. He would agree with the fascist that liberal democracy is spineless;[1] and he would agree with the socialist that in so far as it has a practical morality at all, it is the morality of capitalism. There is thus a dignity and vitality about the two extremes that is lacking in the unheroic centre: a person of Hulme's tem-

[1] The agreement in this case would be accidental. The fascist means that liberal democracy, by toleration, fails to keep down seditious movements; Sorel means that the doctrines and 'myth' of liberalism enervate the individuals in a liberal community.

perament would certainly feel inclined to go to one extreme or the other, and given such a choice there is little doubt that Hulme, with his respect for 'the long note of the bugle', would choose fascism.

This, however, is a false statement of the position: the moralities of communism and fascism are not the only possible bases of a State whose economic arrangements would be in harmony with its moral claims; and a blind faith in progress is not the only alternative to violence. Political policies cannot be pictured as a line of booths strung out from Right to Left with liberal democracy somewhere in the centre. Such a picture ignores the possibility of a Christian polity, to be established not through a cult of violence, but by strengthening some existing features of society. There are not three possibilities, but four, and if Hulme's use of the word 'religious' is to be given due weight, the fourth possibility must be considered. Hulme's arguments against progress, if taken alone and literally, do lead to a pessimistic fascist view, but if we interpret them in the light of his other arguments they lead neither to fascism nor to communism, but away from both. In all Hulme's writing it is clear that he believes that the individual justifies the State, and not that the State justifies the individual. The value of the individual is measured by absolute standards, not by his service to the State; and in the same way the truth of a scientific doctrine, the beauty of a work of art, and the virtue of a good action, are all judged by standards that are not merely standards of public expediency, whether expediency means the greatest happiness of the greatest number, or the military power of the nation.

It is in this sense that Hulme believes in liberty: liberty means freedom to recognize the proper authority in every activity and to take one's proper place in the hierarchy. The strength of every authority lies in its own nature: the strength of the military authority is military, the strength of mathematical authority is mathematical, and no one kind can override another without ultimately injuring both. True, there are problems of interrelation, but these are not solved by making one single authority supreme and giving it the power to control the formation and expression of opinion.

Hulme's position is thus aristocratic, but it implies a kind of democracy among aristocracies. Politics must be democratic in the sense in which science is democratic, and aristocratic in the sense in which science is aristocratic. That is to say, the qualities by which men rise to positions of authority must be the qualities that they are required to use when they reach that authority. Furthermore, the burden of deciding which is the appropriate authority on any question must always rest on the individual man. He must run the risk of making a mistake, and although he must often make use of other people's judgment, he cannot rightly shirk his responsibility by accepting one leader over all. The wish to have one final human authority to decide all questions springs from laziness: that laziness is ineradicable, but it is not to be encouraged. There is nothing to be said for combining the offices of Poet Laureate, Prime Minister, President of the Royal Society, Heavyweight Boxing Champion and Archbishop of Canterbury. Some unifying authority there must be, but the true unifying authority is not the personality of a leader or a king; it is, in the Christian phraseology, the grace of God given to each in his order. To set up a living person in the place of that authority is to set him in place of God.

Men are unequal and divergent in their talents, and for that reason aristocracies are necessary; each man has in some measure the capacity to recognize authority and to exercise it; but it may well be that some functions in society need qualities that cannot be acquired in a single generation, so that some aristocracies, either in principle or in practice, may be hereditary. Within these limitations, a Christian democracy is possible; and these limitations are not arbitrary restrictions, they are simply facts, like the facts on which the claims of democracy are based, and they are there all the time, whether they are recognized or not. Aristocracies that fulfil a proper function within the State cannot be eliminated without leaving a need that will be felt. Sooner or later that need will be supplied, and it is most likely to be adequately supplied if its real nature is recognized.

The kingship, for example, has a function, as the visible symbol of the relation between man, in all his various capacities, and God. If that function is not fulfilled by a king, then it is fulfilled more or less adequately by a president or a national leader. A Christian king is not a national leader combining temporal and spiritual power; his political influence may be small, but his example and responsibility point to the existence of an authority that is higher and more general than that of any parliament or aristocracy. As long as the king does not become a ceremonial fountain-pen of his prime minister, the kingship is the safeguard of all liberty within the State.

Granting all this (and all this seems to follow from Hulme's premisses) we are still left with problems of the relations between States, and between diverse factions within the State. As far as we can look into the future, there is no prospect of a World State, or of entirely harmonious relations between different States. The World State, if it ever appears, will not be the result of direct effort, but the outcome of common interests. The kind of internationalism that persists in spite of wars and revolutions is that of the scientists, who meet in international conferences because they have common interests, not because they are consciously international. The kind of internationalism that tries to hustle people into union, although they are not conscious of any common interests, can only have a superficial and precarious success.

Combined with utopian liberalism there has been a belief that people are driven into war only through the struggle for markets, and by the conspiracies of armament-makers. It has been assumed that men are naturally peaceable, that peace is good, and that violence is justifiable only in the interests of law; and 'law' has been understood to mean the law that embodies the most advanced morality of the time. The outlook assumes that there is a single line of development of mankind, so that it is quite easy to see what is the just law that must be enforced. Sorel dislikes this alleged rejection of force; he claims that in fact there is no unique line of development for mankind, and that there is no universal law that can claim a monopoly of force. This can be admitted: as long as there are different States and different ideologies, there is likely to be war, and both sides will think that they are fighting in the cause of justice. But Sorel goes further: he claims that the liberal-democratic State is the corrupt and deliquescent product of romanticism; it is based not on absolute intrinsic values but on a mixture of hedonism and spineless humanitarianism.

A healthy State must certainly recognize intrinsic values, but Sorel goes on to argue that we can only expect a return of the classical ideal, and its faith in the heroic values, through proletarian violence. Myths are necessary as an incentive to action, and the appropriate myth is the general strike.[1] Sorel does not explain why this should lead to the return of the classical outlook, and his attempt to make violence one of the absolute or objective values is only made plausible by confusing violence and heroism. It ought to be plain enough that willing-

[1] Sorel is not at all clear about the practical implications of his belief. He seems to think that it is possible to believe in his myth and at the same time not believe in it: 'By accepting the idea of the general strike, although we know that it is a myth, we are proceeding exactly as a modern physicist does who has complete confidence in his science, although he knows that the future will look upon it as antiquated. It is we who really possess the scientific spirit, while our critics have lost touch both with modern science and modern philosophy; and having proved this, we are quite easy in our minds.' (*Reflections*, p. 166.)

This scientific analogy is not strictly accurate; the scientist does not deliberately use a theory that does not fit all the relevant facts, and a myth that is known to be inadequate is not a myth at all, but hocus-pocus.

ness to die for a cause is not the same thing as willingness to cut another man's throat, but Sorel blurs the distinction, and Hulme does not clarify it.

Sorel's contention that the struggle against capitalist
morality, if it is to go on at all, cannot be conducted suc-
cessfully in an atmosphere of genteel utopianism, is
undoubtedly true;[1] and the distinction that he draws
between revolutionary violence and the vindictive acts
of cruelty sometimes carried out in the name of justice
is equally valid. There is, however, no need to go on
to a glorification of violence. The temptation to resort
to violence is always strong, just as there is a strong temptation to kick a machine that has broken down. Violence
is easy, it saves us the bother of recognizing the faults in
ourselves, and it satisfies our craving to blame something
outside ourselves. We must recognize this craving as we
recognize the craving for leadership, but we need not
yield to it in its stupid and evil forms. Sorel does not
argue that we should, but this interpretation is sometimes placed on his work, and Hulme's association with
him is liable to make people read the same interpretation
into *Speculations*.

[1] In the general strike of 1926, for example, the labour leaders had not
grasped Sorel's conception of the strike as an episode of war: when they
had launched the strike they suddenly saw the consequences of their
action. They had challenged the whole capitalist system, and they realized too late that they were in danger of winning more than they had
intended. Their own careers, their aims and hopes, had all been fixed
within the capitalist system, and they were alarmed at the prospect of
having to consolidate immense gains. At once, they called off the strike.
A general strike of labour is now illegal, but action by capital equivalent
to a general strike is legal.

No doubt Hulme disliked the kind of person who was a pacifist in 1916, and he disliked and distrusted the ideas that usually went with pacifism, but a religious outlook is not consistent with a glorification of violence. Violence may spring from covetousness or greed quite as often as it does from an outraged sense of justice, and the worship of violence encourages, and is encouraged by, the tendency to look upon all evil as something exterior to ourselves. If we do not recognize the existence of original sin, we invent our own substitute for the devil; we fix on fascism, bolshevism or war itself, and hate it with an intensity that gives us a sense of conscious virtue. But to say that the hatred of war is sometimes based on this kind of illusion is not to say that war is good. Sorel seems to share Hegel's belief that 'War has the deep meaning that by it the ethical health of the nations is preserved and their finite aims uprooted.' The making of absolute pacifism into a supreme article of faith may be a sign of declining national vitality and of blindness to all other intrinsic values, and so may indifference to religion, science, and the arts; or it may be a sign that the morality of the State is wholly out of key with religious morality: but it does not follow that the worship of war and violence will harmonize religious and political morality or restore national vitality.

On this point Hulme's position is simple: he believes that there are evils worse than killing, and misfortunes worse than being killed. Violence is an evil, but not the greatest, and is sometimes necessary if greater evils are to be avoided. If we accept this, it is important to remember that it is necessary to be really ready to fight: the attitude that says, 'Let us be prepared and then we won't have to fight', is evasive and ineffective. It springs from a misgiving and an evasion: a belief that it is wrong to fight, combined with a desire to have all the advantages of fighting. It is ineffective because it deceives no one: it encourages the enemy to strike. The only real deterrent is a genuine willingness to fight.

Sorel's arguments show that all doctrines of complete non-violence are based on illusion, but his cult of violence cannot be accepted by anyone who believes in an attitude properly called religious. To put violence in the place of God is as silly as putting it in place of the Devil or in place of our own faults. Violence will come, as surely as disease, but it is not a thing to work for. The kind of pacifism that is based on false ideas, or on a heretical insistence on private values, or on personal fear, is bad; but a society that worships violence is ill-balanced and unstable, and by any religious standard it is immoral. Even when violence is used in defence of other beliefs, it must be remembered that a victory by violence is a victory for violence. Sorel's contention that moral systems cannot modify each other through discourse and example, but must resort to violence when they differ, overlooks the fact that these moral systems do not exist as consistent wholes in real people; no man wholly believes in 'capitalist ethics', though his class may sometimes act as if it did. A real moral revolution will not be accomplished without some acts of violence, but to assume, as Sorel sometimes does, that violence itself automatically accomplishes a moral revolution, is either to relapse into a form of liberal confidence in human nature, or else to invoke a morality of force.

Sorel, for all his talk about 'absolute values', never makes his values clear. Although he points out the danger of violence without a moral force behind it, the final flavour that emerges from his writings is a faith in violence itself, and the only justification offered is that violence does in fact succeed. But this is doubtful: a democracy may be suppressed by a foreign military dictatorship, or a decadent democracy may be broken up and superseded by a military dictatorship from within, but historically it is equally true that dictatorships do not last for ever. It is difficult to say how much truth there is in Hulme's argument that human nature is infinitely amenable to force and propaganda. Some minds, at least, tend to react *against* the teaching they receive, so that no doctrine, and no view of life, can ever be wholly suppressed by force and propaganda alone. It is doubtful whether violence is effective in the long run, and certainly it is a misuse of terms to call a cult of violence 'religious'.

The valuable part of Sorel's work is not his personal plea for a myth of violence, nor his argument that violence is inevitable, but his general attack on utopianism as a substitute for a real morality. He maintains that it is not possible to know all the conditions of the future: every new organization of society reveals new factors that in turn modify the kind of organization that is needed. He therefore says that the planning of utopias is 'unscientific': the most we can do is to evaluate some of the existing factors, and strengthen them if we think it wise. This was the method of Marx, who isolated the class struggle as a factor. It is a *conservative* method, which points to existing features and tries to maintain them by active effort. The utopian myth, on the other hand, though it may have been useful in the past, is dangerous not only because it turns men's energy away from immediate action, and leads to day-dreaming, but also because it is founded on illusion. The wickedness of jerry-builders and bucketshop proprietors will not automatically disappear under socialism or fascism: much of it will find a new outlet. The political problem is to mitigate the inconvenient effects of this wickedness and to take the fullest advantage of every virtue; the moral problem is to awaken every individual to a sense of moral responsibility. And a sense of moral responsibility cannot rest solely on social prudence, 'the greatest good of the greatest number'. There must be some ultimate intrinsic values by which we can measure the 'greatest good'. Though Hulme never mentions Kant, there is no doubt that he follows Kant in regarding morality as an absolute obligation implicit in the nature of reason.

Kant's doctrine is far tougher than that of utopian liberalism: it aims at a better state, but does not imply a belief in perfectibility. It looks on moral effort as a characteristic of life itself: it is consonant with the doctrines of religion, and it accepts as absolute the moral values of Christianity. Writing with a greater detachment than Sorel or Hulme, and a greater desire to find the truth, and not merely to correct existing errors and over-emphasis, Kant was able to assimilate something of Rousseau's ideals without mistaking them for facts. His essay on perpetual peace was a serious examination of the conditions on which peace was possible, and it rejected the possibility of a universal republic.

Progress, in the sense of a continual surrender of individual or local freedom in return for a corresponding surrender of the sovereign rights of other people and countries with whom we wish to trade, is possible; a group of satisfied and successful nations may find 'collective security', backed by an International Police, the cheapest and most effective way of ensuring peace among themselves and protecting themselves against outsiders. But a change of this kind is mainly a matter of convenience, and it ought not to be confused with moral aims. It represents no real moral progress in the individual, and it may run counter to real moral ideals. In the words of Pascal: 'States would perish if they did not often make their laws give way to necessity. But religion has never suffered this, or practised it.'[1]

Man is radically imperfect: that is to say, he is capable, and always will be capable, of making a definite moral effort to lead a better life, but he will never reach a state of perfection in which that effort will be unnecessary. Sorel and Hulme share this belief with Kant, and they imply that political problems can never be finally solved. Beyond their practical objections to utopianism, there is a moral objection. We have neither the ability to settle the

[1] Fragment 613.

problems of to-morrow nor the right to try. A political programme ought always to be provisional: it should be an attempt to do what is right to-day, and not to build a world in which man can do no wrong. The desire to put things right for ever is based on vanity: behind all utopianism, there is not only a desire to blame 'the system' for the shortcomings of the individual man, but also a fear that future generations will be less wise than ourselves and will need to be protected from error by a rigid, fool-proof and rogue-proof system. The people who are most convinced that they are better than their grandfathers are least convinced that their grandsons will be wiser or better than themselves. In so far as a utopian scheme is a spur to effective action, it is obviously useful, but often it serves a less reputable purpose. The romantic utopian abolishes heaven and the devil, and then invents a new heaven and a new devil, more flattering to himself.

This confusion of politics and religion stultifies both: any religious system has political implications, but the duties and responsibilities that it imposes on the citizen may run counter to his personal interests, or to the interests of his class or his country. Political morality is mainly prudential, and to mistake it for an absolute morality is to undermine the foundations upon which *all* morality rests. 'There is nothing so perilous', says Pascal, 'as what pleases God and Man.'[1]

The desire to escape from responsibility, and the desire to substitute daydreaming for practical activity, are

[1] Fragment 499.

deeply rooted in human beings. Even in religion these desires can find an outlet, but their indulgence at the expense of proper duties is a perversion and a sin. Religion does not, for example, give a mechanical rule to say what kind of violence is permissible, or when it can be rightly used. Tradition and authority are necessary to correct our personal errors, but the good life can never be reduced to the solution of an algebraic problem. Democratic liberalism, purged of its illusions about human perfectibility, and its tendency to blame 'the system' for the faults of the individual man, may be as nearly consistent with Christian morality as any policy in public affairs can be. A totalitarian policy cannot be, for it absolves the individual from his responsibility by making the State the source of all authority; and by rolling all the hierarchies into one it does explicitly what the utopian liberal does unconsciously: it confuses the human with the divine.

Chapter Eleven

HULME AND MODERN POETRY

'What is *not* interesting, is that which does not add to our knowledge of any kind; that which is vaguely conceived and loosely drawn; a representation which is general, indeterminate, and faint, instead of being particular, precise, and firm. . . . What are the external objects of Poetry, among all nations and at all times? They are actions; human actions.'—MATTHEW ARNOLD, Preface to *Poems*, 1853.

Imagery is a more general characteristic of poetry than is metre, but a quarter of a century ago, when Hulme was writing and lecturing, the popular poetry of the day was seldom distinguished by definite visual imagery or by new and accurate analogies. Masefield vigorously insisted on talking of the workaday world, but Yeats was still in the Celtic Twilight; Kipling, Newbolt and Watson were very widely admired for their political poetry, and a smaller public was still loyal to Stephen Phillips, Maurice Hewlett and Mary Coleridge. Poetry was expected to be 'the expression of a charming personality', or a metrical statement of poetical experience or of sentiments that were flattering to the reader. The minor poets of the day were certainly walking in Tennyson's shoes and wearing Byron's cloak: they turned up occasionally in Shakespeare's doublet and Swinburne's elastic-sided boots, but it was sometimes hinted that they had not quite the same insight and inspiration as their predecessors. There was nothing against the fancy-dress, but it did not of itself entitle them to a hearing: the views of George Arliss on politics are not necessarily as interesting or important as those of Wellington or Disraeli. In spite of murmurs, however, most readers expected English poetry to follow the romantic tradition of Shelley and Byron, and as long as the vocabulary and rhythms of that tradition were retained they were not sharply critical of the actual content of the poems.

To attack the degeneration of taste in general would have been useless, and Hulme turned his attention to one particular technical point. According to Hulme, a poem is good if it contains a new analogy and startles the reader out of his habit of treating words as counters. Poetry is always the advance guard in language. The progress of language is the absorption of new analogies. '*Creative* effort means *new* images. . . . Thought is the joining together of new analogies, and so inspiration is a matter of an accidentally seen analogy or unlooked-for resemblance.' Poetry is marked off from prose not by its rhythm or by the sentiments it expresses, but by its vividness: 'The prose writer drags meaning along with a rope. The poet makes it stand up and hit you.'

Plainly this is not the whole truth: it ignores the effects of sound altogether; and it does not explain why some images are memorable and significant, whilst others, equally vivid, are trivial and comic. Although Hulme

often condemns romantic poetry because he dislikes its
attitude, his theory ignores the fact that the merit of
poetry depends to some extent on the moral and intellectual beliefs that it implies. This limitation, however,
served a useful purpose. A theory of poetry that made
all poetic merit depend on accuracy of statement, and
not on the importance of the subject, was a useful side-
issue at a time when poets were trying to persuade their
readers to accept a new outlook and a new attitude in
poetry.

In recent years Hulme's theory has helped to prevent
critics from condemning swans because they were not
geese, but his influence must not be exaggerated. Hulme's
dislike of versified moralizing and Wardour Street poeti-
cality was shared by Ezra Pound, T. S. Eliot, F. S. Flint,
H.D., and other writers; and the Imagist movement,
which they initiated and which has influenced English
poetry for a quarter of a century, might well have developed without the help that Hulme gave it.[1] Stephen
Phillips's *Beautiful lie the Dead* could be called an Imagist
poem, but Phillips had nothing to do with Hulme or
with the official 'movement'. T. S. Eliot knew very
little of Hulme directly until the *Speculations* were published in 1924; F. S. Flint owed more to a reading of the
French *vers-libristes* than to any sympathy with Hulme's
ultimate intentions. The real leader of the movement
was Ezra Pound, and Pound was willing to find a place
in poetry not only for definite visual imagery, but also

[1] Some details of the early history of the Imagist movement are
given in Foster Damon's book on Amy Lowell.

for verbal music and 'the dance of the mind among ideas'.

Hulme's general statements are at first sight very plausible. He says that there are two qualities to distinguish: first, the ability to see things as they really are, and not as you have been taught to see them; second, the ability to hold on through infinite detail and trouble to the exact curve you want, and to avoid falling into the conventional curves of ingrained technique. These are the two essentials of good poetry: it does not matter whether the thing that is seen is important or not. This is the Platonic view: the object of aesthetic contemplation is something framed apart by itself and regarded without memory or expectation, simply as being itself, as end not means, as individual not universal.

The importance of the subject is nothing, the accuracy and detachment everything. When this detachment and accuracy is shown in the realm of the emotions, the result is imagination; when it appears in the contemplation of finite things, it is fancy.[1] A poem is thus the expression of an intuition, in Bergson's sense. 'Now this is all worked out in Bergson, the central feature of his whole philosophy,' says Hulme, and Hulme's conception of the technique and aim of poetry closely resembles the conception of philosophy that is found in Cusanus, Bergson and Husserl. Bergson, for example, assumes that in ordinary perception we do not see things as they are: we see only certain conventional types, and these types are determined by our primary need, which is action, not

[1] *Speculations,* p. 139.

knowledge. He says that the business of the philosopher is to pass beyond this conventional vision; and in a somewhat similar way Husserl claims that the aim of his 'phenomenology' is to allow our experience to reveal its own essence and structure. A resolute preliminary suspension of judgment was necessary: the philosopher must not presuppose common-sense theory or any other theory.

Hulme follows Bergson in assuming that reality is a flux of interpenetrating elements, which we envisage in fixed shapes according to our needs. In Hulme's view, it is the artist who does the work that Bergson ascribes to the philosopher: he tries to see things without reference to any specific need of action. Most of us see what we are interested in: the artist tries to see what there is to be interested in. For practical purposes we separate out some features of the flux and speak of them as if they could really be isolated. Whenever we do this (and we do it whenever we speak in prosaic, scientific terms), we are ignoring the interpenetration. The artist tries to express the interpretation, and it is this that people mean when they speak of art as 'the revelation of the infinite in the finite'. This conception of art is not, of course, wholly new: in some ways it recalls Plato, and it bears a strong resemblance to Schopenhauer's doctrine: 'Art is the pure contemplation of the Idea in a moment of emancipation from the Will.'

According to Hulme, the artist leaves the level where things are crystallized out into definite shapes that can be used, he immerses himself in the flux, and comes back

with a new shape that he tries to fix. He has not *created*
anything: he has *seen* something. 'For instance, the effect
produced by Constable on the English and French
Schools of landscape painting. Nobody before Constable saw things, or at any rate painted them, in that
particular way. This makes it easier to see clearly what
one means by an individual way of looking at things.
It does not mean something that is peculiar to an individual, for in that case it would be quite valueless. It
means that a certain individual artist was able to break
through the conventional ways of looking at things
which veil reality from us at a certain point, was able
to pick out one element which is really in all of us, but
which before he had disentangled it, we were unable to
perceive.'[1]

A good work of art thus reveals something that is in
reality. A new metaphor, a new myth, a new type of
character, all these reveal a feature of reality for which
we previously had no name. Once the feature has been
pointed out, we recognize it again and again. Don
Quixote, for example, and Pickwick, Falstaff, and Caliban, are recognizable types of characters, or aspects of
all our characters, and no other name for them exists.
We may have seen something of the sort before, but we
are likely to notice it more frequently after it has once
been pointed out to us, just as a word seems to turn up
in print surprisingly often just after we have looked up
its meaning. The artist has seen something that is real,
and has made it plain to us; but in order to do this he

[1] *Speculations*, p. 150.

had to be free from the usual way of looking at things.

Some of the greatest artists have been unpractical or immoral; some have done their best work more or less asleep, or drunk, or under the influence of drugs; and children, who are free from the preoccupations of adults, sometimes produce works of art that show deeper insight than their authors are likely to have when they are older. All this follows from the fact that the artist, at one moment of his work, must be free from the prosaic vision that we use for ordinary purposes. The merit of his work depends partly on the technical skill with which he communicates what he has seen, partly on the accuracy of his intuition, and partly on the proportion that he establishes between it and other intuitions. Other things being equal, the quality of his conscious thought and his practical morality may help us to decide the range and sanity of his vision; but it is useless to say: 'He would have been a greater poet if. . . .' A failure on the familiar surface is sometimes the stimulus that leads the artist to an apprehension of reality that is a valuable addition to, or modification of, those he has failed to apply.

This outlook reconciles the two apparently contradictory aspects of art that were described by Keats and Shelley: one, that 'Beauty is truth, truth Beauty', the other that poetry 'is not subject to the control of the active powers of the mind'. Good art is a vision of something that will come to be recognized as a constituent of reality; but this vision can only be reached through the operation of the subconscious, or at any rate inarticulate, powers of the mind. The subconscious work of the imagination, rearranging its limited set of symbols to get a picture of some newly revealed aspect of reality, must always be done before a new work can appear; but there is nothing mysterious or subconscious about the work when it does appear. It is a new perception and act of naming, like the discovery and naming of a potato or a planet.

Hulme is putting forward a programme rather than a theory; he is an apologist rather than a critic; and he does not want to be bludgeoned by references to Milton and Dante. A theory such as Hulme's may be very useful to some artists: it may serve as a buffer to deaden hostile criticism, and enable them to feel, when criticized, that it is a theory that is being criticized, not the particular work. To the artist who is protected in this way, the theory seems obviously right, but the protection of the artist's self-confidence is not the only purpose of a theory of aesthetics, nor is it enough that the theory helps the artist to do good work. Muddled cosmogonies like those of Donne and Milton, and cock-and-bull mythologies like those of Blake and Yeats, have often helped to release the poet from conventional ways of looking and speaking, but they do not rank as scientific metaphysics. A theory that does not apply to Milton or Dante is as bad as a pseudo-science that ignores many of the facts of orthodox science: it may be useful, and it may include something valuable that is omitted from more orthodox studies, but it cannot itself be good criticism or good philosophy.[1]

[1] One must make allowances, of course, for Hulme's journalistic

Hulme himself is far more of a poet than a philosopher; he is not trying to reveal a logical structure and unity in the world, and when he pleads for a logic of images he is pleading for poetry, not metaphysics. But he is not wholly a poet, either. He would like to show that the poet's grasp of reality is as valid as the philosopher's, but instead of sitting down to write poetry, he tries to give poetry the prestige of logic by showing that poetry is a kind of logic. To do this, he first of all restricts the notion of poetry to the operations of the fancy, and then tries to find a theory of logic that can be extended to include this kind of poetry. This is at the root of his interest in Husserl: the prominent place that Husserl gives to what he calls the 'free fancy' in his phenomenology enables Hulme to see a way of dignifying poetic 'fancy', and of discrediting imagination by making it nothing more than a complex operation of the fancy.

This, however, does very little to clarify the problems of criticism. Hulme restricts his attention to the superficial, explicit meaning of poetry, and all his talk of the necessity of a logic of images amounts to nothing more than a plea for the continuation of vivid sensuous poetry. Hulme's 'logic of images' does not cover all the effects of poetry, nor is the distinction that he tries to draw between a logic of counters and a logic of images as sharp as he would wish. Criticism is in some ways intermediate between poetry and science; and the 'logic of

exaggeration. It would be silly to take him *au pied de la lettre* when he says: 'Personally I am of course in favour of the complete destruction of all verse more than twenty years old.'

images' in poetry is never wholly beyond critical discussion. Sometimes, indeed, it seems to be simply a compressed form of the logic of counters. Furthermore, the logic of counters, in so far as it has any real meaning and influences our thought, is never *wholly* free from poetic effects. To say that one logic is objective and the other is not, is plainly silly, for it is a demonstrable fact that people with the proper skill do agree about good and bad poetic logic, just as properly trained logicians agree about good and bad counter-logic. The distinction that Hulme is trying to draw is useful, but like the distinction between gas and liquid, it breaks down at the critical temperature.

Some of the confusion in Hulme's criticism of poetry arises because he keeps talking like a painter, and in principle limits poetry to the accurate description of visible things. 'A man cannot write without seeing at the same time a visual signification before his eyes. It is this image which precedes the writing and makes it firm.'[1] No doubt he merely intended to find a theory that would enable him to condemn all poetry that talks of the infinite and man's unconquerable soul, but instead of condemning this poetry as being untrue or immoral, he tries to prove that it is not poetry at all. This he does by converting his own indifference to music,[2] and his preference for visual imagery, into a theory of poetry. In-

[1] *Notes on Language and Style.*
[2] There are very few references to music in Hulme's writing, and none that show any appreciation of it. The impression of those who knew him was that 'It seemed to him time spent in listening to music would have been better spent in conversation'.

tending to sweep out the 'infinite', he gets rid of everything that is invisible and intangible. Among much that
is acute in Hulme's criticism, we find grotesque assertions based on nothing more than personal predilection.
It is quite possible to share his dislike of Rousseau and
Victor Hugo without sharing his taste in architecture and
sculpture, or approving his lack of taste in music; and it
is possible to share his 'religious' view of man without
believing that it must necessarily find expression in
purely visual poetry and in purely rectilinear 'Byzantine' art. The use of concrete images and geometrical
order is not the only way of expressing a sense of man's
limitations.

Although Hulme looks to art for the expression of a
religious attitude, he denies that poetry is akin to religion, and in his *Lecture on Modern Poetry* he is less concerned with the content of poetry than with poetry as the
means of expression. In his technical criticism of poetry
he keeps very near to Bergson: 'Plain speech is essentially inaccurate. It is only by new metaphors, that is,
by fancy, that it can be made precise,'[1] and again: 'The
great aim is accurate, precise and definite description.'[2]
As a description of one of the qualities of good writing,
whether prose or verse, this is admirable, but Hulme
bases it on a mistaken theory of language: 'Poetry . . .
is not a counter language, but a visual concrete one. It is a
compromise for a language of intuition which would hand
over sensations bodily. It always endeavours to arrest
you, and to make you continuously see a physical thing,

[1] *Speculations*, p. 137.   [2] Ibid., p. 132.

to prevent you gliding through an abstract process.'[1]

When the conventional expression of noble or poetical sentiments is confused with poetry, these strong un-guarded statements may be a useful tonic. But poetry is not a substitute for some other imaginary language. It *is* language, and language is not concerned with hand-ing over sensations bodily. It is a symbolism, not a sub-stitute for actual experience. Hulme's contention (apart from his exaggeration) is that we do not think in words, but in images, and by images he nearly always means visual images 'seen in the mind's eye'. But in fact the problem is not as simple as this: some people think mainly in words, and some mainly in visual images; and some-times we have the curious sensation of thinking without having any communicable symbols at all, whether words or mental pictures. Moreover, language is not only a symbolism, like drawing and gesticulation, which en-ables us to communicate our thoughts and sensations, but also a mechanism through which we relate them and organize them, and it deals not only with visual experi-ences but with all sorts of sensations, intuitions, and thoughts, and the vividness with which it presents them is not necessarily visual:

> From harmony, from heavenly harmony,
>   This universal frame began

or

> The wan moon is setting beyond the white wave,
> And time is setting with me, O!

[1] *Speculations*, p. 134.

In neither of these passages is the imagery directly visual: the lines from Dryden are musical rather than visual, and the second of the lines from Burns only remotely influences the sense of sight, although the effect of the whole depends upon it. Some of the greatest poetry is not *directly* concerned with sensuous images at all, but with relating abstract processes to other sensations, and making us 'realize' them. The process of realizing a truth is distinct from that of knowing it: we suddenly feel its full implications, its relation with all that we know and act on already. We say that we have seen what it means. But this metaphorical use of 'see' ought not to make us say that the only object of poetry is to make us 'see' things in the ordinary sense.

In poetry, visual images are far more common than images that affect the sense of touch or smell, but this does not mark off poetry from prose; for in prose too the eye predominates over ear and nose and fingers. The difference is not that poetry is purely visual, but that the poet makes a more vivid and more far-reaching use of his sensuous images than the prose-writer does. Yet abstract words have their symbolic value no less than the concrete sensuous words that call up a picture. 'The eternal silence of the infinite spaces' that say nothing, and have no message for us, can raise a shuddering horror as poetically as any hairy claw.

When Hulme says that 'All poetry is an affair of the body—that is, to be real it must affect body' and adds that bodies and daggers are needed in tragedy,[1] no doubt

1 *Speculations,* p. 242.

he is speaking for many people besides himself; and if poetry is not to be divorced from action it must certainly be expressed in terms that act upon our senses. But a more general statement of the relation between poetry and action is found in a passage of Newman's, quoted by Sorel in the *Reflections on Violence*: 'Assent, however strong, and accorded to images however vivid, is not therefore necessarily practical. Strictly speaking, it is not imagination that causes action; but hope and fear, likes and dislikes, appetite, passion, affection, the stirrings of selfishness and self-love. What imagination does for us is to find a means of stimulating those motive powers; and it does so by providing a supply of objects strong enough to stimulate them.'[1]

These objects are not always objects of the sensuous world, and though they can sometimes be described directly, more often abstractions are used, not only to give intensity to physical descriptions, but also to evoke a sensation that is not an image of a physical sensation at all. If we dislike this use of abstractions to build up a world that is not a picture of the world of sense, we must reject much of Shakespeare and most of Dante, as well as Smart, Traherne and Milton:

> . . . a dark
> Illimitable Ocean without bound,
> Without dimension, where length, breadth and
>   highth,
> And time and place are lost.

[1] Newman: *Grammar of Assent* (1891 edition, p. 82).

Here the dance of the mind among ideas and abstractions is used as one of the elements of poetry. The mind cannot think coherently beyond the bounds of actuality, but words can raise up a world of possibility beyond those limits, and the sensations that the poet produces in playing with that world may be related to the real and unromantic world. To try to make poetry out of nothing but abstractions is to risk dullness; the poet must present for inspection, as Marianne Moore has said, 'imaginary gardens with real toads in them'; but there is a dullness too in the poem that is nothing but sensuous imagery or nothing but music. The problem is to keep all three components active, to let one fall silent only for a momentary effect, as the 'cello may leave the viola and the violin a clear field until it suddenly re-enters to give a new significance to their movements.

In his *Notes on Language and Style* Hulme seems to recognize that words have properties and suggestions of their own, apart from the object or relation that they signify: 'The very act of trying to find a form to fit the separate phrases into, itself leads to the creation of new images hitherto not felt by the poet. . . . This creation by happy chance is analogous to the accidental stroke of the brush which creates a new beauty not previously consciously thought of by the artist.' It is certainly true that poetry often writes itself in this fashion: after a period of meditation and failure, the poet will sometimes find himself writing long passages or even complete poems that need very little subsequent correction. He feels that the poem is being dictated, and often he can see no difference in quality between passages dictated in this way and passages that are the result of long and painfully conscientious work.

Hulme is inclined to minimize this aspect of poetry. He makes the act of creation, whether in poetry or any other art, sound quite conscious and deliberate. He forgets that the artist is seldom consciously aiming at technical precision when he is at work, he is guided quite as much by his hand as by his head, and it is only later that he sees the point of what he has done. Even a classical poet like Pope admits that the process of learning to write is like training for a sport: we have to learn the rules and tricks of the trade, but do not begin to use them effectively until we know them so well that we have forgotten them.

In all art there is an element of play, a deliberate use of a medium for a purpose that is not the usual one. The mutilation and misuse of words may be poetry (' 'Twas brillig, and the slithy toves') or the free association of images ('The Grand Panjandrum himself with the little round button on top'). The proper use of the word 'fancy' in criticism includes all these activities. Fancy is not only a grasping of sensuous similarities—the sort of thing you get in Pope or Crashaw—it is also a grasping of obscure relationships and associations. If we say that a woman looks as if she had kissed a letter-box, we are being fanciful in Hulme's sense, but this kind of scientific metaphor ('a canary-yellow precipitate', as the chemistry books say) cannot be made the sole basis of poetry.

In poetry the effects of sound, and the general suggestion of similar-sounding words, may be quite as important as the visual images called up by the actual words. A poem in an unknown language, or no language at all, may be poetically enjoyable:

> A rumskin a bobbadilla
> Anna bobba ring tang,
> Nip-chang, fees-chang, chairo
> Pollywash and trimeo.

This is poetry, though it has very little meaning and presents no visual images. Art is partly a playful demonstration of the properties of the medium itself, whether the medium is paint, stone, music, or the sounds of common speech; but in Hulme's account only the visual properties of words are recognized, and only the serious descriptive use of them is admitted.

In all art there is an element that seems to be meaningless: a formal pattern or a pleasing rhythm does not need to be interpreted in order to be enjoyed. In some works —a geometrical design for example, or a Bach fugue— this element may predominate, but as Hulme points out in connection with Byzantine art, even the formal element may have a meaning. Meaning, indeed, in the sense of an effect that could also be produced in some other medium, is never wholly absent, even from music. Most people who prefer Beethoven's music to Wagner's would claim that Beethoven seems to be *saying* something that is wiser and more mature than Wagner. Although we know very little about Beethoven's verbal thoughts, we know that his development was like

Shakespeare's: the early sonatas can be compared with the comedies, the middle symphonies with the histories, and the *Hammerklavier Sonata*, and 'posthumous' quartets with *King Lear* and *The Tempest*.

Music can express not only emotions but also thoughts, and an attitude to the world; and poetry, since it has some of the resources of music as well as some of those of painting, can say two or three things at once. Even when it has a superficial meaning that is 'hard, dry, and classical' it may have a latent content that is very different, and this content may be expressed through the sound of the poem and through the less obvious suggestions of the images. Hulme, who was more concerned with painting than with music, considered only the explicit meaning. In writing poetry, he did not ignore the effects of sound (in a manuscript draft of one of his poems, the accents are carefully marked), but he did not rely on the music of words to carry part of his meaning. He found an image first, and then found the words that said it without making horrid noises. He did not jot down rhythms in his notebooks and then find words to fit them. His sensibility to verbal music was acute enough to make him dislike the implications of the metres and rhyme schemes in use in his day, but beyond this he took no great interest in it, and it found no place in his theories. His only statement on this subject was that poetasters write in metre because poets have done so, and poets because singing and not speech is their aim.

Metre and rhyme, however, can reinforce the poem's meaning, and their very arbitrariness can help the poet by freeing his mind from habitual prosaic courses and putting new ideas and new images into his head. Furthermore, they help to make the poem foolproof; they give it a definite form and surface so that it stays in the memory undistorted and is handed on unaltered. It was for this reason that the Mongols, at a time when they had no written language, issued their laws and military commands in metrical verse.

But the use of these devices is also a restriction: it narrows the range of sound the poet can produce, and it leads to padding and irrelevance. The music may be keyed too high or too low for the poet's purpose; and if the poem is meant to be read and not recited, is the old rigidity necessary? If we can rely on the printed page instead of the memory, is there any need of these precautions? Rhymed and regular poetry is easy to read, for long experience has taught people to read it fairly well. But if some readers can read irregular verse with a proper emphasis and rhythm, does not the new freedom open up new possibilities for the poet? He can concentrate more on imagery (and in poetry intended for silent reading this is natural), or he can use new kinds of verbal music. But the new poetry is no easier to write than the old. It may be said that without definite rules of prosody, it is easier to palm off a prosaic statement of palatable sentiments; but that is not true: the reader with an ear for rhythm can detect a clumsy line in free verse as easily as a finger-counter can detect a defective pentameter.

Hulme's dislike of the standard forms must be distinguished from the positive search for new cadences and sound patterns that was carried on by some of his contemporaries. In the poetic movement inaugurated by Hulme, Flint, Pound and Eliot there were two distinct tendencies; one towards a poetry depending mainly on images, and the other towards new cadences. The two are often lumped together as the free-verse movement, but Hulme was an innovator mainly in the matter of images, and only incidentally in musical form; Flint was more interested in the study of cadence, whereas Eliot's poetry is full of the sort of imagism that Hulme wanted, and is relatively conservative in the matter of verbal music. Eliot's rhythms are nearly all developments of standard rhythms, and much of his poetry is rhymed and uses familiar consonant-patterns.

Hulme's defence of free verse is not based on a liking for cadence or irregular rhythm: it arises from his conception of the proper subject-matter for modern poetry. In his *Lecture on Modern Poetry* he says that the old desire to make poetry imperishable and rigid was a result of the wish to make something durable amid the changing world, something like the Pyramids or the Trajan Column. That desire has now gone, he thinks, and 'We are no longer concerned that stanzas shall be shaped and polished like gems, but rather that some vague mood shall be communicated.' Whereas the old poetry dealt with the siege of Troy, the new deals (as G. K. Chesterton has said) with the emotions of a boy fishing. Furthermore, modern verse is to be read and not chanted: 'We have thus two distinct arts. The one intended to be chanted, and the other intended to be read in the study.

... I am not speaking of the whole of poetry, but of this distinct new art which is gradually separating itself from the older one and becoming independent.

'I quite admit that poetry intended to be recited must be written in regular metre, but I contend that this method of recording impressions by visual images in distinct lines does not require the old metric system.'

The romantic poetry that Hulme disliked sprang from a desire to dramatize life and to exaggerate emotions, and for these purposes regular metres and heavy rhymes were useful. The new poetry that he hoped to see was to be more modest; and it was to aim solely at recording particular sensations: 'The first time I ever felt the necessity or inevitableness of verse, was in the desire to reproduce the peculiar quality of feeling which is induced by the flat spaces and wide horizons of the virgin prairie of western Canada.

'You see that this is essentially different to the lyrical impulse which has attained completion, and I think once and for ever, in Tennyson, Shelley and Keats. To put this modern conception of the poetic spirit, this tentative and half-shy manner of looking at things, into regular metre is like putting a child into armour.'[1]

Thus it seems to Hulme that there is a case for a kind of poetry that would be deliberately trivial, more concerned with exact physical observation and apt metaphor than with noble sentiments and imaginative insight. He flatly denies that poetry is related to religion, he attacks the idea of 'imagination', as used by Coleridge and Rus-

[1] *Lecture on Modern Poetry.*

kin, and he asserts 'the particular verse we are going to get will be cheerful, dry and sophisticated, and here the necessary weapon of the positive quality must be fancy'.[1]

As a counter-blast to romantic vapourings, and as a description of one part of poetic technique, this is excellent, but as a theory of poetry, and as a forecast, it is poor stuff. The art of poetry cannot flourish unless people can appreciate poetry that is more concerned with a lady's shoe than with the starry heavens; but religion cannot flourish unless it has a language, and by Hulme's own argument that language must be poetry. As intuitions of the outer world need to be expressed in words, so also do moral and spiritual perceptions. Poetry is not religion, nor is it a substitute for religion: it is a medium through which we can express, among many other things, a religious intuition of the world; and without it religion is as inarticulate as physics would be without its mathematics. When we begin to write poetry, we are led to subjects such as the nature of man; and therefore the insight and sentiment that Hulme tried to keep out of poetry cannot be kept out. The device of defining imagination as a kind of more elaborate fancy does not succeed even with its author. Hulme claims that his 'classical' test of poetry does not depend at all on our sense of the importance of its subject-matter, but this is no more than a device for condemning poetry he does not like. As Pascal says: 'We only consult the ear because the heart is wanting. The rule is uprightness.'[2] Feelings about

1 *Speculations*, p. 137.   2 Fragment 30.

227

the value of human life, about suffering and love, about the value of simple enjoyment, and the nature of death, all the feelings Hulme distrusted whenever he recognized them, persist in coming. They can be modified by a changed outlook, but they are never abolished, and they demand expression in words.

If we turn to Hulme's own poetry, we find that it was far less trivial and particular than he believed. The infinite, kicked out of the front door, comes in at the back, and Hulme, without knowing it, writes poems that deal with important and universal subjects. We see this happening in a short poem called *Above the Dock*:

> Above the quiet dock in midnight,
> Tangled in the tall mast's corded height,
> Hangs the moon. What seemed so far away
> Is but a child's balloon, forgotten after play.

This certainly satisfies some of Hulme's criteria: it gives a definite picture and a neat analogy; it deals with simple and familiar things; but it is wrong to say that it does not drag in the infinite. In all Hulme's poems, the 'infinite' things—beauty, sky, moon and sea —appear, but where a romantic poet would try to make familiar things seem important by comparing them with moon or sea, Hulme reverses the effect and makes the infinite things seem small and homely by comparing them with a red-faced farmer, or a child's balloon, or a boy going home past the churchyard. This is the opposite of the romantic method, and it is easy enough to parody, but when it is done well its effects are as notable as those of romanticism, and perhaps not as different from them as Hulme thought.

The difference between Hulme's poetry and professed romantic poetry is not that the subject of Hulme's poetry is unimportant, but merely that its *explicit* subject is concrete and trivial. The underlying feeling and the latent meaning are as important as any 'emotion of the infinite' or romantic sense of wonder. But this is true of all good poetry: Hulme's criteria are among the technical tests of poetry, but these are not the only tests: the judgment of poetry cannot be wholly divorced from intellectual and moral judgments. Each of Hulme's poems implies a belief about the relation of religion to life, as a passage from Wordsworth might do, even if it were not one of the 'great' passages. A denial of the romantic view of life may be hard and sophisticated, but it is not unimportant. When Hulme, at the end of his description of the world as chaos, without order or purpose apart from the mind that sees it, tries to show how this view is acceptable to him, he falls into prose that is very near to poetry: 'A melancholy spirit, the mind like a great desert lifeless, and the sound of march music in the street, passes like a wave over that desert, unifies it, but then goes.'

This is the poetry of stoicism, not Christianity, but it is serious and imaginative, and it cannot be called cheerful, dry and fanciful.

Chapter Twelve

THE TRAGIC VIEW

'Now, when he was courting a woman's love and wanting her
to love him, Niels Lyhne of Lönborghof, who was twenty-
three, bent forward a little in his walk, had nice hands and small
ears and was by nature a little timid;—he wanted her to love him
and not the idealized Nicholas of his dreams, who had a proud
walk, assured manners, and was a little older; he now took a
lively interest in this Niels with whom he had formerly associated
as with some less presentable friend. He had been too busy adorning
himself with what he lacked to have time to notice what he possessed; but now with the passion of a discoverer he began to
gather himself together out of the memories and impressions of
his childhood, out of the vivid moments of his life, and with
happy astonishment he saw how it fitted together, piece by piece,
and built itself up into a quite differently intimate personality
from the one he had run after in his dreams. And also far more
genuine and strong and energetic.—J. P. JACOBSEN, *Niels Lyhne*.[1]

The main theme of Hulme's work is the defence of what
he calls the religious view. If we regard only those elements on which Hulme insists most strongly, it might
be said to be a pessimistic view, stoical perhaps, but not
Christian; but these elements must be taken in conjunc-

1 Quoted by J. B. Leishman in the introduction to his translation of
Requiem and other poems, by R. M. Rilke.

tion with others which, because they were widely known, Hulme felt no need to stress. The whole outlook is not new, and it might be better to call it tragic rather than classical or religious; but it is important, and its importance is more widely recognized to-day than it was in Hulme's time. The word tragic itself is liable to be misunderstood: there is nothing gloomy or pessimistic in the tragic view of life. Pessimism is our first reaction from a sentimental romantic view, and it turns easily into an attitude of cynicism or despair. The tragic view recognizes from the beginning all those facts that lead to disappointment and bitterness, and therefore it leaves room for a gaiety that is not at the mercy of circumstances. There are signs of such an attitude to-day not only in politics and philosophy, but also in modern English poetry and in the novels, plays and poems of Franz Kafka, Hugo von Hofmannsthal and Rainer Maria Rilke.

The tragic view is necessary because the romanticism of Victor Hugo, the sentimental optimism of liberal pacifists, and the utopian faith in automatic progress are no longer tenable, and many people who had placed their hope in them find themselves reduced to a despair that would be pitiful if it were not silly. We feel that scientific discoveries threaten the security of our moral existence, and shake all our certainties into nothing. The world for which we are in some measure responsible has grown from a village to an empire, our sympathies have grown with it; but we are baffled by the problems of co-operation, and we have lost confidence in our own judgments. The optimism that went hand in hand with nineteenth-century science has disappeared; we are no longer confident that in the light of science alone we can grow straight and healthy. Science answers one question only to let us see another and harder question waiting.

There is nothing strange or pitiable in this: it is our own nature to ask questions and seek difficulties to overcome; but for some people the zest has gone out of the search, they are afraid of what they may discover. When we look into our own motives, the human soul shows the same endless complexity as the atom. We learn to use our knowledge of it to heal the obviously sick, but at the same time we take away the foundations of our confidence: we look into ourselves with a kind of metaphysical horror, knowing that all our motives have causes, that our conscience is twisted and controlled by accidental happenings, and that our conclusions often bear no relation to what is right and true.

What the psychologist does for the individual, the social scientist does for the community. He reveals ideas, theories, morals, and standards of art and poetry, as the outcome of man's economic needs: he discredits the idea of disinterested truth and justice as the psychologist discredits that of liberty and virtue. Science, which set out cheerfully to smooth away our obstacles, ends by smoothing away our motives. It gives us no final and certain knowledge, it does not tell us what things are worth doing, and it suggests that sometimes, when we thought we were being altruistic and honest, we were really acting from deep-seated motives on behalf of ourselves or our class, and in the light of our own morality these motives seem hardly creditable. In such a state of mind, it seems that nothing is worth while, and that all effort is futile.

A crisis of the same kind may happen to anyone who is concerned with words. There comes a moment when he can no longer speak coherently, because he sees that all the meanings of words are vague and uncertain. What reason have we to assume that grammar, syntax, logic, style, correspond to any reality in the world or in the minds of other people? How can we make any assertion that is not shot through with uncertainty, ambiguity and error? Hugo von Hofmannsthal, in *A Letter of Lord Chandos*, represents a young and famous poet writing to Bacon to 'excuse himself to this friend for his total cessation from literary activity'. 'My case is shortly this. I have completely lost the faculty for either thinking or speaking coherently about anything whatsoever. To begin with, it became impossible for me in discussing any elevated or universal theme, to utter those words of which most men make habitual and unreflecting use. I endured inexplicable discomfort at having so much as to pronounce such words as "spirit", "soul", or "body". I experienced an inner powerlessness to pass judgment on the pleasures of the court, the events of Parliament, or what you will. . . . Abstract words, which are a necessity of our tongue, crumbled in my mouth like some decaying fungus. . . .'

Hofmannsthal is right in placing the scene of this

crisis in another age, for it is not peculiar to our own time. It is one of the themes of Shakespeare's later plays, for example; but it is peculiarly pressing in our time, and there are some people who relate it to the declining birth-rate of Western Europe. They say that in the history of every civilization a time comes when the race loses its confidence in its gods, its values and its mission; and then, in some way not understood, it begins to die out, and less civilized races take its place. In Western Europe to-day they see a decline in courage, faith, and hope that seems to them to be exactly like the decline that led to the fall of Athens, Sparta, and Rome.

And yet all this is nonsense: like all the other problems of self-consciousness, the difficulty arises from having asked too much and from having fixed our absolute in ourselves. Our language can never be exact and perfect; but this should lead to new energy and determination, not merely to indifference and despair. To aim towards perfection, whether in knowledge, speech or action, is right; but to expect to be rewarded by attainment is to misunderstand the whole nature of human life and activity. It is this error that leads to disillusion, and the disillusion has nothing to do with the decay of a race and the death of its gods. It is a stage on the way to health, as Hofmannsthal saw; and we can pass beyond it to a new certainty and confidence. When we can see clearly what our own problem is, we can put it into words and so escape from it. If it seems that our social world is less moral than that of earlier ages, it is because our inventions have given us greater control of the material world, and therefore a greater field for our responsibility. If our science has for the moment outrun our other certainties and left them confused and ineffectual, it is because our optimism was based on a false conception of science and of man. Our new self-consciousness, our trick of questioning our own motives, is an instrument of Hulme's critique of satisfaction: it shows that our confidence was misplaced, but it does not destroy the grounds for confidence. The man who says he cannot love a woman because he knows his own motives, or cannot like a poem because it is the outcome of historical forces, is to be helped but not pitied.

For such people, something more than intellectual scepticism is involved; they really do feel that life is not worth living: but it is an intellectual error, or a lack of intellectual persistence, that has led them to this attitude. They say that science has taken away their certainties. In the mechanical sciences we run no risk of making this mistake: we hold fast to the simple fact that the existence of the atom and the photon does not disprove the existence of the solid rock; the theory of relativity does not disprove the existence of our clocks and measuring rods, it merely tells us how to use them. Yet to hold hard to the concrete fact and deny the theory is no solution of our difficulties. It is only through question and doubt that our knowledge can grow: the only durable certainty is built on sure foundations of despair, whether in intellectual knowledge or in morals. The people who say that they are disillusioned are sincere, but they have not seen far enough; they know they could not have been disillusioned if they had not started with illusions, but they have not clearly seen the nature of their own errors.

If we ignore real facts about ethics and the nature of man, our purposes are bound to be frustrated sooner or later, and this frustration is the theme of tragedy. Tragedy starts by recognizing the existence of evil, not only in the outside world but in ourselves. It is not a daydream escape from reality, like the dreams in which we imagine that we can fly, or that we have infinite power and fascination. It recognizes our limitations, and makes them acceptable. In this it is no more pessimistic than mechanical science. The aim of natural knowledge is to show us the obstructions in the external world, to reveal their nature so that we can turn them, to show the hidden incompatibilities in our own desires so that we can make a choice and avoid frustration; but obstructions remain, as long as life and consciousness remain, and the business of tragic poetry is to make us recognize the fact and accept it as naturally as we accept the fact of gravitation. Tragic poetry does not forbid us to laugh, any more than the law of gravitation forbids us to fly. It teaches us the conditions we must accept if we choose to laugh; and if we accept these conditions we can see the world as Jacobsen's Niels Lyhne saw it when he outgrew his dreams and became a reasonable man.

Tragic poetry that deals with these matters is imaginative, in Coleridge's sense, and it is possible to claim with some show of reason that nearly all important imaginative poetry implies that tragic view. What makes the discussion of imagination and fancy worth while is that critics do, in the main, agree as to which passages are to be called imaginative, and which fanciful. Most readers will agree that Pope's couplet about words and leaves is fanciful:

> Words are like leaves; and where they most abound,
> Much fruit of sense beneath is rarely found;

and they will agree that when Beddoes speaks of windless pestilence,

> Transparent as a glass of poisoned water
> Through which the drinker sees his murderer smiling,

his description is imaginative. In *The Decline and Fall of the Romantic Ideal*, F. L. Lucas uses these examples, and a passage from *The Scholar-Gipsy*, to show that imagination is not merely a matter of multiple resemblances; and the examples seem to be conclusive: but the interesting thing is that both of the imaginative passages express, beneath the surface, a tragic view of life. There is no need to assume a mysterious, indefinable essence to account for their fascination. Both of them profess to be speaking about finite things, and both imply an important judgment about the world or life in general, though this judgment never becomes explicit.

There is a familiar kind of imaginative poetry in which the whole poem is an extended metaphor for something that is never mentioned explicitly; and in the similes and metaphors that impress us most we often feel that both of the things compared really stand for something else that is not even mentioned. Although the poet seems to speak only of concrete and sensuous things, his words apply to the nature of the world, or to the intrinsic limitations of thought and feeling. He says that one thing is like another; but the simile is not imaginative unless it draws attention to qualities that belong to something quite different. $A = B(= C)$ is the typical statement of this kind, and in the middle of what seemed to be a straightforward statement about A's and B's the reader suddenly feels that something more far-reaching has been said. This second statement may not have been part of the poet's conscious intention, and it may not be plainly understood by the reader, for words often have their effect long before we are conscious of all their meanings.

In the passage from *Death's Jest-Book*, the reader is startled at the sudden presentation of an image that suggests far more than the poet stops to mention. The glass of water may be poisoned, even when it seems clear and transparent, and behind simplicity there may be malice smiling. One can go further, and say, as Beddoes often says explicitly, that life itself is like that, with death and evil latent in all delight and innocence. This may not be a plain statement of the tragic view, but it is the tragic view seen through the eyes of a romantic.

Again, there is a similar hidden meaning behind the passage in which Arnold tells the carefree scholar-gipsy, 'born in days when wits were fresh and clear', to leave the modern world 'with its sick hurry, its divided aims',

> As some grave Tyrian trader from the sea,
> Descried at sunrise an emerging prow

Lifting the cool-hair'd creepers stealthily,
   The fringes of a southward-facing brow
      Among the Ægæan isles;
And saw the merry Grecian coaster come,
   Freighted with amber grapes and Chian wine,
   Green, bursting figs, and tunnies steep'd in brine—
And knew the intruders on his ancient home,

   The young light-hearted masters of the waves—
      And snatch'd his rudder, and shook out more sail;
      And day and night held on indignantly. . . .

It is not merely that both scholar and Tyrian trader are
fleeing from a foreign world. The simile involves differences as well as likenesses, and the differences are essential to the poem. The carefree scholar is compared to the
grave Tyrian, the melancholy modern thinker to the
'young light-hearted masters of the waves'. There is an
implied assertion that to be carefree is to be grave in the
only valuable sense, and that to be torn by uncertainties
and doubts is to be frivolous. This is part of the tragic
view, but it insinuates itself all the more effectively into
our minds because it is kept in the background, and never
made explicit. By itself, it might be as distasteful as it is
true, but it is welcomed when it comes as a concealed
implication of a simile that is itself apt and acceptable.

   The couplet from Pope, however, is not imaginative,
for although leaves are like words, and fruit is like sense,
in half a dozen ways, there is no hidden reference in
these resemblances: nothing is said or implied except
that A is like B, and there the matter ends. The passage

is fanciful but not imaginative. Only where the comparisons reach out beyond the things that the poet names, does fancy become imagination. We need not be wholly aware of this extension to feel its force: words act on us with all their meanings and associations before we become conscious of them, and the poet himself is likely not to notice them until he has written down the words. It is often this sense of exceptionally intricate interrelations with exceptionally wide application that makes imagination different from fancy. It is not, as Hulme suggests,[1] that imagination deals with feelings and fancy with infinite things, but that imaginative writing implies a theory about the world, even when it seems to talk of finite things.

In Ruskin's *Modern Painters* there is a passage that says something very similar, but with a certain amount of romantic bugaboo: 'There is in every word set down by the imaginative mind an awful under-current of meaning, and evidence and shadow upon it of the deep places out of which it has come. It is often obscure, often half told, for he who wrote it, in his clear seeing of the things beneath, may have been impatient of detailed interpretation, but if we choose to dwell upon it and trace it, it will lead us always securely back to that metropolis of the soul's dominion from which we may follow out all the ways and tracks to its farthest coasts.'[2]

Hulme dislikes this passage because it seems to make the imagination too serious a thing, and he dislikes still

1 *Speculations*, p. 134.
2 *Modern Painters*, Part III, Sect. 2, Chap. iii, §5.

more a later passage: 'Imagination . . . cannot be but serious; she sees too far, too darkly, too solemnly, too earnestly, ever to smile. There is something in the heart of everything, if we can reach it, that we shall not be inclined to laugh at. . . . Those who have so pierced and seen the melancholy deeps of things, are filled with the most intense passion and gentleness of sympathy.'[1]

There certainly seems to be an unwarranted assumption here: there is no reason for supposing that 'the deeps of things' are melancholy; you may feel that they are melancholy, and you will certainly feel that they are melancholy if you are an honest artist but nevertheless romantic, for you will discover that the truth is not what you hoped it might be. Your disillusion, however, is no excuse for making a general principle of your own emotion and saying that imagination cannot but be solemn. Ruskin is right in saying there is an 'undercurrent of meaning' in imaginative art, and he is right in seeing this undercurrent as a disappointment to romantic preconceptions, but he is wholly wrong in asserting that the truth is therefore melancholy.

Insight brings gentleness, certainly, for it springs from sensibility; but it may also bring indignation. The two are not contradictory except to the romantic who has, in the last resort, no absolute principles to justify either. The incapacity for action that is supposed to follow from intelligence and insight is really the result of a collision between romantic preconceptions and an obscure vision of the truth. Tragic insight does not end in helpless

[1] *Modern Painters,* Part III, Sect. 2, Chap. iii, §9.

acquiescence in the world as it is; it recognizes the rightness and necessity of action, as it recognizes other facts; and it does not look for impossible results. It must not be confused with the false stoicism which accepts as inevitable some things that could well be altered, and ought to be altered.

In his wish to contradict romantic notions, Hulme goes too far in his condemnation of Ruskin. 'Accurate, precise and definite description' is not the sole criterion of poetry: it is one of the technical criteria of some kinds of poetry. In spite of Hulme's statement that the importance of the subject does not matter, serious imaginative poetry such as *Hamlet* or *The Tempest* is superior to *As You Like It* or *The Knight of the Burning Pestle*, not merely because it is technically better, but because it shows greater sympathy, insight and knowledge, and talks about more important things. A criterion that would put Hulme's short poems on the same level as *King Lear* is idiotic, and Hulme realizes that comprehensiveness is as important as accuracy: but in his haste to correct the error of those who judge everything by the importance of the explicit subject, he wildly overstates his case.

When he claims that the 'highest' verse need not be serious, he shows the same over-emphasis. The explicit meaning of the highest verse need not be serious, but beneath the surface there is, as Ruskin says, something that we shall not be inclined to laugh at. In the *Notes on Language and Style*, there is a phrase that shows that Hulme clearly recognized the difference in level between 'serious' and 'comic' verse: 'Humour and expression—a joke analysed and viewed as the decadent form into which all forms of literary expression can be shown to pass by degeneration of function.' It is quite true to say that in England to-day the joke is a far more popular form than the imaginative poem, and it is equally true to say that it is nearly always an inferior way of coping with any important situation. Imaginative poetry is often said to be obscure or mysterious by people who do not want to recognize what it implies, but it is far more true to say that most jokes proceed by obscuring a difficult situation and switching off the sympathy and intelligence, whereas imaginative poetry makes the whole situation clearer and more actual. A successful joke enables you to recognize a fact without thinking or feeling any more about it, a successful imaginative poem forces you to take account of the fact so that it governs your thought and action. The joke is the natural device of the man who wants to retain a false view of the world, but is nevertheless compelled to face an awkward fact.

In this sense, again, Ruskin is right: the 'highest' verse is serious, even if it is superficially comic. He is wrong only when he assumes that to be serious is to be melancholy. In trivial matters, the joke is an entirely legitimate device; the English habit of talking of 'a sense of humour' as if it were the same thing as a sense of proportion is neither evasive nor unreasonable. But it is important, if we are going to use jokes, to make sure that our general attitude is sound. There is something unhealthy about a man, a family, or a nation, that needs to joke all the time; and there is also something unhealthy and ill balanced about anyone short of a genius who never makes a joke at all.

The romantic needs to make jokes in real life, but cannot tolerate them in art because they are out of key with the melancholy he sees in 'the deeps of things'. In tragic art there is no such all-pervading melancholy: there is pity, and terror, and a sense of human limitation, but there is also a place for comedy. Indeed, comedy is an essential part of tragedy: you cannot portray the limitations of humanity without stumbling on the absurd. The heroine weeps, and all her thought is on the highest level, but as she weeps she snuffles and has to blow her nose, and this is more truly tragic than her weeping, but it is also comic; and this kind of comedy is found in Shakespeare as it is in Tchekov. Caliban is funny, but he is also horrible and terrifying. He is an animal, but he is also a man, and part of ourselves.

All comedy is pathetic if you let yourself realize the situation. Tchekov portrayed the tragi-comedy of people who were full of romantic ideals, yet failed and made themselves ridiculous over small things. A situation of this kind is not funny if you stand too near: all farce is pathetic for the actors. But for the spectators this particular situation is tragic *because* it is funny. The romantic man is willing to fail if he can fail heroically and grandiloquently, but he is not willing to be made to look an ass: yet it is in looking an ass that he becomes a genuine tragic character; for he carries his own doom in himself.

He is condemned to failure by his own wild, impossible aspirations, his delusions about the nature and possibilities of man, his undisciplined pride and ambition. He has made himself the equal of the gods, and his failure is grotesque. There is always something sad, as well as funny, in the sight of a man aiming high and tripping over a dead cat.

Grotesque situations of this kind are foreign to romantic comedy and romantic melodrama, but they are always found in classical tragedy. Fancy, in Coleridge's sense—a resemblance with some points of difference—is thus more natural to classical tragedy than to romantic melodrama. It is a *part* of the imaginative vision; for the 'points of difference' are deliberate and significant: they point to human limitations.

Although fancy in this sense may be part of tragic poetry, it is not the whole. Imagination, as Coleridge understands it, is still essential. 'A literature of wonder must have an end as inevitably as a strange land loses its strangeness when one lives in it,'[1] says Hulme, but romantic wonder has little to do with imagination, and there is another kind of wonder that Hulme does not mention. Romantic wonder is comparative: it compares an extraordinary thing with an ordinary, and is amazed and startled. The other kind of wonder looks into the ordinary thing and sees its internal relations. It is amazed not at the relative size of things but at similarities and differences, and when a poet has looked at things with this kind of wonder he must use analogies between one thing

[1] *Speculations,* p. 140.

and another to express a similarity of feeling, and so to persuade the reader to accept the one because he accepts the other.

This kind of wonder is found in a great deal of poetry that is not romantic in Hulme's sense, in the poetry of Rilke for example. Many of Hulme's opinions are found in Rilke, but Rilke is more balanced and more mature. He too distrusts utopianism in politics and exaggerated claims on behalf of poetry, but he does not rush to the opposite extreme and say, for example, that poetry is nothing but intuition, and that all intuitions are equal. He admits the need for comprehensiveness as well as accuracy. Although his method resembles that of the imagists, he is more patient, he sees more, and sees more deeply, and his images have a wider and deeper significance. Rilke willingly looks at the whole of life and death in tragic terms, and praises them as a reasonable man must do, in spite of all ugliness, cruelty, and uncertainty.

Hulme says that poetry is not concerned with religion and that it is written to amuse bankers; but the poetry and prose of the last twenty years that has expressed the tragic view has been as 'serious' and has dealt with subjects as 'important' as Dante or Shakespeare. Tragedy cannot avoid important subjects, and often those subjects are more baffling than anything Hulme cared to face directly. The root of tragedy lies not merely in the fact that man is innately wicked as well as innately good, but also in the fact that he does not know for certain what is wickedness and what is virtue, and must nevertheless act and accept responsibility. 'The greatest pain of purgatory', says Pascal, 'is the uncertainty of the judgment. *Deus absconditus*';[1] and this is true of our life from day to day: each man must decide for himself what his obligations are.

In the novels of Franz Kafka, as in Rilke's poetry, we find this sense of tension and uncertainty. When, in *The Trial*, Kafka's hero is under arrest by powers that he does not understand, but which are plainly not the powers of the political or legal world, he does not even know what charge is brought against him, nor how he could defend himself. The absolute values are there, but we cannot know them. In the end, we do not know whether the hero was a good man or a bad man: and he does not know himself. Moral and religious authority exists, but the burden of recognition is on the individual: that is the condition of life and the dramatic tension of tragedy. Kafka startles and terrifies: we knew already that the questions were hard to answer, and that we did not know the rules by which to answer them; but we made a guess and hoped that good intentions would save us. But Kafka says that we can never know the rules, and questions whether the intentions were good; yet he leaves us with an intense conviction that these questions are immensely important. The burden of decision rests on the individual; we cannot know the right answer for certain; the one thing we know for certain is that the possible answers are not all equal.

In other modern writers, too, we find this insistence

1 Fragment 517.

on the tragic view of life, and on man's responsibility in a world in which he cannot foresee the judgment of his action. But this writing is not pessimistic: it is plain and truthful, and it brings not weariness and despair but new energy and new enjoyment. The poems of Gerard Manley Hopkins, for example, do not express uncertainty about religion; they are simply tragic poems: the uncertainty is part of the religion, for even in religion there is no final certainty. In this it is like philosophy: 'Metaphysics', said Scheler, 'is not an insurance company for the benefit of the weak and those in need of support.' There is this difference, that the liturgy and scriptures of religion can be interpreted to meet the needs, experience, and ability of all; but the understanding of its ritual is not the same for the grown man as it is for the child, and its parables do not excuse the strong for accepting no more than the responsibilities that belong to the weak. Religion offers strength, and the guidance of tradition and authority; it offers a place for humility, but not for intellectual or moral or aesthetic laziness. The recognition of reality and the acceptance of its responsibilities remains an obligation of the individual, and he is sustained by the knowledge that there is a reality to be recognized, though it can never be known completely.

When we have grown accustomed to illusions, reality is hard to bear. The child's world of make-believe only slowly yields to the real external world. The inner world that is expressed in make-believe has its own claims; and our business is to recognize the forces that move us, not to give way to them without knowing. The imaginative art of any age includes a picture of the inner world, and of man's relations to the outer world. It is no easier to be clear-sighted and truthful about the inner world than it is to be clear-sighted and truthful about the external world of material science, and we do not learn anything about the forces of this inner world by giving way to them any more than we learn about gravitation by falling down a cliff.

There is a place in poetry for fantasy and escape, just as there is a place in life for play and make-believe. Nonsense is bad when it is taken for sense, and dream-satisfaction is bad when it takes the place of a real and necessary effort. Fantastic poetry and make-believe become dangerous only when we indulge in them at the expense of reality; and cricket and mountaineering are bad only when we allow them to replace our sense of duty in politics and religion. Disinterested activity without any known objective is one of the main sources of any real progress, and the play of poetic imagination is such an activity. Poetic intuitions, like good actions, are valuable in themselves, but they also lead on to further knowledge and action. They are the leaves and petals of the tree, not tinsel decorations. They are good in themselves, but their virtue does not end there. Even the impulse to sing and dance, like the song of birds and the dance of the young hare, leads on to something beyond itself, and poetic intuitions can serve 'to make action urgent and its nature clear'. But disinterested activity, in poetry as in philosophy and science, is stultified if we decide beforehand what kind of result we expect; without that temporary abandonment of preconceived certainties, the activity will fail. It is like learning to swim: we feel that we are going to drown if we leave hold of our support, but we must have the courage to let go, to feel that it does not matter if we do drown, and then we shall float.

We cannot do this, nor can we guard against the errors that may follow from abandoning ourselves to fantasy, simply by a faith in human destiny; even when we abandon ourselves we must recognize that there is right and wrong beyond the individual judgment, and that we ourselves are fallible. In the history of imagination, there are periods of regression, of stagnation, and of advance on false trails, as there are in the history of science. There are other times when there is a beneficial change in the kind of art that is made and appreciated. Hulme's work helps us to understand the change that is happening in our time. He claims that in rejecting the whole of religious beliefs we have forced ourselves into an untenable position in politics, in poetry, and in philosophy. He does not claim to be systematic: he even denies that a completely comprehensive and consistent logical position is possible; but his outlook is neither irrational nor anti-intellectual nor quietist.

Words, when we use them with all their significance and suggestion, are rich with the accumulated experience of the past, and if we use them rightly we can make them say far more than we can say in 'scientific' terms, and with far greater effect. But although we cannot depict reality in our counter language, we must go on trying to: that is a condition of our logical thought, and only logical thought is more or less foolproof. But we must not expect that kind of thought to express 'intuitions of organic wholes'; that is the function of poetry. Philosophy, itself compelled to use logical language, must recognize the scope and value of poetry, which it has sometimes neglected; but it cannot become poetry, as Bergson seems to wish: its business is to extend and sharpen the use of the abstract scientific words, not to abandon them. Some of the things that poetry says succinctly can be analysed into logical signs, but without the succinct expression we can no longer grasp the whole intuition. We are compelled to choose between a language that has a narrow scope and is foolproof, and one that has a wider scope but is more liable to lead to error. Philosophy must fail when it sets itself the objectives of poetry, and poetry, though at its best its statements are often literally and scientifically true, does not depend on that kind of accuracy for its value. Both have their uses, but one is restricted and the other is uncertain. Both, however, leave room for development, and perhaps no speech belongs wholly to one category or is ever wholly free from the faults of the other.

All this is part of the tragic view, and we can accept it as lightheartedly and gaily as the *andante* of Haydn's Quartet in E Flat Major breaks into *menuetto*, for it is based on a view that is serious but not solemn or self-pitying. It leaves no place for boastfulness or evasive cynicism or any of the other sentimentalities. In the tragic view, all doctrines of perfectibility are seen to be dangerous, whether in politics, philosophy or aesthetics. It is not merely that we are sometimes unlucky, and that we fail in our highest and most sustained endeavours: it is that this failure is intrinsic to our nature. As long as we are sensitive, thinking, moral creatures—as long as we are aiming, as we must aim, at perfection—we must find that any ultimate objective that we set ourselves is unattainable or unsatisfactory. That which is humanly good, or true, or beautiful, consists not in a final revelation and justification, but in particulars. There is no finality except in religion; and, for Hulme, religion is final only in so far as it forces man back on a recognition of his own limitations. 'It is the closing of all the roads, this realization of the *tragic* significance of life, which makes it legitimate to call all other attitudes shallow.'

It is a dramatic peroration, but it is not quite true. Something does escape from this closing of all the roads: the doctrine of perfectibility is dangerous, but man does make a little progress, tentatively and precariously; some forms of society are better than others; and it is not only by tradition and discipline that anything decent is got out of the ordinary man. Between sentimental optimism and stoical pessimism, there is a middle way that offers guidance to every man and makes demands upon him according to his ability. It is a road that lacks the melodramatic appeal of any form of extremism, but it is not a compromise. It involves, as Hulme saw, the recognition of values that are good for their own sake, and not merely for their contribution to human survival or to the fulfilment of a personality. Democracy and democratic progress are bound to fail if they do not rest on the religious or tragic outlook; but within the framework of a Christian polity, whose economy reflected the moral principles it professed, a form of democracy would be not only possible but also necessary, for democracy is the form of government that recognizes most openly the responsibility of the individual and the fact that all government rests on the consent of the governed. Progress towards such an end is not impossible, nor is it utopian to ask for it, for it is not based on any assumption that human nature can be radically changed. Hulme perhaps was tending towards some such belief, and although in his published writing he is often nearer to the pessimism of Hobbes than to Christianity, his arrogant manner need not force us to follow his own path, and we can be grateful to him for pointing out some of the errors that lie on the other side.

THREE POEMS BY T. E. HULME

*

THE MAN IN THE CROW'S NEST

Strange to me sounds the wind that blows
By the masthead in the lonely night.
Maybe 'tis the sea whistling—feigning joy
To hide its fright
Like a village boy
That, shivering, past the churchyard goes.

SUSAN ANN AND IMMORTALITY

Her head hung down
Gazed at earth, finally keen,
As the rabbit at the stoat,
Till the earth was sky,
Sky that was green,
And brown clouds passed
Like chestnut leaves along the ground.

A City Sunset

Alluring, earth-seducing, with high conceits
is the sunset that coquettes
at the end of westward streets.

A sudden flaring sky
troubling strangely the passer-by
with vision, alien to long streets, of Cytherea
or the smooth flesh of Lady Castlemaine. . . .

A frolic of crimson
is the spreading glory of the sky
heaven's wanton
flaunting a trailed red robe
along the fretted city roofs
about the time of homeward-going crowds
—a vain maid, lingering, loth to go. . . .

LECTURE ON MODERN POETRY

I want to begin by a statement of the attitude I take towards verse. I do that in order to anticipate criticism. I shall speak of verse from a certain rather low but quite definite level, and I think that criticism ought to be confined to that level. The point of view is that verse is simply and solely the means of expression. I will give you an example of the position exactly opposite to the one I take up. A reviewer writing in *The Saturday Review* last week spoke of poetry as the means by which the soul soared into higher regions, and as a means of expression by which it became merged into a higher kind of reality. Well, that is the kind of statement that I utterly detest. I want to speak of verse in a plain way as I would of pigs: that is the only honest way. The President told us last week that poetry was akin to religion. It is nothing of the sort. It is a means of expression just as prose is, and if you can't justify it from that point of view it's not worth preserving.

I always suspect the word soul when it is brought into discussion. It reminds me of the way that the medieval scientists spoke of God. When entirely ignorant of the cause of anything they said God did it. If I use the word soul, or speak of higher realities, in the course of my speech, you will know that at that precise point I didn't know of any real reason and was trying to bluff you. There is a tremendous amount of hocus-pocus about most discussions of poetry. Critics attempting to explain technique make mysterious passes and mumble of the infinite and the human heart, for all the world as though they were selling a patent medicine in the market-place.

There are two ways in which one can consider this. The first as a difficulty to be conquered, the second as a tool for use. In the first case, we look upon poets as we look upon pianists, and speak of them as masters of verse. The other way is to consider it merely as a tool which we want to use ourselves for definite purposes. One daily paper compared us to the Mermaid Club, but we are not. We are a number of modern people, and verse must be justified as a means of expression for us. I have not a catholic taste but a violently personal and prejudiced one. I have no reverence for tradition. I came to the subject of verse from the inside rather than from the outside. There were certain impressions which I wanted to fix. I read verse to find models, but I could not find any that seemed exactly suitable to express that kind of impression, except perhaps a few jerky rhythms of Henley, until I came to read the French *vers-libre* which seemed to exactly fit the case.

So that I don't want any literary criticism, that would be talking on another level. I don't want to be killed with a bludgeon, and references to Dante, Milton and the rest of them.

The principle on which I rely in this paper is that there is an intimate connection between the verse form and the state of poetry at any period. All kinds of reasons are given by the academic critics for the efflorescence of verse at any period. But the true one is very seldom given. It is the invention or introduction of a new verse form. To the artist the introduction of a new art form is, as Moore says, like a new dress to a girl; he wants to see himself in it. It is a new toy. You will find the burst of poetic activity at the time of Elizabeth put down to the discovery of America. The discovery of America had about as much effect on the Courtier poets at that time as the discovery of a new asteroid would have had on the poetic activity of Swinburne. The real reason was, I take it, that the first opportunity was given for the exercise of verse composition by the introduction of all kinds of new matter and new forms from Italy and France.

It must be admitted that verse forms, like manners, and like individuals, develop and die. They evolve from their initial freedom to decay and finally to virtuosity. They disappear before the new man, burdened with the thought more complex and more difficult to express by the old name. After being too much used, their primitive effect is lost. All possible tunes have been played on the instrument. What possibility is there in that for the new men, or what attraction? It would be different if poetry, like acting and dancing, were one of the arts of which no record can be kept, and which must be repeated for each generation. The actor has not to feel the competition of the dead as the poet has. Personally I am of course in favour of the complete destruction of all verse more than twenty years old. But that happy event will not, I am afraid, take place until Plato's desire has been realized and a minor poet has become dictator. Meanwhile it is necessary to realize that as poetry is immortal, it is differentiated from those arts which must be repeated. I want to call attention to this point—it is only those arts whose expression is repeated every generation that have an immutable technique. Those arts like poetry, whose matter is immortal, must find a new technique each generation. Each age must have its own special form of expression, and any period that deliberately goes out of it is an age of insincerity.

The latter stages in the decay of an art form are very interesting and worth study because they are peculiarly applicable to the state of poetry at the present day. They resemble the latter stages in the decay of religion when the spirit has gone and there is a meaningless reverence for formalities and ritual. The carcass is dead, and all the flies are upon it. Imitative poetry springs up like weeds, and women whimper and whine of you and I alas, and roses, roses all the way. It becomes the expression of sentimentality rather than of virile thought.

The writers who would be able to use the old instrument with the old masters refuse to do so, for they find it inadequate. They know the entirely empirical nature of the old rules and refuse to be cramped by them.

It is at these periods that a new art form is created; after the decay of Elizabethan poetic drama came the heroic couplet, after the decay of the couplet came the new lyrical poetry that has lasted till now. It is interesting to notice that these changes do not come by a kind of natural progress of which the artist himself is unconscious. The new forms are deliberately introduced by people who detest the old ones. Modern lyrical verse was introduced by Wordsworth with no pretence of it being a natural progress; he announced it in good set terms as a new method.

The particular example which has most connection with what I have to say is that of the Parnassian school about 1885: itself beginning as a reaction from romanticism, it has come rapidly to decay; its main principle of an absolute perfection of rhyme and form was in harmony with the natural school of the time. It was a logical form of verse, as distinct from a symbolical one. There were prominent names in it, Monde, Prudhomme, etc., but they were not very fertile; they did not produce anything of great importance; they confined themselves to repeating the same sonnet time after time, their pupils were lost in a state of sterile feebleness.

I wish you to notice that this was not the kind of unfortunate accident which has happened by chance to a number of poets. This check to the Parnassian school marked the death of a particular form of French poetry which coincided with the birth and marvellous fertility of a new form. With the definite arrival of this new form of verse in 1880 came the appearance of a band of poets perhaps unequalled at any one time in the history of French poetry.

The new technique was first definitely stated by Kahn. It consisted in a denial of a regular number of syllables as the basis of versification. The length of the line is long and short, oscillating with the images used by the poet; it follows the contours of his thoughts and is free rather than regular; to use a rough analogy, it is clothes made to order, rather than ready-made clothes. This is a very bald statement of it, and I am not concerned here so much with French poetry as with English. The kind of verse I advocate is not the same as *vers-libre*, I merely use the French as an example of the extraordinary effect that an emancipation of verse can have on poetic activity.

The ancients were perfectly aware of the fluidity of the world and of its impermanence; there was the Greek theory that the whole world was a flux. But while they recognized it, they feared it and endeavoured to evade it, to construct things of permanence which would stand fast in this universal flux which frightened them. They had the disease, the passion, for immortality. They wished to construct things which should be proud boasts that they, men, were immortal. We see it in a thousand different forms. Materially in the pyramids, spiritually in the dogmas of religion and in the hypostatized ideas of Plato. Living in a dynamic world they wished to create a static fixity where their souls might rest.

This I conceive to be the explanation of many of the old ideas on poetry. They wish to embody in a few lines a perfection of thought. Of the thousand and one ways in which a thought might roughly be conveyed to a hearer there was one way which was the perfect way, which was destined to embody that thought to all eternity, hence the fixity of the form of poem and the elaborate rules of regular metre. It was to be an immortal thing and the infinite pains taken to fit a thought into a fixed and artificial form are necessary and understandable. Even the Greek name ποίημα seems to indicate the thing created once and for all, they believed in absolute duty as they believed in absolute truth. Hence they put many things into verse which we now do not desire to, such as history and philosophy. As the French philosopher Guyau put it, the great poems of ancient times resembled pyramids built for eternity where people loved to inscribe their history in symbolic characters. They believed they could realize an adjustment of idea and words that nothing could destroy.

Now the whole trend of the modern spirit is away from that; philosophers no longer believe in absolute truth. We no longer believe in perfection, either in verse or in thought, we frankly acknowledge the relative. We shall no longer strive to attain the absolutely perfect form in poetry. Instead of these minute perfections of phrase and words, the tendency will be rather towards the production of a general effect; this of course takes away the predominance of metre and a regular number of syllables as the element of perfection in words. We are no longer concerned that stanzas shall be shaped and polished like gems, but rather that some vague mood shall be communicated. In all the arts, we seek for the maximum of individual and personal expression, rather than for the attainment of any absolute beauty.

The criticism is sure to be made, what is this new spirit,

which finds itself unable to express itself in the old metre? Are the things that a poet wishes to say now in any way different to the things that former poets say? I believe that they are. The old poetry dealt essentially with big things, the expression of epic subjects leads naturally to the anatomical matter and regular verse. Action can best be expressed in regular verse, e.g., the Ballad.

But the modern is the exact opposite of this, it no longer deals with heroic action, it has become definitely and finally introspective and deals with expression and communication of momentary phases in the poet's mind. It was well put by Mr. G. K. Chesterton in this way— that where the old dealt with the Siege of Troy, the new attempts to express the emotions of a boy fishing. The opinion you often hear expressed, that perhaps a new poet will arrive who will synthesize the whole modern movement into a great epic, shows an entire misconception of the tendency of modern verse. There is an analogous change in painting, where the old endeavoured to tell a story, the modern attempts to fix an impression. We still perceive the mystery of things, but we perceive it in entirely a different way—no longer directly in the form of action, but as an impression, for example Whistler's pictures. We can't escape from the spirit of our times. What has found expression in painting as Impressionism will soon find expression in poetry as free verse. The vision of a London street at midnight, with its long rows of light, has produced several attempts at reproduction in verse, and yet the war produced nothing worth mentioning, for Mr. Watson is a political orator rather than a poet. Speaking of personal matters, the first time I ever felt the necessity or inevitableness of verse, was in the desire to reproduce the peculiar quality of feeling which is induced by the flat spaces and wide horizons of the virgin prairie of western Canada.

You see that this is essentially different to the lyrical impulse which has attained completion, and I think once and for ever, in Tennyson, Shelley and Keats. To put this modern conception of the poetic spirit, this tentative and half-shy manner of looking at things, into regular metre is like putting a child into armour.

Say the poet is moved by a certain landscape, he selects from that certain images which, put into juxtaposition in separate lines, serve to suggest and to evoke the state he feels. To this piling-up and juxtaposition of distinct images in different lines, one can find a fanciful analogy in music. A great revolution in music when, for the melody that is one-dimensional music, was substituted harmony which moves in two. Two visual images form what one may call a visual chord. They unite to suggest an image which is different to both.

Starting then from this standpoint of extreme modernism, what are the principal features of verse at the present time? It is this: that it is read and not chanted. We may set aside all theories that we read verse internally as mere verbal quibbles. We have thus two distinct arts. The one intended to be chanted, and the other intended to be read in the study. I wish this to be remembered in the criticisms that are made on me. I am not speaking of the whole of poetry, but of this distinct new art which is gradually separating itself from the older one and becoming independent.

I quite admit that poetry intended to be recited must be written in regular metre, but I contend that this method of recording impressions by visual images in distinct lines does not require the old metric system.

The older art was originally a religious incantation: it was made to express oracles and maxims in an impressive manner, and rhyme and metre were used as aids to the memory. But why, for this new poetry, should we keep a mechanism which is only suited to the old?

The effect of rhythm, like that of music, is to produce a kind of hypnotic state, during which suggestions of grief or ecstasy are easily and powerfully effective, just as when we are drunk all jokes seem funny. This is for the art of chanting, but the procedure of the new visual art is just the contrary. It depends for its effect not on a kind of half sleep produced, but on arresting the attention, so much so that the succession of visual images should exhaust one.

Regular metre to this impressionist poetry is cramping, jangling, meaningless, and out of place. Into the delicate pattern of images and colour it introduces the heavy, crude pattern of rhetorical verse. It destroys the effect just as a barrel organ does, when it intrudes into the subtle interwoven harmonies of the modern symphony. It is a delicate and difficult art, that of evoking an image, of fitting the rhythm to the idea, and one is tempted to fall back to the comforting and easy arms of the old, regular metre, which takes away all the trouble for us.

A LECTURE ON MODERN POETRY

The criticism is sure to be made that when you have abolished the regular syllabled line as the unit of poetry, you have turned it into prose. Of course this is perfectly true of a great quantity of modern verse. In fact, one of the great blessings of the abolition of regular metre would be that it would at once expose all this sham poetry.

Poetry as an abstract thing is a very different matter, and has its own life, quite apart from metre as a convention.

To test the question of whether it is possible to have poetry written without a regular metre, I propose to pick out one great difference between the two. I don't profess to give an infallible test that would enable anyone to at once say: 'This is, or is not, true poetry,' but it will be sufficient for the purposes of this paper. It is this: that there are, roughly speaking, two methods of communication, a direct, and a conventional language. The direct language is poetry, it is direct because it deals in images. The indirect language is prose, because it uses images that have died and become figures of speech.

The difference between the two is, roughly, this: that while one arrests your mind all the time with a picture, the other allows the mind to run along with the least possible effort to a conclusion.

Prose is due to a faculty of the mind something resembling reflex action in the body. If I had to go through a complicated mental process each time I laced my boots, it would waste mental energy; instead of that, the mechanism of the body is so arranged that one can do it almost without thinking. It is an economy of effort. The same process takes place with the images used in prose. For example, when I say that the hill was clad with trees, it merely conveys the fact to me that it was covered. But the first time that expression was used was by a poet, and to him it was an image recalling to him the distinct visual analogy of a man clad in clothes; but the image has died. One might say that images are born in poetry. They are used in prose, and finally die a long, lingering death in journalists' English. Now this process is very rapid, so that the poet must continually be creating new images, and his sincerity may be measured by the number of his images.

Sometimes, in reading a poem, one is conscious of gaps where the inspiration failed him, and he only used metre of rhetoric. What happened was this: the image failed him, and he fell back on a dead image, that is prose, but kept an effect by using metre. That is my objection to metre, that it enables people to write verse with no poetic inspiration, and whose mind is not stored with new images.

As an example of this, I will take the poem which now has the largest circulation. Though consisting of only four verses it is six feet long. It is posted outside the Pavilion Music-hall. We instinctively shudder at these clichés or tags of speech. The inner explanation is this: it is not that they are old, but that being old they have become dead, and so evoked no image. The man who wrote them not being a poet, did not see anything definitely himself, but imitated other poets' images.

This new verse resembles sculpture rather than music;

it appeals to the eye rather than to the ear. It has to mould images, a kind of spiritual clay, into definite shapes. This material, the ὕλη of Aristotle, is image and not sound. It builds up a plastic image which it hands over to the reader, whereas the old art endeavoured to influence him physically by the hypnotic effect of rhythm.

One might sum it all up in this way: a shell is a very suitable covering for the egg at a certain period of its career, but very unsuitable at a later age. This seems to me to represent fairly well the state of verse at the present time. While the shell remains the same, the inside character is entirely changed. It is not addled, as a pessimist might say, but has become alive, it has changed from the ancient art of chanting to the modern impressionist, but the mechanism of verse has remained the same. It can't go on doing so. I will conclude, ladies and gentlemen, by saying, the shell must be broken.

Appendix III

NOTES ON LANGUAGE AND STYLE[1]

NOTES FOR A PREFACE

I believe that while the world cosmically cannot be reduced to unity as science proclaims (in the postulate of uniformity), yet on the contrary poetry can. At least its methods follow certain easily defined routes. (Any one can be taught how to use poetry.)

Real work, history and scientific researches, the accidental, the excrescences, like digging, and necessary just as digging is. Poetry the permanent humanity, the expression of man freed from his digging, digging for poetry when it is over.

---

1 These notes were excluded from the *Speculations* edited by Herbert Read 'mainly for economic reasons, but also, I must confess, because at the time of editing that volume their corporate value did not immediately emerge from an extremely illegible script'. In July 1925 Mr. Read published about half of them in *The Criterion*. In the present selection nothing of importance has been omitted, and the order of Hulme's manuscript has been closely followed. (The notes are on loose sheets of paper, partly sorted into folders.) A few slips in spelling have been corrected, and contractions have been expanded, where these would be more tiresome in print than they are in manuscript, but I have not tried to remove occasional solecisms or to change notes into grammatical sentences. The meaning is clear enough as it stands, and any alteration would involve a distortion of the tone.—M.R.

NOTES ON LANGUAGE AND STYLE

CLUMSINESS OF PROSE—RELATION OF LANGUAGE AND THE IDEA EXPRESSED

Analysis of the attitude of a man reading an argument

(i) Compare in algebra, the real things are replaced by symbols. These symbols are manipulated according to certain laws which are independent of their meaning. N.B. At a certain point in the proof we cease to think of x as having a meaning and look upon it as a mere counter to be manipulated.

(ii) An analogous phenomenon happens in reasoning in language. We replace meaning (i.e. *vision*) by words. These words fall into well-known patterns, i.e. into certain well-known phrases which we accept without thinking of their meaning, just as we do the x in algebra. *But* there is a constant movement above and below the line of meaning (representation).[1] And this is used in dialectical argument. At any stage we can ask the opponent to show his hand, that is to turn all his *words* into visions, in realities we can see.

Seeing 'solid' things

One facet of the idea may be expressed in this way. Refer back to note on the use of x in arithmetic and its analogy in expression. Habitually we may say that the reader takes words as x *without* the meaning attached. Aphra[2] sees each word with an image sticking on to

[1] Hulme illustrates this by a little sketch of a curve rising above a fixed horizontal line (the level of *meaning*) and falling again.
[2] Hulme was going to write a book about a character called Aphra.

272

it, never a flat word passed over a board like a counter.

Perhaps the nearest analogy is the hairy caterpillar. Taking each segment of his body as a word, the hair on that segment is the vision the poet sees behind it.

It is difficult to do this, so that the poet is forced to use new analogies, and especially to construct a plaster model of a thing to express his emotion at the sight of the vision he sees, his wonder and ecstasy. If he employed the ordinary word, the reader would only see it as a segment, with no hair, used for getting along. And without this clay, spatial image, he does not feel that he has expressed at all what he sees.

The ordinary caterpillar for crawling along from one position to another. The hairy one for beauty, to build up a solid vision of realities.

All emotion depends on real solid vision or sound. It is physical.

But in *rhetoric* and expositional prose we get words divorced from any real vision. Rhetoric and emotion —here the connection is different.

So perhaps literary expression is from *Real to Real* with all the intermediate forms keeping their *real* value. In expositional reasoning, the intermediate terms have only counter value. Give an example of *counter* prose (boy's letter to paper).

Watching a class: the difference between their attitude to geography and that to mathematics. Probably having only spatial imagination, the geography is quite clear and comprehensible. If the mathematics could be got into the same flat form upon a map, with only relative distances to be observed, then their difficulties would vanish.

This suggests that the type of all reasoning is that of arranging counters on the flat, where they can be moved about, without the mind having to think in any involved way. (cf. this with note in the old book, about chessboard.)

The ideal of modern prose is to be all counters, i.e. to pass to conclusions without thinking.

Visual Poetry

Each *word* must be an image *seen*, not a counter.

That dreadful feeling of cheapness when we contemplate the profusion of words of modern prose. The true ideal—the little statue in Paris.

The contrast between (i) a firm simple prose, creating in a definite way a fairy story, a story of simple life in the country (in the old country). Here we have the microcosm of poetry. The pieces picked out from which it comes. Sun and sweat and all of them. Physical life and death fairies. And (ii) on the other hand, genteel poetry like Shelley's, which refers in elaborate analogies to the things mentioned in (i).

Gibbering ghosts and Morris's tales seem *real*, as (i). Transmigration of souls seems a drawing-room thrill, compounded of goodwill and long words.

Style

With perfect style, the solid leather for reading, each sentence should be a lump, a piece of clay, a vision seen;

rather, a wall touched with soft fingers. Never should one feel light vaporous bridges between one solid sense and another. No bridges—all solid: then never exasperated.

A man cannot write without seeing at the same time a visual signification before his eyes. It is this image which precedes the writing and makes it firm.

The piece from Morris as an example of poetry always being a solid thing. Seen but not words.

Criticism

Rising disgust and impatience with the talking books, e.g. Lilly and the books about Life, Science, and Religion. All the books which seem to be the kind of talk one could do if one wished.

Rather choose those in old leather, which are *solid*. Here the man did not talk, but saw solid, definite things and described them. Solidity a pleasure.

It is seeing the real clay, that men in an agony worked with, that gives pleasure. To read a book which is *real clay* moulded by fingers that had to mould something, or they would clutch the throat of their maddened author. *No* flowing on of words, but tightly clutched tense fingers leaving marks in the clay. These are the only books that matter—and where are they to be found?

Style short, being forced by the coming together of many different thoughts, and generated by their contact. Fire struck between stones.

Mechanism of Creation

Get rid of the idea that out of vacuo can come writing. Generally following certain practical ends, we throw out writing—comes out as the one in the many. Not as a pure intellectual machine. A cindery thing done, not a pure thought made manifest in some counter-like way.

The idea is nothing: it is the holding on to the idea, through the absolutely transforming influence of putting it into definiteness. The holding on through waves.

That extraordinary difficulty in shaping any material, in moving from the idea to the matter. Seen even in simple matters like going to the tailor's. The difference between the idea and the choice. Material is never plastic. The extraordinary difficulty of the living material. Seen in everything, even in railway meetings, in people, in everything. Write essay on it.

The resistance of the ὕλη, ἐνεργής. The process of invention is that of gradually making solid the castles in the air.

Self-delusion

(i) Whence comes the excitement, the delusion of thinker's creation?

(ii) All inventions spring from the *idea*, e.g. Flaubert and the *purple* bases of Madame Bovary.

(iii) I have a *central* idea like that quite *unworked* out into detail.

(iv) I see a book *worked out* from the same central idea and I unconsciously imagine that I have worked it out myself, and that I could easily have been the author.

(v) But in the working out is required the multiplicity of detail that I lack. The central idea is nothing.

At last come to think that all expression is vulgar, that only the unexpressed and silent. . . .

Dead Analogies

All styles are only means of subduing the reader.

(i) New phrases made in poetry, tested, and then employed in prose.

(ii) In poetry they are all glitter and new coruscation, in prose useful and not noticed.

(iii) Prose a museum where all the old weapons of poetry kept.

(iv) Poetry always the advance guard in language. The progress of language is the absorption of new analogies. (Scout, so nearest to flux and real basic condition of life.)

Expression (I)

If I say: putting in the 'finer touches', it expresses what I mean by the refinement of language.

But the damnable thing is that if I use that phrase to another person, it produces no equal effect on him. It is one of the rounded counters of language and so has the least possible meaning. What to me is an entirely physical thing, a real clay before me, moulded, an image, is when used nothing but an expression like 'in so far, etc.'.

The pity is that in this all the *meaning* goes.

NOTES ON LANGUAGE AND STYLE

A word to me is a board with an image or statue on it. When I pass the word, all that goes is the board, the statue remains in my imagination.

Transfer physical to language

Dome of Brompton in the mist. Transfer that to art. Dead things not men as the material of art. Everything for art is a thing in itself, cf. the café at Clapham as a thing in itself.

And the words moved until they became a dome, a solid, separate world, a dome seen in a mist, a thing of terror beyond us, and not of us. Definite heaven above worshippers, incense hides foundations. A definite *force majeure* (all the foundations of the scaffolding are in us, but we want an illusion, falsifying us, something independent of foundations). A long pillar.

Aphra took the words, and they grew into a round smooth pillar and the child wondered and the merchant caused. Putting a few bricks together to imitate the shape of a dome, but the mist effect, the transformation in words, has the art of pushing it through the door.

Example of Plastic Imagination

The two tarts walking along Piccadilly on tiptoe, going home, with hat on back of head. Worry until could find the exact model analogy that will reproduce the extraordinary effect they produce. Could be done at once by an artist in a blur. The air of absolute detachment, of being things in themselves. Objects of beauty with the qualification as the basis of it. Disinterestedness, as though saying: We may have evolved painfully from the clay, and be the last leaf on a tree. But now we have cut ourselves away from that. We are things-in-themselves. We exist out of time.

Language (I)

(i) Delightful sensation of power in looking at it, as a vehicle, a machine whose ages we can see. The relics of the extravagant fancies and analogies of dead and forgotten poets.

Regard each word as a picture, then a succession of pictures. Only the dead skeleton remains. We cut the leaves off. When the tree becomes a mast, the leaves become unnecessary. But now only the thick lines matter, and the accompanying pictures are forgotten.

(ii) An agricultural implement. Philosophy expressed in farmer's language. All the predominant metaphors are naturally agricultural, e.g. field of thought, flood, stream. Keep present in mind when we look at nature, the curious place of language which is founded on it and *subordinate* to it. When I see a stream now (such as Waterloo Bridge) I imagine it carrying down with it the impermeable language and the *begriffe* of philosophy.

If only the making and fixing of words had begun in the city stage in the evolution of society and not in the nomadic.

(But ideas expressed would have been the same. So thought and language not identical.)

Language (II)

The fallacy that language is logical, or that meaning is. Phrases have meaning for no reason, cf. with nature of truth.

(i) The metaphysical theory. Watching a woman in the street. Is the idea expressed anything like? So——

(ii) The idea is just as real as a landscape and there is the same difficulty in getting it on to paper. Each word is a different twist to it, something added. Each of the fifty possible sentences that will express it changes its character.

(iii) Another question: growing conviction of the Solidity of Ideas, as opposed to language.

Very often the idea, apart from the analogy or metaphor which clothes it, has no existence. That is, by a subtle combination of allusions we have artificially built up in us an idea, which apart from these, cannot be got at. As if a man took us on a rocky path and said look—and we saw the view. i.e. the analogy is the thing, not merely decoration. i.e. there is no such thing as.

Language (III)

Large clumsy instrument. Language does not naturally come with meaning. Ten different ways of forming the same sentence. Any style will do to get the meaning down (without childish effect). There is *no* inevitable simple style as there ought to be.

Language a cumbrous growth, a compound of old and new analogies. Does this apply to thought? Is there *no* simple thought, but only styles of thought?

Poetry is neither more nor less than a mosaic of words, so great exactness required for each one.

Language (IV)

(i) Thought is prior to language and consists in the simultaneous presentation to the mind of two different images.

(ii) Language is only a more or less feeble way of doing this.

(iii) All the connections in language, this term including not only prepositions, but all phrases (ready made), which only indicate the precise relation or attitude or politeness between the two simultaneously presented images.

(iv) Connect this with the old scorn, denoted by the black edge theory, cf. Rue de la limite. And hence see the solution of the difficulty, and the use of words for literary purposes, always inferior.

Thought

As merely the discovery of new analogies, when useful and sincere, and not mere paradoxes.

The things bring a kind of going straight, write them as analogy and call it literature, cf. marching in step, the great procession (analogy of creative and sexual pleasure).

Creation

Thought is the joining together of new analogies, and so inspiration is a matter of an accidentally seen analogy or unlooked-for resemblance. It is therefore necessary to get as large as possible change in sense impressions, cf. looking in shop windows, and war-game. The more change of shapes and sights there is the more chance of inspiration. Thoughts won by walking.

Fertility of invention means: remembrance of accidental occurrences *noted* and arranged. (cf. detective stories.)

Expression (II)

Think of sitting at that window in Chelsea and seeing the chimneys and the lights in the dusk. And then imagine that by contemplation this will transfer itself bodily on to paper.

This is the direct opposite of literature, which is never an absorption and meditation. But a deliberate choosing and working-up of analogies. The continued, close, compressed effort.

The demand for clear logical expression is impossible, as it would confine us to the use of flat counter-images only.

If you only admit that form of manipulating images as good, if you deny all the other grasps, hands, for the cards, all solid images, all patterns, then you can be clear, but not otherwise.

Expression (III)

(i) People who think, pen in hand. Like people who write at twenty, for *Eton College Chronicle*. Writers first, and then afterwards perhaps find thought.

(ii) Think in air. And then years afterwards acquire knack of writing.

Expression (IV)

The chessboard of language expression, where the two players put down counters one after the other. And the player who became interested in the pieces themselves and carved them, and gazed at them in a kind of ecstasy.

Humour and Expression

A joke analysed and viewed as the decadent form into which all forms of literary expression can be shown to pass by degeneration of function (a suitable analogy for this).

(i) The surprise at the end. Resembles novel building.

(ii) Analogies in poetry, like the likenesses of babies, to be taken half seriously, with a smile.

CONTEMPT FOR LANGUAGE

Black Border

All literature as accident, a happy escape from platitude. Nothing new under the sun. Literature like pitching, how to throw phrases about, to satisfy a demand. An exercise for the time being, no eternal body to be added to. So learn phrases 'ringed with gold', 'in a lens', etc.

To excite certain mild feelings of delight in the reader, to produce a pleasant warm feeling in brain as phrases run along.

Enlightenment when first see that literature is not a vision, but a voice, or a line of letters in a black border.

Vision the sight of the quaint shadows in things, of the lone trees on the hill, and the hills in life; not the deed, but the shadow cast by the deed.

The art of literature consists exactly in this *passage from the Eye to the Voice*. From the wealth of nature to that *thin* shadow of words, that gramophone. The readers are the people who *see* things and want them expressed. The author is the Voice, or the conjuror who does tricks with that curious rope of letters, which is quite different from real passion and sight.

The prose writer drags meaning along with the rope. The poet makes it stand on end and hit you.

Prose

A sentence and a worm are the most stupid of animals and the most difficult to teach tricks. Tendency to crawl along; requires genius, music, to make them stand up (snake charmer).

Uncomfortable vision of all words as line. String lying on paper. Impossibility of getting mystery out of this. Words seen as physical things. Pull gently into rows. Want to make them *stand up*. Must invent new plan.

Words seen as physical things like a piece of string, e.g. walking on dark boulevard. Girl hidden in trees passes on other side. How to get this.

Always a border round, to isolate the sentence as a thing in itself, a living worm to be taught tricks.

NOTES ON LANGUAGE AND STYLE

FACILITY IN MANIPULATION

Phrases

Two people sitting talking at table. Delight in having counters ready to hand. (French.) Must not be taught how to *make* counters but a list of them.

(i) Collection of phrases. Words fit in and out of phrases. A *cadre* for grammar. Impossibility of grammar because can't think of end of sentence first. *Learn list* of sentences then fix grammar for them as do in English. Get grammar by ear.

(ii) No language but collection of phrases, but phrases on *different* subjects. One wanders as over a country. No fixed guide for everything. Start Good morning.

(iii) All one tense for past. *Je suis allé.*

Sentences

Sentences as units. Given a large *vocabulary of sentence units*, not of words, we are fluent and can express what we want.

Model sentences learnt perfectly. Perhaps three or four in each Berlitz lesson. Gradually get a definite *armoury* of sentences which will help you and be sufficient to you in conversation.

Physical need some people have to be able to make a comment, to exchange comments. Hence proverbs are the most popular authors. cf. with reading in W.C.

Never, never, never a simple statement. It has no effect. Always must have analogies, which make an other-world through-the-glass effect, which is what I want.

Danger that when all these notes are arranged, the order will kill them in commonplace. When isolated at least there is hope they suggest great unities, which I am at any rate at present quite unable to carry out.

All theories of how to teach a language, all in the air, all null and void, if *each day* you do not learn at your finger's-ends some new phrases. One new *word* and ten phrases as to how to employ it.

Each night. What new phrases. What new *cadres* for the word I already know?

Question of preposition etc. at end of sentence. *Il le faut le faire payer.* Do we think of end first?

In learning foreign language and teaching your own, learn how little is your knowledge of your own. Hesitating for a phrase in your own language. Very few of us learn all the *possible phrases* in our own language, and we must have them all at the tips of our fingers to write well.

So adapt same method to *English.* Read and Read, and copy the phrases like the one about 'microscopic detail magnified'.

THE IMAGINARY WORLD AND A STANDARD OF MEANING

Literature always possible. Compared with peasant, it only deals with imaginary world. Even my attempt to get to reality (no long words) is in the end only another adjustment of the imaginary toy. Fields left un-altered.

Literary people work in imaginary land, which all of us carry about in desert moments.

Not sufficient to find analogies. It is necessary to find those that add something to each, and give a sense of wonder, a sense of being united in another mystic world.

One must have something to overawe the *reader*. The fact outside him, e.g. in boasting. Take case of '*Oh, Richard, oh mon roi.*'

All literature and poetry is life seen in a mirror; it must be absolutely removed from reality, and can never be attained.

The exact relation between the expression and the inside image: (i) Expression obviously partakes of the nature of cinders, cf. Red girl dancing. (ii) But on other hand, vague hell image common to everybody makes an infinite of limited *hard* expression.

> Over a large table, smooth, he leaned in ecstasies,
> In a dream.
> He had been to woods, and talked and walked with
>   trees
> Had left the world
> And brought back round globes and stone images
> Of gems, colours, hard and definite.
> With these he played, in a dream,
> On the smooth table.

(cf. the red dancer in his head.)

Expression (Metaphysical)

The red dancer on the stage. A built-up complex of cinders, so not due to any primeval essence. Cinders as foundations for (i) philosophy (ii) aesthetics.

The old controversy as to which is greater, the mind or the material in art.

Each dancer on the stage with her effects and her suggestions of intensity of meaning which are not possible, is not herself (that is a very cindery thing) but a synthesized state of mind in me. The red moving figure is a way of grouping some ideas together, just as powerful a means as the one called logic which is only an analogy to *counter-pushing*.

This can be considered more seriously. A picture like this, the comic dancer, fading away into the margin (this the basis of all art), not [this][1] which gives the limitations, the furniture, etc

Must be imaginary world. Trick it out with fancies. Analogies must be substituted for what suggests something, a cloud of fancies, e.g. Waterloo Bridge in the early morning.

The only intellectual pleasure in recognizing old friends.

(i) At a race. Look first and see the horses in the paper described. Then excited about result.

(ii) Picture gallery (*a*) recognition of *names*. (*b*) progress to recognition of characteristics. Galleries full of strange names no interest.

1 Hulme has two little sketches, one a small central squiggle with half a dozen radiating strokes, the other a small rectangle like a frame.

(iii) Climate and landscape. The only pleasure in comparison, e.g. Waterloo Bridge and Canada by the river in the morning.

Ideal

Typical Phenomena: the yellow girl leaning from the window in the morning. The Baptist meeting seen through the drawing-room window in the evening.

For the first, if it reminds me of an inexpressible vague something, I must first have been educated into the idea that there was such a vague something.

Observe this something is quite different to the emotional crises of ordinary people when they speak of love and hate. There must be something on which we can hang up our hat. Better something to which, when for a surging moment we have a feeling (really the cinders drunk for a minute) we can *refer* it.

Literature as the building-up of this *state of reference*. Must avoid the word, the Ideal, like a plague, for it suggests easy comprehension where there is no easy comprehension. It is used by Baptist young men to mean quite other things: it has *moral* contamination.

Ideas Staged

In a sense all ideals must be divorced, torn away from the reality where we found them and put on a stage. They must appear separate and far from all dirt and laughter at their low and common relations. They must be posed and moved dramatically, and above all, their gestures must express their emotions. This is the art of literature, the making of this *other* world.

They must wear high-heeled shoes which make them appear free movers, and not sprung from that low thing Earth. The separation of the high heel and the powdered face is essential to all emotions, in order to make a work of art.

Intensity of Meaning

'By thine agony and bloody sweat.' By common effort, all this many times repeated, gives an *intensity of meaning*. This 'intensity of meaning' is what is sought for.

Christian Mystics and Physical Expression

Read them as analogous with own temper. For the expression of states of soul by elaborate physical landscape analogies, cf. my own walking in the evening by the Thames. Also the Neo-Platonic philosophers. It is the physical analogies that hold me, true kindred spirits in that age, in own poetry, not the *vain* decorative and verbal images of the ordinary poets.

Feminine Form

The beauty of the feminine form, which came to be looked upon even by the halest of the four, as a typical vesture or symbol of Beauty herself, and perhaps also as the 'sovran shrine' of Melancholy.

Rossetti saw the spiritual element in face and form, and desired the spirit through his desire of the body, and at last did not know the one desire from the other, and pressed on, true mystic as he was, in ever-narrowing circles, to some third thing that seemed to lie behind both desires. 'Soul is form and doth the body make.'

Eve blur

Tennyson seems to have waited for his expression to come to him—to have brooded before a scene with its orchestra of sounds, in a kind of intense passiveness— until the thing beheld *became greatly different from what it was at any other moment or to any other man.*

DWELLING ON A POINT

Perhaps the difficulty that is found in expressing an idea, in making it long, in dwelling on it, by means of all kinds of analogy, has its root in the nature of ideas and thought itself.

Dancing as the art of prolonging an idea, lingering on a point.

This clearly seen gives the relation between the author's and the reader's position. Both can see the points (as visions in their heads), e.g. Moore's hypostatization of the ideas as real. But I am quite unable to dwell on this point at the length of ten pages.

The author is the man who dwells on a point for the edification of the reader, and for his pleasure, thus prolonging the pleasure and luxury of thought in the mind of the reader.

Method: (i) quotation; (ii) analogies from all possible subjects.

Write down examples:

(i) Prose—of making a tremendous deal out of a point which can be noted down in one sentence. But perhaps the sentence only represents it to the writer. To get the same effect on the reader as it produces on him, he must work it up into a froth, like stirring eggs.

(ii) Dwelling on a point in poetry. The main function of analogy in poetry is to enable one to dwell and linger upon a point of excitement. To achieve the impossible and convert a point into a line. This can only be done by having ready-made lines in our heads, and so getting at the result by analogy.

The inner psychology of a poet at such a creative moment is like that of a drunkard who pushes his hand forward along a table, with an important gesture, and remains there pondering over it. In that relaxing gesture of pushing comes the inner psychology of all these moments.

Gradually one learns the art of dwelling on a point, of decorating it, of transforming it, until it produces in the reader the sense of novelty.

READER AND WRITER

Personal

The popular idea of poet as in communion with the infinite, cf. account of Yeats walking in the woods, but remember Tennyson and his hair. (The deed and poem always greater than the man.)

The rubbish that authors write in their casual moments, when they talk. We haven't heard the kind of interview Shelley and Keats would have given.

Reason why Whitman did not go to the goldfields and become a frontiersman actually. His hatred of the particular, and desire to be the average American citizen. Desire to find romance even in Brooklyn. Often at theatres, and a journalist and carpenter. When had made money would go for long holidays in the woods and by the sea. Always seen on bus-tops.

The bodily activity and position most favourable to thought requires coolness, comfort, and a table, a strenuous effort. Can't think without words or pencil.

Object and Readers of Poetry

Poetry after all for the amusement of bankers and other sedentary arm-chair people in after-dinner moods. No other. (Not for inspiration of progress.) So no infinite nobleness and function about that. (For one person in a thousand hence uselessness of school teaching.)

Entirely modern view of poet as something greater than a statesman, cf. Frederic the Great.

In old days merely to amuse warrior and after banquet.

(i) amuse banker.

(ii) for use of clerks in love to send to sweethearts.

(iii) temporary moods (in theatres) of cultivated artificial people.

(iv) songs of war.

NOTES ON LANGUAGE AND STYLE

Author and Reader

Just as Aristotle asserts that Matter the unlimited contains Forms embedded in it, and that they are not thrust upon it from some ideal world, so all the effects that can be produced by the literary man (here assuming his apprenticeship and marshalling of isolated moments to produce a mystic separation, aided by old metaphors), are to be found dormant, unused in the reader, and are thus awakened.

The Reader

The new art of the Reader. (i) The relation between banker and poetry. (ii) Sympathy with reader as brother, as *unexpressed* author.

Literature a method of sudden arrangement of commonplaces. The *suddenness* makes us forget the commonplace.

Complete theory, what was thought, in the old book, of relation between the poet and the reader seen suddenly at a glance in listening to boys going home from music-hall whistling a song. Chelsea Palace. Here a new way (a mental dance) found for them of synthesizing certain of their own emotions. (Even so with personal psychological poetry, mere putting down is for the reader a form of expression.)

Always seek the causes of these phenomena in their lowest elements—their lowest terms, i.e. literati in Chelsea.

The Writer

The effort of the literary man to find subtle analogies
for the ordinary street feelings he experiences leads to
the differentiation and importance of those feelings.
What would be unnoticed by others, and is nothing
when not labelled, becomes an important emotion. A
transitory artificial impression is deliberately cultivated
into an emotion and written about. Reason here creates
and modifies an emotion, e.g. standing at street corners.
Hence the sudden joy these produce in the reader when
he remembers a half-forgotten impression. 'How true!'

What is the difference between people who can write
literature and people who can merely appreciate it. The
faculty of disillusionment and cynicism, of giving the
show away, possessed by readers. What is the necessary
quality for creation?

Literary man always first completely disillusioned and
then deliberately and purposely creative of illusions.

A writer always a feeble, balanced, artificial kind of
person. The mood is cultivated feeling all the time. The
vibrant and tense fingers, drawing up rhythm, which one
knows could be broken at any moment by anyone coming into the room.

Do these doubts, as to authors, vitiate in any way the
work they produce?

Poetry not for others, but for the poet. Nature infinite,
but personality finite, rough, and incomplete. Gradually
built up.

Poet's mood vague and passes away, indefinable. The
poem he makes selects, builds up, and makes even his

own mood more definite to him. Expression builds up personality.

The life of the literary man being always aiming at the production of these artificial deliberate poises in himself, and so at the creation of his own chessboard.

But what of the relation of this to ordinary life and people? They have their own hereditary (sentimental) chessboards, which remain the same until changed by the survival of some of those of the literary man. The earnest striving after awkward and new points of view, such as that from a balloon, the useful seen from the non-useful attitude.

Literature as red counters moving on a chessboard, life as gradual shifting of cinders, and occasional consciousness.

Unfortunately can now see the trick, can see the author working his counters for the peroration. So very few more possible enthusiasms left. Grit and toothache still to be in any heaven or Utopia.

Literature as entirely the deliberate standing still, hovering and thinking oneself into an artificial view, for the moment, and not effecting any real actions at all. Sunsets no consolation in harvest-field.

(Lovers' sentimental fancies in letters.)

A POEM

It was formerly my idea that a poem was made somewhat as follows: The poet, in common with many other people, occasionally experienced emotions which strangely moved him. In the case of the greengrocer this was satisfied by reading Tennyson and sending the lines he seemed to have experienced to his beloved. The poet, on the contrary, tried to find new images to express what he felt. These lines and vague collections of words he gradually built up into poems. But this I now see to be wrong; the very act of trying to find a form to fit the separate phrases into, itself leads to the creation of new images hitherto not felt by the poet. In a sense the poetry writes itself. This creation by happy chance is analogous to the accidental stroke of the brush which creates a new beauty not previously consciously thought of by the artist.

The form of a poem is shaped by the intention. Vague phrases containing ideas which at past moments have strongly moved us: as the purpose of the poem is narrative or emotional the phrases become altered. The choice of a form is as important as the individual pieces and scraps of emotion of which the poem is made up. In the actual making accidental phrases are hit upon. Just as musician in striking notes on piano comes across what he wants, the painter on the canvas, so the poet not only gets the phrases he wants, but even from the words gets a *new* image.

Creative effort means *new* images. (Lobster and me.) The accidental discovery of effect, not conscious intellectual endeavour for it.

The theory that puts all phrases in a box and years later starts to arrange *all wrong*. Don't. Start creating *at once*, and in this very process new ideas spring up, accidentally. So *condemn* card system, red tape leads to nothing. The living method of arranging at once in temporary notebooks.

CROWDS

Drama

The effect produced by multitude (i) one by one as they left the hall; (ii) policemen's dance.

Actors can add to a comedy. All gestures unreal, but add to comedy and subtract and annoy in tragedy.

Music

Fortuitous assemblage of noises.

The mechanical model, music seen for an instant once during a hymn as smooth rolling.[1]

Conductor's baton and foundation in body rhythm.

Music in its power of seeming to hold an audience or crowd together into an organism. When plays low in park the atmosphere seems to fall to pieces and crowd becomes units again. cf. Band and Bard.

Sound a fluid beaten up by conductor.

Breaking of waves. Listening is like the motion in a ship.

Big Crowds

(i) Not found in streets which are routes, except in those which are meeting-places, as Oxford Street.

1 Hulme has a small sketch of one circle rolling inside another.

(ii) The old market-places, the gymnasia of the Greeks, Plato, and the pretty youths.

(iii) Churches and theatres to catch the prolific mood. Davidson and railway stations.

(iv) Secular churches in street, to sit, rest and look.

BEAUTY, IMITATION, AND ECSTASY

Tradition

Poetry always founded on tradition. So light-haired woman with upturned face in Regent Street. A bright moon in dark sky over Paddington. All books, history, etc., after all only a record of the opinions of a class, the artificial moments and poses of literary men. The other classes and little worlds inarticulate (cf. villages).

When artistic impressions of miners and artisans seen (Millet) they do not in any way have anything to do with the emotions of the miner, do not in any way dignify his life. Are only blurs in light and shade. There is no *depth* in the mirror.

Beauty

Art creates beauty (not art copies the beauty in nature: beauty does not exist by itself in nature, waiting to be copied, only organized pieces of cinders). Origin of this view, course of etchings has made cranes and chimneys at night seem beautiful.

Landscape makes the ordinary man think pieces of wood beautiful. 'Just like a picture.'

So one purpose of art to make people like the merely healthy. Necessary to correct false bias in favour of guilt. Plain steel. (Should make all art seem beautiful.)

Beauty is usefulness seen from another point (cf. distant railway line, *not* the one you yourself are on). Point of view above, birds' eye, because *new*. The waiting engine in the trees, *one* line, red light, like animal waiting to kill.

Culture seeks romantic in far regions. Seeks passions and tragedies in peasants. Tolstoy. Then sees it in prostitutes. Why not abandon it all and take supernatural for art.

Whitman had a theory that every object under the sun comes within the range of poetry. But he was too early in the day. No use having a theory that motor-cars are beautiful, and backing up this theory by working up emotion not really felt. Object must cause the emotion before poem can be written. Whitman's theory, that everything in America must be glorious, was his snare, because it was only a theory.

Minor poets, with their romantic jewels, make same mistake from other side—a lost poetic content. Lexicon of beautiful is elastic, but walla-walla not yet poetically possible.

Continual effort necessary to think of things as they are, the constraint necessary to avoid great tendencies to use big words and common phrases without meaning. cf. Nietzsche and his ambition to say everything in a paragraph.

NOTES ON LANGUAGE AND STYLE

Imitation

Tendency to begin a tale 'It began in the E.M. restaurant' and similarly with poems. The imitation makes one imagine that one is producing stuff of the same calibre and the same effect on other people.

Stupid little poems about flowers and spring, imitations. No *new* emotion in them. Or the infinitely fascinating man (fiction), cf. G. Moore's novels, the infinitely beautiful woman.

Poetasters write in metre because poets have done so, poets because singing, not talking, is the obvious mode of expressing ecstasy. Whitman went wrong through deficiency of selective process. Even Turner had to shroud his railway train in vapour.

What is the exact difference which would be produced if chess or cinders were stated by Andrew Lang. How is the childishness made to disappear? Perhaps they don't state a thing baldly but hint at rounder and counter-like figures behind it.

People anxious to be literary men think there is no work, just as haymaking—but just as monotonous grinding it out. Concerned in the field with ecstasy, but the pains of birth and parturition are sheets and sheets of paper.

W. B. Yeats attempts to ennoble his craft by strenuously believing in supernatural world, race-memory, magic, and saying that symbols can recall these where prose couldn't. This an attempt to bring in an infinity again. Truth that occasionally have moments of poetic feeling in W.C. and other places, banging of doors, etc.

The beauty of London only seen in detached and careful moments, never continuously, always a conscious effort. On top of a bus, or the sweep of the avenue in Hyde Park. But to appreciate this must be in some manner detached, e.g. wearing workmen's clothes (when not shabby but different in kind) then opportunity for conscious reflection. It is the stranger that sees the romantic and the beautiful in the commonplace, cf. in New York, or in strange city, detached and therefore able to see beauty and romance.

Moments of enthusiasm due to a selection seen as a possible *continuously* happy future.

All attempts at beauty necessarily consciously made, open to reaction of the man who talks of 'nature', etc.

Life as a rule tedious, but certain things give us sudden lifts. Poetry comes with the jumps, cf. love, fighting, dancing. The moments of ecstasy.

Literature, like memory, selects only the vivid patches of life. The art of abstraction. If literature (realistic) did really resemble life, it would be interminable, dreary, commonplace, eating and dressing, buttoning, with here and there a patch of vividness. Zola merely selects an interesting group of sordid pieces.

Life composed of exquisite moments and the rest shadows of them.

The *gaps*—hence chess.

Drink

They followed the road with the knowledge that they were soaring along in a supporting medium, possessed

of original and profound thoughts, themselves and sur-
rounding nature forming an organism of which all the
parts harmoniously and joyously interpenetrate each
other.

Heroes occasionally, drink influence only for a time
like effect of church or music.

The literary man deliberately perpetrates a hypocrisy,
in that he fits together his own isolated moments of
ecstasy (and generally deliberate use of big words without personal meaning attached) and presents them as a
picture of higher life, thereby giving old maids a sense
of superiority to other people and giving mandarins the
opportunity to talk of 'ideals'. Then makes attempt to
justify himself by inventing the soul and saying that
occasionally the lower world gets glimpses of this, and
that inferentially he is the medium. As a matter of fact
being certain moments of ecstasy perhaps brought on
by drink. Surely obvious that drink and drugs have
nothing to do with a higher world (cf. Q and his little
safe yacht, a kind of mechanical ladder to the soul
world).

All theories as toys.

INDEX

Abruzzi, Duke of the, 16

Absolute values, 51, 54, 55, 89, 93, 96, 110, 112, 114, 116, 122, 131, 132, 135, 138, 140, 167, 172, 174, 177, 178, 187, 193, 197, 201, 202, 241, 247, 252; *see also* Intrinsic values

Action Française, 18, 102

Adams, F. S., 14*n.*

Angelico, Fra, 43

Aquinas, St. Thomas, Thomism, 122, 130, 146

Archaic art, 74

Aristocracy, 194, 195, 196

Aristotle, 78

Arliss, George, 207

Arnold, Matthew, 120, 238; *Preface to Poems* (quoted), 206; *Scholar-Gipsy,* 237, 239; (quoted) 238

Auden, W. H., 177; (quoted) 249

Augustine, St., of Hippo, 45, 48

Bach, J. S., 111, 166, 222

Bacon, Francis, 48, 233

Baudelaire, Charles, 18, 154

Beaton, Cecil, (quoted) 222

Beddoes, T. L., 238; (quoted) 237

Beethoven, L. van, 222

Bergson, Henri, 13, 16, 17, 18, 19, 20, 34, 68, 69, 78 *et seq.,* 117, 123, 130, 134, 135, 138, 143*n.,*

150, 165, 209, 210, 216, 251; *Introduction à la Métaphysique,* Hulme's translation (quoted), 79, 81, 82, 83

Berkeley, George, 49

Berlin Aesthetic Congress, 19

Bevan, Mrs. Robert (Stanislawa de Karlowska), 32, 34

Black, William, (quoted) 161

Blake, William, 213

Bologna Philosophical Congress, 16, 17

Bolshevism, 199

Bomberg, David, 20, 24, 25

Brussels, 16

Brodzky, Horace, 32*n.*

Brooke, Rupert, 19, 22

Bruno, Giordano, 48, 49, 60, 78, 81, 149

Brzeska, Sophia, 32

Bürger, G. A., 153

Burns, Robert, 218; (quoted) 217

Byron, Lord, 60, 154, 162, 206, 207

Byzantine art, 21, 57, 59, 65, 74, 75, 76, 216, 222

Cambridge, 14, 15, 19

Cambridge Magazine, The, 33, 104; (quoted) 105, 107, 108, 109, 112, 113

Cambridge Platonists, 93

INDEX

INDEX

308

INDEX

INDEX